THE LADY LAUREATES

Women Who Have Won the Nobel Prize

Second Edition

by

OLGA S. OPFELL

The Scarecrow Press, Inc.
Metuchen, N.J., & London
1986

Acknowledgments of permissions to reprint appear on page iv.

AS
911
.N9
O63
1986

Library of Congress Cataloging-in-Publication Data

Opfell, Olga S.
    The lady laureates.

    Bibliography: p.
    Includes index.
    1. Nobel prizes. 2. Women--Biography. 3. Women
authors--Biography. 4. Women scientists--Biography.
I. Title.
AS911.N9O63 1986   001.4'4   85-19670
ISBN 0-8108-1851-5

For John

and in memory of

Johanne and Georg

In preparing the first edition of this book I received invaluable help from Karen O'Connor, Ruth Loring, and Elsie Waerndt. For this new edition, Ruth Loring has again provided many suggestions. I also thank Edward Hee, Dr. Helen Koritz, Brother Edward Guinn, and Margareta Ehrèn.

ACKNOWLEDGMENTS

I gratefully acknowledge the following debts for permission to reprint certain materials:

To the Nobel Foundation, Stockholm, for quotations from various volumes of their annual Les Prix Nobel, which is copyrighted © by the Nobel Foundation, and for the portraits reproduced herein of the laureates. To the Elsevier Scientific Publishing Company of Amsterdam for quotations from various volumes of their Nobel Lectures series which they provide translated into English.

To Ginn and Company, Lexington, Mass., for the use of various passages from The Memoirs of Bertha von Suttner. To Macmillan Publishing Co., Inc., for quotations from Twenty Years at Hull-House by Jane Addams, copyright © 1910 by Macmillan Publishing Co., Inc., renewed 1938 by James W. Linn.

To Francis B. Randall, executor of the estate of Mercedes M. Randall, for various quotations from the published and unpublished papers of Emily Greene Balch, located in the Swarthmore College Peace Collection.

To Eva Andéns Advokatbyrâ, Stockholm, and to Doubleday & Company for quotations from The Story of Gösta Berling by Selma Lagerlöf. Excerpts from The Wonderful Adventures of Nils by Selma Lagerlöf, copyright © 1907, 1913 by Doubleday & Company, Inc., are reprinted by permission of the publisher and of Eva Andéns Advokatbyrâ, Stockholm. Excerpts from The Diary of Selma Lagerlöf, translated by Velma Swanston Howard, copyright © 1936 by Doubleday & Company, Inc., are reprinted by permission of the publisher.

To Hughes Massie Limited, London, for two excerpts from Grazia Deledda's The Mother, translated by Mary G. Steegmann, Macmillan Publishing Co., Inc., 1920.

To University of Pennsylvania Press for lines of Gabriela Mistral's poetry from Some Spanish-American Poets, translated by Alice Stone Blackwell, Appleton, 1929; to Joan Daves for lines from Selected Poems of Gabriela Mistral, translated by Doris Dana, Johns Hopkins University Press, 1971, copyright © 1961, 1964, 1970, 1971 by Doris Dana; to Franciscan Herald Press for lines from Marie-Lise Gautier-Gazarian's Gabriela Mistral, copyright © 1975 by Franciscan Herald Press; and to New York University Press for lines from Gabriela Mistral: The Poet and Her Work by Margot Arce de Vasquez, translated by Helen Masslo Anderson, copyright © 1964 by New York University.

To Farrar, Straus & Giroux, and to Jonathan Cape Ltd., London, for several lines of poetry from O the Chimneys by Nelly Sachs. Translated from the German by Michael Hamburger, Christopher Holm, Ruth and Matthew Mead, and Michael Roloff. Copyright © 1967 by Farrar, Straus & Giroux, Inc.

To Curtis Brown Ltd. and to Doubleday & Company, Inc., for brief portions of Madame Curie by Eve Curie, translated by Vincent Sheean, copyright © 1937 by Doubleday & Company, Inc.

CONTENTS

ALFRED NOBEL

Alfred Nobel, the great inventor, wrote about himself, "Alfred Nobel, a miserable halflife, ought to have been choked to death by a philanthropic physician as soon as, with a howl, he entered life." For almost 63 years he brooded about his delicate health.

The brooder was that ultimate paradox, a misanthrope who optimistically hoped for the future of mankind. The Nobel Prizes for which he so generously provided reflect that idealism. Some critics, however, find it ironic that the inventor of dynamite, the lonely millionaire who made his fortune from explosives that were put to terrible use in two world wars, should specifically designate a peace award. Actually, perhaps 90 per cent of that fortune came from the civilian use of his explosives in tunnel blasting, mining, and road building.

There were still more paradoxes. Nobel was a recluse by nature, who built a great industrial empire over five continents. He was an expatriate who loved his homeland. He was a man of brilliance, whose heart was broken by an ignorant Austrian girl he met in a flower shop.

The irony really began with Alfred Bernhard Nobel's birth in Stockholm on October 21, 1833, at the time his father, the ambitious Immanuel Nobel, was going into bankruptcy. Nothing daunted, Immanuel moved on to St. Petersburg to start an engineering workshop, which prospered when the Crimean War broke out and the Russian government gave him large orders for his inventions, land and submarine mines. His wife and sons followed him to St. Petersburg in 1842. Here the sickly, introspective young Alfred, like his brothers, Ludwig and Robert, was privately tutored. He became enormously proficient in chemistry and languages--he could speak five. But when the war ended, Immanuel Nobel was overextended and suffered a second bankruptcy in 1859.

Alfred had worked in his father's Russian factory and

traveled extensively. Now he returned to Sweden with his parents. In 1863 he set up a small nitroglycerin plant in Heleneborg near Stockholm. The next year the factory blew up, killing his younger brother, Emil. In spite of this tragedy, which caused his father to have a stroke, Alfred Nobel continued to devote himself to research on nitroglycerin. When he combined it with kieselguhr, he produced dynamite. In 1875 he combined nitroglycerin with gun cotton to create blasting gelatin. Thirteen years later he invented ballistite.

Nobel was also a business genius who girded the earth with a chain of explosives factories. As overseer of this empire, he traveled constantly, setting up headquarters in Paris. Some of his immense wealth also came from the Nobel brothers' exploitation of the Baku oil fields.

Nobel never married, and he died alone at his home in San Remo, Italy, on December 10, 1896. "I am not aware," he had once written, "that I have deserved any notoriety and I have no taste for its buzz." This complex man had a profound interest in literature and some literary talent of his own. He wrote poems, a couple of novels, even a satiric comedy, but they were never published.

The Will of Alfred Nobel

"The whole of my remaining realizable estate shall be dealt with in the following way:

"The capital shall be invested by my executors in safe securities and shall constitute a fund, the interest on which shall be annually distributed in the form of prizes to those who, during the preceding year, shall have conferred the greatest benefit on mankind. The said interest shall be divided into five equal parts, which shall be apportioned as follows: one part to the person who shall have made the most important discovery or invention within the field of physics; one part to the person who shall have made the most important chemical discovery or improvement; one part to the person who shall have made the most important discovery within the domain of physiology or medicine; one part to the person who shall have produced in the field of literature the most outstanding work of an idealistic tendency; and one part to the person who shall have done the most or the best work for fraternity among nations, for the abolition or reduction of standing armies and for the holding and promotion of peace congresses.

"The prizes for physics and chemistry shall be awarded by the Swedish Academy of Sciences; that for physiological or medical works by the Caroline Institute in Stockholm; that for literature by the Academy in Stockholm; and that for champions of peace by a committee of five persons to be elected by the Norwegian Storting. It is my express wish that in awarding the prizes no consideration whatever shall be given to the nationality of the candidates, so that the most worthy shall receive the prize, whether he be a Scandinavian or not.

"Paris, November 27, 1895

Alfred Bernhard Nobel"

THE NOBEL PRIZES

Alfred Nobel hated lawyers. With his far-flung industrial empire he was involved in constant litigation and court-
room disputes, and he usually felt that he came out the loser.
So no lawyer was present that November day in 1895 when the
lonely millionaire sat down in his rue Malakoff mansion to
draw up his will in his own handwriting. In early December
he appended his final signature in front of four witnesses, none
of them lawyers, at the Swedish Club in Paris. As Ragnar
Sohlman said, his fundamental idea was "that the main part of
his estate should be set aside for a fund, the income from
which should be distributed annually in the form of prizes in
five different fields of human endeavor."

Nobel's handwriting was exceptionally clear, but the
legal form of his will was not satisfactory. His estate was
scattered in eight countries, his domicile was questioned, and
above all some of his heirs contested the provisions. After
four years of sometimes bitter negotiations, young Sohlman,
one of Nobel's most trusted assistants, worked his way through
the entanglements, greatly helped by the inventor's nephew
Emanuel, who won over the contesting heirs. In 1900 the
charter and by-laws of the Nobel Foundation were officially
sanctioned, with specific directions for the prize distributors.

When Nobel wrote his will, Norway was still united to
Sweden, but after the union was dissolved in 1905, the Nobel
Foundation decided to continue honoring his wish that the Norwegians be entrusted with the Peace Prize. A Nobel Institute
in Kristiania (called Oslo after 1925) was set up just after the
dissolution.

The statutes of the Nobel Foundation govern the prize-
awarding bodies--the Swedish Academy (literature), the Royal
Academy of Sciences (physics and chemistry), the Faculty of
Medicine of the Caroline Institute (physiology or medicine),

and the Nobel Committee of the Storting or Parliament
(peace.)* In addition, there are five Nobel Committees (including the prize-awarding Norwegian Committee) to prepare
and advise and four Nobel Institutes to provide research stations and libraries.

Every fall invitations to nominate candidates are sent
out by the prize-awarding institutions to "statutorily com-
petent" individuals.   These include previous Nobel laureates;
members of the prize-awarding bodies, and the Nobel Committees; professors in the various prize fields at specifically
mentioned universities; presidents of representative authors'
organizations; members of certain international parliamentary
or legal organizations; and members of parliaments and governments.

On February 1 the painstaking committee work begins.
By early fall the Nobel Committees present their choices to
the prize-awarding institutions.   Secret votes are cast in
October or November.   Often the awards in peace and literature have been hotly debated.   But whatever the reaction, the
results make world headlines.

Every year the glitter of Nobel Week cuts across the
cold gloom of Stockholm in December.   The laureates and
their families arrive from far-flung places for endless interviews and much sightseeing in spite of only five hours of
daylight.   Until 1923 the Nobel ceremonies were held in the
auditorium of the Royal Academy of Music.   Since then, with
three exceptions, they have taken place in the Koncerthus
(Concert Hall).

Hours beforehand, crowds begin gathering outside.
Late in the afternoon the laureates arrive at a scene of
splendid pomp and elegance.   To trumpet flourishes and the
strains of the Royal March they follow the Swedish royal
family into the auditorium.   With the King below them in
front row center, they are then seated in red velvet chairs
on a flower-banked stage, with an excellent view of an illuminated bust of Alfred Nobel.   Trumpets continue to sound

---

*On January 1, 1977, the committee was renamed the Nor-
wegian Nobel Committee.   Its members are elected by the
Norwegian Parliament, but there is no mention in Nobel's
will that they themselves must belong to Parliament.

as Swedish dignitaries speak and the King* hands out diplomas, gold medals, and the Nobel check.

After the ceremony 800 of the 2000 or more guests move on the Stadshus (Town Hall), the most impressive building on Stockholm's skyline. Since it floats on an arm of Lake Malaren, its strong brick tower, topped with three golden crowns, is stunningly reflected in the water. The Stadshus has one of Europe's most sumptuous banqueting rooms-- Gyllene Salen (the Golden Hall), decorated with golden mosaics. The dominant figure everybody first notices is that of a colossal woman, Stockholm (the Queen of Malar), who receives homage from the East and the West. Here at the long head table the laureates and their families dine with the royal family. And here each laureate gives an acceptance speech. After the banquet, dancing goes on till long after midnight in Gyllene Salen or Blå Hallen (the Blue Hall), an ornate covered court with marble floor and stairway.

The following day the laureates are expected to give a Nobel lecture. Not all have done so. But the science laureates have always carried out this obligation. Sometimes lectures have been postponed.

Across the border in Norway on the same December 10, an impressive ceremony takes place in the Aula, or Assembly Hall, decorated with Edvard Munch murals, at the University of Oslo. In the presence of the King of Norway[†] and the royal family, members of the Norwegian Storting, and assorted dignitaries, the chairman of the Nobel Committee hands out the Peace Prize. Later the Committee gives a banquet. The next day the "champion of peace" delivers his lecture.

In addition to the regular Nobel Prizes, there is now a Prize in Economic Sciences in Memory of Alfred Nobel, instituted by the Central Bank of Sweden at its tercentenary in 1968 and adjudicated and awarded by the Swedish Royal Academy of Sciences. The bank places an annual amount, equal to a Nobel Prize, at the disposal of the Nobel Foundation. This presentation is also made on Nobel Day. So far no women economists have been honored.

---

*Oscar II (1872-1907), Gustav V (1907-1950), Gustav VI (1950-1972), and Carl XVI Gustav (1972-   ).
†Haakon VII (1905-1957) and Olav V (1957-   ).

WOMEN AND THE PRIZES

To feminists the figures seem somewhat overweighted. In 84 years, 20 women and 483 men (three of whom declined) have won Nobel Prizes in peace, literature, and science. These figures do not take into account the 14 organizations, headed by men, that have won peace Prizes, nor the 20 men who have been honored with the Prize in Economic Sciences. In the face of such numbers, the 20 women must be considered extraordinary.

Marie Curie	1903	Physics[a]
Bertha von Suttner	1905	Peace
Selma Lagerlöf	1909	Literature
Marie Curie	1911	Chemistry
Grazia Deledda	1926[b]	Literature
Sigrid Undset	1928	Literature
Jane Addams	1931	Peace[c]
Irène Joliot-Curie	1935	Chemistry[d]
Pearl Buck	1938	Literature
Gabriela Mistral	1945	Literature
Emily Greene Balch	1946	Peace[e]
Gerty Cori	1947	Physiology or Medicine[f]
Maria Goeppert-Mayer	1963	Physics[g]
Dorothy Crowfoot Hodgkin	1964	Chemistry
Nelly Sachs	1966	Literature[h]
Betty Williams & Mairead Corrigan	1976[i]	Peace
Rosalyn Yalow	1977	Physiology or Medicine[j]
Mother Teresa	1979	Peace
Alva Myrdal	1982	Peace[k]
Barbara McClintock	1983	Physiology or Medicine

---

[a]shared one half of the award with Pierre Curie (other half went to Henri Becquerel); [b]awarded in 1927; [c]with Nicholas Murray Butler; [d]with Frédéric Joliot-Curie; [e]with John Raleigh Mott; [f]shared one half of the award with Carl Cori (other half went to Bernardo Houssay); [g]shared one half of the award with Hans Jensen (other half went to Eugene Wigner); [h]with Shmuel Yosef Agnon; [i]awarded in 1977; [j]awarded

(cont. on p. xv)

A glance at the list of the lady laureates shows that there have been three long-time gaps between them--fifteen years between Marie Curie and Grazia Deledda, seventeen years between Gerty Cori and Maria Goeppert-Mayer, and ten years between Nelly Sachs and Betty Williams and Mairead Corrigan. Actually, the Williams-Corrigan award was delayed a year, and so October, 1977 brought the amazing announcements that three women had gained Nobel Prizes. Never before had two women been named in a single year, let alone three of them!

When on December 10, 1975, a glittering array of laureates descended on Stockholm for the seventy-fifth anniversary celebration of the establishment of the Nobel Prizes, only one woman stood among them. At that time Dorothy Crowfoot Hodgkin was the sole representative of a small band of only 14 lady laureates. Among her more than seventy-five male scientific colleagues she observed that she was used to being the only woman at scientific meetings. "After all," she mused, "women have come rather late to science." And, someone else has remarked, women have to be twice as determined and to work twice as hard as men. Too often lady scientists have come smack up against what Betsy Ancker-Johnson calls the "conspiracy of discouragement."

In the field of peace women nominees have been infrequent, probably because women have lacked the official, often political status to put them in direct line for the Prize. As for literature, some critics have pointed out that the modest list of six female laureates is not in proportion to the role literary women have played in this century.

But women are increasingly represented in the prize-awarding institutions. For many years Selma Lagerlöf and Elin Wägner were the only female members of the Swedish Academy, which has always numbered 18. Kerstin Ekman and Gunnel Valquist have succeeded them. In 1984 the Royal Swedish Academy of Sciences had 262 Swedish members and 123 foreign members. Before the Nobel awards were established, only two women, Eva Ekeblad and Ekaterina Romanovna Daykova (Russian), had been members, both in the eighteenth century. In 1910 Marie Curie was honored, and in 1945, Lisa Meitner (classed as a Swedish member 1952). No

------

(cont.) one half of the prize (other half shared by Roger Guillemin and Andrew Schally); [k]awarded one half of the prize (other half shared by Alfonso Garcia Robles).

native-born women were named again until 1975. Since that
date Aina Elvius, Inga Fischer-Hjalmars, Kerstin Fredga,
Marianne Rasmussen, Kerstin Lindahl Kisseling, and Cecilia
Jarlskog have been listed in the academy roster. From outside Sweden, Katherine Esau and Mary Leakey were elected
in 1971 and 1980.

In 1984 the Caroline Institute, with almost 4000 students, had 750 teachers, including 136 full professors, of
whom eight were women. Two of them, Kerstin Hall and
Birgitta Zetterström-Karpe, were members of the Caroline
Institute's 50-member "Nobel Församling" (Nobel Assembly).

In Norway, Aase Lionaes became a member of the
Peace Committee in 1949 and served as committee chairperson from 1973 to 1978. In 1984, Gidske Andersen (deputy
chairperson) and Else Germeten sat on the five-member
Nobel Committee.

In Alfred Nobel's day women's place was supposed to
be in the home, and higher education was barely open to
them. Until 1921, when a new Swedish Marriage Code came
into force, a woman--married or not--was ruled by a guardian.
A wife's guardian was her husband; an unmarried woman's
guardian was her father or brother. The new code gave the
married woman equal legal and economic footing with her
husband within the family. Swedish feminists point out that
several European countries gave women fundamental civic
rights earlier than Sweden. They attribute the lag to the fact
that industrialization came later to their country.

In the first 28 years of the Nobel Foundation's existence, women had no equal opportunity in education. Then
in 1928 girls were given the same right as boys to enter the
public secondary schools, which prepared for the leaving examination and university studies. Earlier, girls who wanted
the leaving examination could obtain it only in private schools.
Nonetheless, since 1928, many girls of the lower classes
have not been able to obtain a higher education because of
economic difficulties.

In the heady glow of Norwegian independence, Norwegian women were given the vote in 1907. But Swedish
women, who had had a national organization fighting for their
rights since 1902, were not granted suffrage until 1921, the
same year they were emancipated by the Marriage Code.

Alfred Nobel certainly was not prejudiced against women achievers. A lifelong bachelor, he was particularly devoted to his mother, Caroline. Some biographers suggest that a frustration in love during his youth contributed to his notable melancholy. So far as is known, he had only one affair, the 18-year-long liaison with the ungrateful erstwhile flower girl, Sophie Hesse, 23 years his junior, whom he vainly tried to polish and educate. Of all the lady laureates he knew only Bertha von Suttner and admired her greatly. More than one Nobel biography has hinted that if Bertha had not been in love with Artur von Suttner, Nobel would eventually have proposed to the stunning young countess he hired as secretary and manager of his household.

Nobel, who could be witty and cosmopolitan when he chose, did enjoy the company of brilliant and attractive women. Certainly he would have appreciated the variety of the lady laureates: seven Americans (two of them naturalized United States citizens with birthplaces in Prague, then part of Austria-Hungary, and Kattowitz, then part of Germany), one Norwegian, one Austrian, one German, one Italian, one Chilean, one Albanian-Indian, one Englishwoman, two Swedes, two Irishwomen, two Frenchwomen (one born in Warsaw). They were deeply religious women, and they were agnostics and atheists. They were recipients of the Prize when young, like Mairead Corrigan and Betty Williams at 33 and 34 and Marie Curie at 36, and old, like Emily Balch at 79, Alva Myrdal at 80, and Barbara McClintock at 81. Eight were single women, 12 wives, and 11 mothers. Two of them were divorced, but one had made a happy second marriage. The two divorcees also had to cope with mentally retarded daughters. But most of the Nobel mothers have had healthy and bright children, who became successful teachers and scientists. Certainly, as their mothers pursued their careers, these children learned a remarkable self-reliance.

During their own childhoods the future Nobelists showed differing temperaments. Some were lonely, some timid and self-conscious, others outgoing and well-adjusted. Many were tutored and most attended private schools. Four had no formal education whatever, but all the scientific lady laureates have had doctorates. In many cases the women were greatly influenced by an outstanding father or mother, or both. Yet parents were not always wealthy or eminent--the glory of Selma Lagerlöf's father rose from his exuberant, warm personality.

As adults, however, the lady laureates have shared some hobbies and beliefs. Many have been devoted to gardening. Generally, the women scientists have been athletic. Most of the prizewinners have shown strong humanitarian drives and affirmed feminist sympathies, especially such eloquent spokespersons as Rosalyn Yalow and Alva Myrdal. Ironically, at the time they won their awards, Bertha von Suttner, Marie Curie, Grazia Deledda, and Irène Joliot-Curie did not have the right to vote.

Several battled ill health, and four were ill when they received their Prize. The youngest died at 58, the oldest at 94. Generally, the lady laureates have died in their 60s.

As mother and daughter, Marie Curie and Irène Joliot-Curie could claim the closest of relationships. Jane Addams and Emily Balch were longtime friends and co-workers in peace. For years Selma Lagerlöf corresponded with the much younger Nelly Sachs and helped her flee from Nazi Germany to Sweden. And almost at the moment of meeting each other, Betty Williams and Mairead Corrigan formed their partnership. Otherwise, the contacts have been more or less peripheral. Marie Curie and Gabriela Mistral met through the Committee of Intellectual Cooperation of the League of Nations, and Pearl Buck once spoke at a banquet honoring Emily Balch.

The Time Lines (beginning on page 277), show the chronological overlaps. Often in a single year important events occurred in the lives of several lady laureates. Take 1914, when 71-year-old Bertha von Suttner died. Eighteen-year-old Gerty Cori (née Radnitz) entered medical school, 22-year-old Gabriela Mistral won the Poetic Games in Santiago, and four-year-old Dorothy Crowfoot Hodgkin was being transplanted from Egypt to England.

Other years show similar patterns. The happenings, the achievements are the subject of this book.

The Peace Prize

Lay Down Arms
BERTHA VON SUTTNER

Baroness Bertha Sophia Felicita von Suttner always insisted that Alfred Nobel had wanted her to receive the first Nobel Prize for Peace in 1901. That first Prize went instead to 83-year-old Henri Dunant, founder of the International Red Cross, and to 79-year-old Frédéric Passy, head of the French Peace Society and co-founder of the Interparliamentary Union. Head held high, Bertha shook off her disappointment and graciously congratulated these aged winners. Actually she thought that Passy, "the most highly regarded of all the pacifists," alone deserved the honor since he had worked toward abolishing war, Dunant only toward ameliorating its conditions. This was the same strong stand she took throughout her long career as the first important female peace agitator of the modern era.

Bertha von Suttner had to wait four more years. She saw the Peace Prize go to men who were her friends and co-workers--Elie Ducummun and Albert Gobat in 1902, William Randal Cremer in 1903--and to the Institute of International Law in 1904. Then by 1905 Bjørnstjerne Bjørnson, the Norwegian poet and Nobel laureate, who had been influenced by the inventor's nephew Emanuel and by some of his friends, urged her selection "as a duty to Alfred Nobel's memory." She was the second woman to win a Nobel medal. Sharing her Physics Prize, Marie Curie had preceded her in 1903. Bertha's award was for herself alone.

This Austrian aristocrat made additional claims that she had inspired Nobel's decision to write a Peace Prize into his will. But some of his friends pointed out that he had been interested in peace long before he met her. As a youth he had worshiped the idealistic Shelley, and throughout his life, especially in his late years, he kept in touch with many peace idealists. Bertha von Suttner and Nobel met only a very few times and during the 20 years of their friendship exchanged perhaps 30 letters of importance, only one half devoted to peace.

1

Baroness Bertha von Suttner

Certainly the two friends differed on approach.   He could never accept her absolute ideas on compulsory arbitration and widespread disarmament.   When they first met, he told her, "I wish I could produce a substance or a machine of such frightful efficacy for wholesale devastation that wars should thereby become altogether impossible."   Much later he suggested to the Baroness that various governments should contract annual agreements on the peaceful settlement of their differences.   Such proposals hardly satisfied her.   All the same, the indomitable Bertha, who had asked him to do something for the peace movement, always believed that the provision in his will for a peace award was his answer.

When the Peace Prize finally came to her, Bertha lay abed in Wiesbaden, Germany, completely exhausted.   Unable to go to Kristiania, she had to receive the Prize in absentia. This stout 62-year-old widow was physically far removed from the slim and lovely young countess who had met Nobel in Paris 29 years earlier.   She may have reflected that except for the stubborn opposition to her shown by the elder Baron and Baroness von Suttner, she might never have met him at all.

Her love affair, with those unyielding parents on one side, was the stuff of novels.   At 30, Bertha Kinsky was mourning the unexpected death of her fiancé, Prince Adolf von Wittgenstein.   Almost penniless, she had to take a post as governess-companion to the four young daughters of the Baron and Baroness von Suttner.   In their sumptuous mansion in a Vienna that whirled to Strauss waltzes, she fell in love with her pupils' handsome and elegant brother, Artur Gundaccar, a musically talented sometime law student, who was a complete charmer.   "When he entered a room," wrote Bertha, "it immediately grew twice as bright and warm as it was before."   He was seven years her junior, but fully reciprocated her feelings.

The elder Stuttners, however, refused to consider Bertha as a daughter-in-law.   She was too old for their son, she had no dowry.   They were hardly sympathetic either to Bertha's somewhat unusual background.

She was born in Prague, then part of the Austrian empire, on June 9, 1843, the posthumous daughter of the Feldmarschalleutnant Count Kinsky von Chinitz und Tettau of the Austrian Imperial Army.   But the young Bertha was unacceptable at the Hapsburg court because her mother, the daughter

of a cavalry officer, was not of equivalent rank.   There was
one other child, Artur, who wound up as a ne'er-do-well.
Throughout her life Bertha had little to do with her brother.

Her mother, Sophia Wilhelmine Kinsky, née von Körner, a passionate gambler who believed herself clairvoyant,
squandered away the small Kinsky fortune at gaming tables
in the famous German spas of Baden-Baden, Bad Homburg,
and Wiesbaden and at casinos in Rome, Venice, and Paris.
Next to gambling she was obsessed with attending parties for
the military and the nobility.   Bertha was brought up as a
social butterfly to dance and coquette in clouds of tulle.   Educated only by a governess, she became along the way a "ravenous
devourer of books. "   In later years she would say that in the
first half of her life she accepted without question the militaristic traditions that informed the aristocratic society of which
she was a product.   In her memoirs she would describe her
youthful self as "piously loyal to the military and completely
unconcerned about the horrors of war. "   Indeed, at the end of
the Franco-Prussian War, during a visit to Berlin, she stood
in the sunshine on an Unter den Linden balcony watching the
entrance of the victorious troops returning from France.
Bertha admired the "fluttering banners, scattered flowers,
triumphal arches" and considered it all a "lofty, historic festival of joy. "

There was then absolutely nothing in Bertha's past that
appealed to Artur's parents.   They determined to rid their
household of this troublesome governess.   With icy coldness
his mother asked her to answer that particular advertisement
appearing in Die Neue Freie Presse, Vienna's most prominent
daily newspaper: "A very wealthy, cultured, elderly gentle-
man, living in Paris, desires to find a lady, also of mature
years, familiar with languages, as secretary and manager of
his household. "   Ten years Nobel's junior, Bertha barely fit
the description, "also of mature years. "   But from her travels
with her mother she had picked up a remarkable fluency in
French, English, and Italian.   Of all the replies, Nobel decided on hers.   Only after his letter of acceptance came did
Bertha learn that her prospective employer was the famous
inventor of dynamite.

Nobel, of course, did not know that the 33-year-old
woman he had chosen for the job was beautiful and elegant
and possessed a stunning figure.   When he met her at the
station in Paris one April day in 1876, he was taken by her
good looks and charm.   Some biographers have even specu-

lated that had not events played out otherwise he might have proposed to her. Bertha found him "rather below the medium height, with dark, full beard, with features neither ugly nor handsome." She considered his expression "rather gloomy, softened only by kindly blue eyes." In his voice she heard "a melancholy, alternating with a satirical tone." She concluded, "Sad and sarcastic, such was his nature." A suite for her in the elegant Nobel mansion in the rue Malakoff had still to be carpeted and furnished. Until it was ready Bertha stayed at the Grand Hotel. Her only alternatives to homesickness and heartache were Nobel's daily visits. They discussed his business plans and chatted about "the problems of time and eternity."

In just one week he was called to Sweden for the opening of a dynamite factory, and Bertha was left alone. Three days later she received a telegram from Artur von Suttner: "I cannot live without thee." She was in a particularly susceptible mood and impulsively sold her one remaining piece of good jewelry, a diamond cross, to buy a railroad ticket to Vienna. In the highly sentimental fashion of the day she sent a note to Artur, asking him to come to the Hotel Canova to receive word about the Countess Kinsky. When he arrived, they fell sobbing into each other's arms.

Artur's parents, however, remained completely unapproachable. After a secret marriage on June 12, bride and groom fled across the Black Sea to the semi-Oriental world of the Caucasus, where they were befriended by the Princess Dadiani of Mingrelia. Bertha had first met the Princess, "a dazzling beauty of the genuine Georgian type," at Bad Homburg and had continued to see her in Paris at the time "la Contessina" was taking singing lessons from Maître Duprez. Rather naively, the Suttners expected Artur to find a position at the Russian court because the princess, called "Dedopali," was one of many Caucasian rulers who had surrendered their sovereignty for Russian protection. But the hoped-for employment never came. Bertha and Artur were forced to earn their living with music and language lessons. Still they considered the Caucasian excursion "a long honeymoon." When war broke out between Russia and Turkey, their pupils disappeared. Fervently taking up the cause of the Slavs, Artur began writing letters about the war to Die Neue Freie Presse. On her mother's side Bertha was descended from the freedom poet, Theodor Körner. Now she too felt the literary urge. Her first piece was a feuilleton, "Fächer and Schürze" (Fans and Aprons), which she sent off

to the old Presse in Vienna. It was accepted with an hono-
rarium of 20 florins. As more articles poured out, Bertha
continued to use the pseudonym of B. Oulot, formed from the
nickname, Boulotte, the Suttner girls had given her.

After the war the many migrations began, from Tiflis
to Kutais to Gordi to Zugdidi. Later Bertha described the
"serious difficulties" of such trips. "We had often ridden
over the edge of abysses and crossed narrow, swaying
bridges; had reached ferries on which the ferryman refused
to take us over on account of the dangerously swollen state
of the water. "

Artur tried his hand at different jobs such as working
in a wallpaper factory and directing the construction of a
country house for the Princess Dadiani's son-in-law. And
Bertha graduated to sentimental novels. The best of them
was Es Löwos, a poetical description of her life with Artur.
She always referred to him as "My Own, " he to her as "My
Löwos. " In between jobs Artur tried his hand at novels too,
for from his war correspondence he had discovered a talent
for light, picturesque description.

Most importantly, together they began studying authors
such as Charles Darwin, Herbert Spencer, Ernst Haeckel,
and William Buckle, whose History of Civilization impressed
them the most. Now they were both convinced that they had
left "the superficial life" for good. In Inventarium einer
Seele (Inventory of a Soul), her first serious book, Bertha
took stock of these writers on evolution, observing that a
society achieves progress through arbitration and peace. In
that same book she openly admitted that she and Artur had
freed themselves from orthodox religious faith.

After nine long years of silence, the elder Suttners
finally forgave and forgot, and Bertha and Artur were invited
to live at Harmannsdorf, the towered summer castle in lower
Austria, which now became a year-round home. They filled
their days with study, writing, festivities, and country ex-
cursions in a delightful pony cart drawn by donkeys.

The next year, spending most of their royalties, they
were in Paris. Here Bertha introduced Artur to Alfred
Nobel, with whom she had sporadically corresponded since
leaving his employ so precipitously. Nobel entertained them
graciously, but there was no special talk of peace. He did
take them to the salon of Mme. Juliette Adam, the well-

known representative of the "spirit of revanche. " War clouds
were again looming, and Bertha was shocked at the way Mme.
Adam and her circle welcomed the prospect.

That winter of 1886 Bertha became deeply interested
in the new International Peace and Arbitration Association.
Founded in England by Hodgson Pratt, it was working to
establish an international arbitration tribunal, where nations
might settle their differences.   Bertha was so impressed
with its goals that she added a chapter about the association
to the galley proofs of her second serious book, Das Mas-
chinenzeitalter (The Age of the Machine), 1888. Under the
pseudonym of "Jemand" (Everyman), it was cast in the form
of a lecture series on Bertha's own era, given by a professor
about A. D. 3000.   The professor attacks "the militarily and
politically pious" as well as "the spiritually pious, " who support the most dogmatic religion.   Finally he declares that
war mentality arises from an official attitude of hostility to
life.

Now the peace movement began gathering momentum
through the establishment of private peace societies and the
Interparliamentary Union, an organization of parliamentarians
from all over the world.   By the spring of 1887 Bertha von
Suttner decided to help the movement even further by writing
a novel to show the brutality of war and its awful consequences.
To prepare for Die Waffen Nieder (Lay Down Arms) she read
"big-volumed histories, " rummaged through old magazines,
and interviewed grizzled veterans.   With her facts as accurate as possible, she threw herself into the story, living intensely its every page.   "What a woman suffers when she
knows that a beloved husband is engaged in war I could now
more easily imagine, for the depth of my own conjugal love
sufficed to put me mentally in such a situation. "

Her aristocratic heroine is Martha Tilling, whose
first husband Arno falls as a brave officer at the Battle of
Magenta in 1859.   Martha begins to hate war and later marries another officer, Friedrich, who shares that hate. (Bertha said that Artur "sat as model for this character. ")   Because of conventional patriotism Friedrich takes part in the
Austrian campaign against the Danes in Schleswig-Holstein
in 1864.   Then he is wounded in the Austro-Prussian War in
Bohemia.

His letters to Martha are full of horrors:

> Fighting in the open country is terrible enough, but
> fighting amongst human dwellings is ten times more
> cruel.   Crashing timber, bursting flames, stifling
> smoke, cattle run mad with fear; every wall a for-
> tress or a barricade; every window a shothole.   I
> saw a breastwork there which was formed of corpses.
> The defenders had heaped up all the slain that were
> lying near in order from that rampart to fire on the
> assailants.   I shall surely never forget that wall in
> all my life.   A man, who formed one of its bricks,
> penned in among the other corpse-bricks, was still
> alive and was moving his arm.

In a later letter Friedrich, claiming he no longer de-
ceives himself about the "cruel worship of the war god Mars,"
writes:

> The liturgy of the bulletins and the ritual of his-
> toric phraseology no longer appear to me as a
> divine revelation; the mighty organ voice of the
> cannon, the incense-smoke of the powder has no
> charm more for me.   I assist at the terrible wor-
> ship perfectly devoid of belief or reverence and
> can now see nothing in it except the torture of the
> victims, hear nothing but their wailing death cries.

Soon he resigns from the army.   In 1870, by now acquainted
with the peace movement, the couple is settled in Paris.   But
at the outbreak of war between France and Prussia, Friedrich
is mistaken for a Prussian spy and shot.

Turned down by many publishers, who feared that the
novel might give offense, especially in militaristic Germany,
Bertha von Suttner finally persuaded E. Pierson, her Dresden publisher, to bring out Die Waffen Nieder at the end of
1889.   It became such an instant success that optimistically
Bertha decided the peace movement must be triumphant.
Nobel was among the first to send her a congratulatory letter,
praising "your admirable masterpiece" with its "charm of
style and grandeur of ideas."   Another who admired it was
Leo Tolstoy, who wrote: "The abolition of slavery was preceded by the famous book of a woman, Mrs. Beecher Stowe;
God grant that the abolition of war may follow upon yours."

Many critics however, were outraged that this descend-
ant of a long line of military counts should condemn what had
won her ancestors glory.   On the other hand, Bertha's cham-

pions contended she had given the peace movement an effective
slogan and a coherent philosophy.

Flushed by the novel's general success, the Suttners
spent the winter of 1890-91 in Venice, where they helped
found an Interparliamentary Union group. By 1891 they were
fully catapulted into the peace movement. Under the name
of World Peace Congresses, the private peace societies had
been meeting on an annual basis since 1885. Now Bertha von
Suttner was seized with a burning desire to have Austria
represented at the Peace Congress in Rome in November, 1891.
As late as September she was inviting readers of Die Neue
Freie Presse to join an Austrian Society for the Friends of
Peace: "This is the way affairs stand: Armies millions
strong--divided into two camps clashing their arms--are
awaiting only a signal to spring at each other; but in the mutual trembling dread at the immeasurable horror of the
threatening outbreak may be found some security for the
delay. "

Acceptances poured in, among them one from the composer, Johann Strauss. The Society was founded with triumph.
The girl who had suffered stage fright during singing lessons
in Paris now found herself the first woman in history to
speak from the Roman Capitol. When it was time for her to
appear, she was fully poised: "Quite calmly, unconcernedly,
in glad exaltation I said what I had to say, and a storm of
applause followed my words.... I had something to say,
which seemed to me important, and which I knew would be a
welcome and joyous message to the like-minded persons who
surrounded me ... and so I spoke without any uneasiness,
with the assurance of an ambassador who has definite and
good tidings to communicate. "

In Rome the delegates' most important decision was
to found in Bern, Switzerland, a central bureau of the peace
societies. Generously the baroness gave the new bureau the
money she had earned from an Italian translation of Die
Waffen Nieder.

Meanwhile, as Bertha radiated pride, Artur founded
and became president of the Union for Resistance to Anti-
Semitism. Her own next move was to help found an Interparliamentary group in Austria. Then in 1892, during an
interlude between lecturing and writing, she and a young
Austrian supporter, the 28-year-old Alfred Hermann Fried,
launched a monthly magazine with the same title as her

famous anti-war novel. Fried himself was destined to win
a Nobel Prize in 1911.   After a while the journal started appearing under the imprint of E. Pierson.   It became the
official organ of the Bureau of the International Parliamentary
Conference, the International Peace Bureau in Bern, and the
Austrian Peace Society.   For it Bertha von Suttner wrote
reports, critiques, appeals, news items, and interviews.   In
1893 she added one more title to her name--vice-president
of the bureau in Bern.

     She remained editor of Die Waffen Nieder until 1899,
when it closed its doors, and then became a collaborator on
Die Friedens-Warte (The Peace Lookout), where she continued
her "Footnotes to Contemporary Affairs," which she had begun
in 1892.   Up until 1914 she kept her eye on the dangerous
game politicians were playing and in fact predicted the coming
tragedy.

     Her career was ever widening.   In the 1890s the Inter-
parliamentary Union, pressing for arbitration and disarmament, was developing into an authoritative agency.   The
peace societies were also fighting for international federation, arbitration, and disarmament.   But they lacked a political arena and had to restrict their activities to journalism
and propaganda.   Her nose to the wind, Bertha von Suttner
turned to international journalism.   Quickly she was recognized as the first woman political journalist of exceptional
quality.   Her articles appeared in Die Neue Freie Presse,
the Berliner Tagblatt, the Frankfurter Zeitung, and other
well-known newspapers.

     Now she began writing quite regularly to Nobel about
the peace movement.   When she asked him for a contribution
to her Austrian Peace Society, he sent a check.   But, perhaps forgetting that the peace movement had already announced
three concrete objectives, he indicated that it needed a "definite program" more than money.   Meanwhile the baroness
urged him to attend the fourth World Peace Conference in
Bern in 1892.   He spent less than one day at the congress,
but did invite the Suttners to visit him at his hotel by the
Lake of Zürich and to go sailing with him in his tiny aluminum motor boat.

     A few months later he wrote them that he intended to
found a prize for the person who accomplished the most for
the cause of peace.   In Nobel's original version the prize
would be awarded only once every five years in line with his

first belief that it should not be given more than six times.
For, he reasoned, if in 30 years the world had not mended
its ways, there would be a reversion to barbarism. The
Peace award, with the original ideas somewhat altered, was
written into Nobel's will in 1893 and again into his last will
in 1895.

After the Bern congress Bertha von Suttner helped establish the German Peace Society in Berlin. That was only
one of her innumerable projects.   She was almost overactive.
In a reckless outpouring of energy she was writing, organizing, lecturing, and attending conferences of the peace societies and the Interparliamentary Union, where she showed
such a special talent for fostering harmony and reconciliation
that the Scandinavians dubbed her "conciliatrix." In the process she became a great propagandist.   Once when Fridtjof
Nansen was scheduled to speak in Vienna about his polar ex-
pedition, she persuaded him to include some words on behalf
of the peace movement and thus won quite a few cohorts.
On many other occasions the Baroness von Suttner cleverly
slipped in unexpected peace overtures. She herself had become an increasingly effective lecturer although some critics
complained that "Peace Bertha" did not know when to stop
talking.   In recognition of her organizational talents Passy
called her "notre général en chef."

The Suttners were childless, but often, especially back
at Harmannsdorf, out of public scrutiny, they treated each
other with the playful abandon of children. Artur accompanied her everywhere, but almost like a prince consort remained discreetly in the background.   Faithfully they attended
every International Peace Congress except the one in Chicago
in 1893.

Probably Bertha reached her high point at the Peace
Congress at The Hague in 1899.   It was called by the young
Russian czar, Nicholas II.   Artur had brought her the good
tidings one August day in 1898 as she sat in the summer-
house at Harmannsdorf.   Carrying the mail to her he
shouted, "I am bringing the most magnificent, the most sur-
prising news today!" After reading and discussing the official invitation printed in their newspaper, the von Suttners
felt they were living one of the "loveliest hours" of their
lives.

They worked hard for the Czar's manifesto, arranging
public meetings, forming committees, and propagandizing

through newspaper articles. Bertha hailed it as "the finest
goal which fate could have offered me after my hopes and
longings over the years." Arriving at The Hague on May 16,
she wrote in her diary: "The city steeped in the magic of
spring. Radiant sunshine. Lilac perfumes in the cool air."

At the formal opening session the Dutch foreign minister greeted the representatives of 26 governments, almost all
of them members of the nobility. In one of the only 15 places
reserved for journalists sat Bertha von Suttner, the only
woman in the hall. Eventually she would write a book, Die
Haager Friedenskonferenz, Tagebuchblätter (Journal of The
Hague Peace Conference), 1911. The proceedings were held
behind closed doors, but the pacifists, who could not participate in the conference itself, tried to make personal contacts
with the delegates. When Bertha von Suttner was not attending
the sessions, she and Artur were busy entertaining and being
entertained by old and new friends of peace. Occupying a
position halfway between press and society, Bertha kept a
salon, which became the center of the peace lobby. Always
she sought out the most important delegates, believing that
the peace idea could best be realized if the governing classes
were influenced.

She had expected the Conference to be "the fulfillment
of a lofty, ambitious dream" and to mark the beginning of a
new era of peace. Yet while it was still in session the
British Parliament was voting Ł4 million for the Boer War.
Only a short while before, China and Japan had gone to war,
the Turks had murdered thousands of Armenians, Italy had
taken arms against Abyssinia, Britain and the United States
had threatened to fight over Venezuela, and the Spanish-
American War had broken out. The Conference was hardly
over when Western nations began taking retaliatory measures
against the Boxer Rebellion in China. Bertha von Suttner
always maintained, however, that the fight against war should
be relentlessly pursued under just such conditions. In 1899
she was happy to point to some recent small successes in
mediation-arbitration between the United States and Britain,
France and Brazil, and Argentina and Chile.

Like many other pacifists, Bertha was sadly disappointed
in the compromises and watering down of ideas at The Hague.
On July 4, "a melancholy day," she confided to her diary:
"Cold, cold are all the hearts--cold is the draft that penetrates
through the rattling windows. I am chilled to the bone!" She
was also disturbed that the Conference, which accepted the

Red Cross Geneva Convention and set up additional rules
about war wounded and prisoners of war, should be so concerned with "humanizing" war rather than with abolishing it
altogether.

She was, however, pleased by the work of the arbitration committee, which discussed four ways to settle international conflicts--mediation, diplomacy, investigative commissions, and organized arbitration.   Most of all she felt encouraged by the decision to set up a permanent international
arbitration court at The Hague.   Later she wrote many articles and organized many meetings to popularize the idea of
such a court.   The Baroness von Suttner lived to see the
Hague Tribunal receive its own Palace of Justice in 1913
through the generosity of Andrew Carnegie.   Ahead lay its
most significant role, following World War I, in resolving
various disputes under international law.

After the Hague conference Bertha von Suttner plunged
into public relations activities and turned out scores of
pamphlets.   Her diary indicates though that she found life at
Harmannsdorf somewhat boring if not disquieting.   The quarry
business there was going from bad to worse.   Artur, who
controlled the family's affairs after his father's death in
1898, lived constantly in fear of bankruptcy and of having to
sell the family acres.   The Suttners worked themselves to
the limit and always against time in an attempt to save the
estate.

That strain was complicated by a brief period of jealousy when Bertha was afraid that Artur was showing more
than an avuncular interest in his young and beautiful niece,
Marie Luise, with whom he took walks in the castle park.
It was, however, a trifling experience, soon forgotten.

Then on December 10, 1902, the sixth anniversary of
Nobel's death, Bertha von Suttner's world broke in two.   After
having been ill off and on for a year, Artur died.   The free
thinker Bertha drew a large cross on the last written leaf of
her diary.   On the new page she wrote, "Have lost everything!"
Soon though she pulled herself together and worked on as
Artur had urged her to do.   Things got worse at Harmannsdorf, and she moved to Vienna.

In December, 1905, the year Norway gained its independence from Sweden, the Baroness von Suttner could not
go to Kristiania to accept her Nobel Prize medal, diploma,

and check (which came at a fortuitous time) from the newly
elected King Haakon. She lay completely exhausted after lecture tours in 31 cities of the German Reich. At Wiesbaden
she refused at first to accept a telegram, forwarded from
Vienna, because of excess charges. Fortunately, she did
pay the amount and so received her formal notification from
the Norwegian Nobel Committee. In her diary for December
1 she wrote: "Sleepless night. Strange that it should bring
me despondency instead of joy. But it is a splendid thing.
Came to the decision not to travel to Kristiania. Not up to
it. Would probably suffer a breakdown in health." It especially pained her that Artur had not lived to see the day. A
month later she commented, "Silent and lonely tears for me,
despite my Nobel Prize, a lonely old fool."

Since December 10 fell on a Sunday, the Norwegian
Parliament was not in session. But to conform to the statutes, the Nobel Committee invited members of Parliament
to attend the inauguration of the new Norwegian Nobel Institute building, where the Peace award was announced.

Bertha von Suttner waited until spring to deliver the
lecture expected of every laureate. Introduced by Bjørnson,
she spoke on "The Evolution of the Peace Movement" to an
audience consisting of the King, Queen Maud, members of
the Norwegian Storting (Parliament), and distinguished guests.
She was dressed in black and her voice was husky with emotion as she talked slowly and concisely, using no gestures
or changes of facial expression. Her large clear eyes were
magnetic enough. Following her lecture, Jørgen Gunnarson
Lovland, Norway's foreign minister and chairman of the
Nobel Committee, gave a banquet for the Baroness and declared that her call "Lay down arms!" would be to her eternal honor.

After her triumph in Kristiania, Bertha von Suttner
continued to write and lecture on peace, moving easily from
workers' clubs to aristocratic circles. One newspaper commented that "she lisped on against war, clad in elegant
black, weighted down by gemstones, with an intriguing fan
in her hand, fine diction, and outstandingly good posture."
She wrote another sentimental novel, Der Menschheit Hoch-
gedanken (When Thoughts Will Soar), with a peace theme
and a plea for raising the status of women. She had, of
course, made it her life's work to get members of her sex
to understand they had a duty to fight for the cause of peace.

Nicholas II called a second Peace Congress at The
Hague in 1907, and again Bertha von Suttner attended. But
she was bitterly disappointed that the agreements dealt with
the limitations of war rather than its abolition. Likewise,
she became disillusioned with Theodore Roosevelt, who she
felt played an important role in the conference decision not
to stop the armaments race. She did not understand his
reasoning that any prohibition would be futile without a system of international police. In her Nobel lecture she had
quoted the American President: "It remains our clear destiny to strive in every practical way to bring nearer the
time when the sword shall not be the arbiter among nations."
But she had also commented, "Although the supporters of
the existing structure of society, which accepts war, come to
a peace conference prepared to modify the nature of war, they
are basically trying to keep the present system intact."

As it turned out, Roosevelt would follow her as a
Peace prizewinner, being honored for his successful negotiations to end the Russo-Japanese War. Just before she won
her award Bertha had talked seriously with him in Washington, D. C., when she went to the United States to attend the
Peace Congress in Boston. She returned in 1912 for a six-
month lecture tour across the country. This time she was
greeted with great enthusiasm in over 50 cities and towns
and enjoyed being feted. The New York Evening World expressed surprise at her appearance--"And yet this powerful
lady looks just the kindly, sensible hausfrau, with soft, simply done gray hair, plump unwrinkled face, and a motherly
smile." She was received by President Taft, William Jennings
Bryan, and J. Pierpont Morgan, and was named a member of
the advisory committee of the Carnegie Peace Foundation.
The Carnegie connection resulted in a welcome gift, a personal letter from Andrew Carnegie informing her that from
January 1, 1913, she was to receive a monthly pension from
the foundation to guarantee her a worry-free old age.

The "powerful lady" continued to correspond with
famous statesmen and leaders and became a special friend
of Prince Albert of Monaco, who entertained her lavishly.
She was named honorary vice-president of the International
Peace Bureau in Bern. She played a prominent part in the
Anglo-German Friendship Committee formed at the 1905
Peace Congress. She wrote and lectured on behalf of the
International Club set up at the 1907 Hague Peace Conference.
Again and again, in her lectures she declared, "Europe is

one," implying that unity was the only way to prevent world
catastrophe. She also warned against using aviation as a military instrument.

As Bertha von Suttner grew older, she started showing
more than a touch of vanity. She needed little urging to catalogue the achievements that had won her international fame.
Along with the honors, however, came letters that tore her
heart, letters from Austrian military men eager for the approaching war. Many of them called her a traitor.

In between all her duties she studied her diaries and
wrote her <u>Memoiren</u> (Memoirs) in two volumes, finishing
them in 1908, but cutting them off in 1902, the year Artur
died. She added a euphoric supplementary chapter about her
first trip to America, writing that it was ahead of Europe in
its women's movement, its social movement, and in technical
arts, popular education, democratic spirit, and comforts.
In her second volume Bertha von Suttner declared quite simply of the peace cause that "it is the one important thing."

On her seventieth birthday, she was notified that she
had been named honorary president of the International Peace
Bureau. Two months later, already affected by her last illness, the Baroness von Suttner was honored at the Peace
Congress in The Hague as the "generalissimo" of the peace
movement. In the spring of 1914 she declined an operation
for a malignant tumor in her stomach. In May she still took
an active interest in preparations for the twenty-first Peace
Conference scheduled to be held in Vienna in September.
She died on June 21, 12 days after her seventy-first birthday and just one week before the archducal assassination at
Sarajevo. Her loyal maid Kathi and Alfred Fried remained
with her to the end, and Fried reported her last words as,
"Lay down arms. Tell that to many, many people."

Again and again she had warned that the rulers of
Europe were paving the way to catastrophe. She had noted
in her diary in April, 1913: "All in all it seems to me
that the great European disaster is well on its way. If so
many seeds have been sown, surely the weeds will sprout up
soon and surely so much stockpiled gunpowder will explode."

Despite her Cassandra role, Bertha von Suttner would
have been crushed by World War I. But had she lived beyond
it, she most certainly would have hailed the League of Nations
and the Kellogg-Briand Pact. Far beyond her time the Coun-

cil of Europe, the European Economic Community, and the United Nations were cast in her mold. As her biographer Beatrix Kempf suggests, all these can be traced back "to the early pioneering days, to the 'castles in the air' of a group of idealists in the nineteenth century, many of whom were in touch with Bertha von Suttner, if they were not her comrades-in-arms."

Like Artur, she was cremated at Gotha, and her ashes were left in the columbarium. The war put an end to any plans for a monument. Today the aristocratic face of Bertha von Suttner graces the Austrian 1000-schilling banknote. But outside her country she is undeservedly forgotten.

Peace and Bread
JANE ADDAMS

"War is not a natural activity for mankind," said Jane Addams. For this passionately held conviction she suffered deeply. Thus to her friends and admirers the Nobel Peace Prize was an especially deserved accolade. It came in 1931, eleven years after her name had first been proposed to the Nobel Committee. Actually in 1920, when Emily Greene Balch wanted to nominate her, many of her circle felt the time was not right. Vilified during the war, their saint was then being branded a Communist.

During the next decade her name was regularly submitted, and several campaigns were waged with her knowledge. By 1931, however, she had regained her position as one of America's great women. Unfortunately, that December she lay so ill in a Baltimore hospital, awaiting an operation for a tumor, that she could not attend the award ceremony. It shocked her followers that she had to share the Prize with Dr. Nicholas Murray Butler, the president of Columbia University in New York. Butler was a conservative internationalist, who had fully supported American entry into the war in 1917. Like his co-laureate, he was unable to sail to Oslo, and the American minister to Norway had to accept the shared Prize.

Halvdan Koht, member of the Nobel Committee and professor of history at the University of Oslo, was not afraid of emphasizing Jane Addams' wartime stand. "She held fast to the ideal of peace even during the difficult hours when other considerations and interests obscured it from her compatriots and drove them into conflict. Throughout the whole war she toiled for a peace that would not engender a new war, becoming, as she did so, the spokesman for the pacifist women of the world. Sometimes her views were at odds with public opinion both at home and abroad. But she never gave in, and in the end she regained the place of honor she had had before in the hearts of her people."

18

Jane Addams

The 71-year-old laureate recovered from her operation,
but was never strong enough to go to Oslo to give a Nobel
lecture. Her prize money, really a windfall in an early year
of the Depression, she donated entirely to the Women's International League for Peace and Freedom. She explained,
"The real cause of war is misunderstanding. Let this money
be spent in the cause of international understanding." In fact,
the Women's League and her beloved Hull-House were the
only words she wanted engraved after her own name on her
tombstone.

She was a slim, unknown young idealist of 29 when
she and her college friend, Ellen Gates Starr, founded Hull-
House in Chicago in 1899. She had become a heavyset, world-
famous idealist of 55 when the Women's League was founded
at the Hague Conference in 1915. Between that year and
1919, when the League was set up in permanent form, a scur-
rilous press made Jane Addams its constant target.

The young woman who came to Hull-House was a complex personality. She had had a happy rural childhood in
Cedarville, a prairie town in northern Illinois. Her father,
John Huy Addams, was a prosperous miller known for his
devotion to fine principles. A state senator for eight terms,
he became the friend of Abraham Lincoln in Springfield.
Once he showed his daughter a slim packet of letters all
bearing Lincoln's whimsical salutation, "My dear double-D'd
Addams."

In later years that daughter, Laura Jane, born September 6, 1860, would identify strongly with the prairie
President. The family soon dropped the name Laura in favor of Jane, which quickly became the diminutive Jenny.
When she was barely two years old, Jenny lost her mother.
Pretty Sarah Addams, born Weber, passed on to this youngest child her stout humanitarian instincts. In her loneliness
little Jenny was coddled and protected by three sisters, Mary,
Martha, and Alice, and a brother, James Weber. Another
reason for the spoiling was that tuberculosis of the spine left
her with a slight curvature. From then on the small, skinny,
gray-eyed girl walked a bit pigeon-toed and cocked her head
slightly to one side.

At eight Jenny acquired a stepmother, a sophisticated
widow named Anna Haldeman, who brought two more sons to
the Addams household. Harry later became a surgeon and
married Alice, and George, almost Jenny's exact age, be-

came her favorite playmate.   Later he showed romantic feelings she could not return.

Jenny was not precocious at school, but did well
enough.   The major influence in her life was her handsome
and imposing father, whom she adored.   Obeying his wishes,
she gave up her dream of attending Smith College and went
dutifully to nearby Rockford Seminary for Women.   Here she
bloomed as class president and editor of the school magazine.
In her twentieth year she spoke on "Bread Givers" at the
First Junior Exhibition of Rockford Seminary and luminously
charted the course her life was to take: "We then, the class
of 1881 ... are not trying to imitate our brothers in college;
we are not restless and anxious for things beyond us, we
simply claim the highest privileges of our time and avail ourselves of the best opportunities.   But while on the one hand,
as young women of the nineteenth century, we gladly claim
these privileges and proudly assert our independence, on the
other hand we still retain the old ideal of womanhood--the
Saxon lady whose mission it was to give bread unto her household.   So we have planned to be 'Bread-givers' throughout
our lives; believing that in labor alone is happiness, and that
the only true and honorable life is one filled with good works
and honest toil, we have planned to idealize our labor...."

At graduation she was the valedictorian.   She had
taken extra courses to qualify for a bachelor's degree, and
a year later when the seminary became Rockford College for
Women, she returned to collect her degree.

Like many others in that first generation of American
college women, eager to make something of their lives, but
a bit uncertain and easily discouraged, Jane went through a
period of ill health and depression once she was out of school.
No sooner had she recovered than her father died suddenly.
Despite her enormous heartache, she enrolled at the Women's
Medical College in Philadelphia.   But after a few months her
health broke down again.   Convinced by family and friends
that she could shed her depression if her back problem were
cured, she put herself under the care of her stepbrother
Harry Haldeman, who successfully operated on her.   For
some time she had to wear a brace.

During a trip to Europe in 1883-85 with her stepmother
and a party of friends she kept busy visiting cathedrals, studying foreign languages, and sopping up culture.   Then once in
London's East End, as part of a tourist group, she watched

with sinking heart the Saturday midnight auction of decaying
fruits and vegetables.   She would never forget the "two huge
masses of ill-clad people clamoring around two hucksters'
carts" or "the myriads of hands, empty, pathetic, nerveless
and workworn, showing white in the uncertain light of the
street, clutching forward for food which was already unfit
to eat. "   Nor would she forget the man who tore into a tossed
cabbage with his teeth and devoured it unwashed and uncooked.
For the next few weeks she was afraid to look down narrow
streets and alleys for fear they would show similar horrors.

During two frustrating winters in Baltimore with her
stepmother and two somewhat happier summers in Illinois
she kept looking for something to do with her life.   In 1888,
on another trip to Europe with Ellen Gates Starr, she found
the answer.   Gradually she had become convinced

>that it would be a good thing to rent a house in a
>part of the city where many primitive and actual
>needs are found, in which young women who had
>been given over too exclusively to study might re-
>store a balance of activity along traditional lines
>and learn of life from life itself; where they might
>try out some of the things they had been taught and
>put truth to 'the ultimate test of the conduct it dic-
>tates or inspires. '

Not really a new dream.   As a little girl, accompany-
ing her father to a nearby town, where he had business in a
mill close to the poorest quarter, Jenny had caught her first
sight of real squalor:

>I remember launching at my father the pertinent
>inquiry why people lived in such horrid little houses
>so close together, and that after receiving his ex-
>planation I declared with much firmness when I
>grew up I should, of course, have a large house,
>but it would not be built among the other large
>houses, but right in the midst of horrid little houses
>like these.

But in 1886 Jane Addams had not mentioned her plan
to anybody or done anything about it.   Then one day in Madrid she realized with horror that she had watched the killing
of five bulls and several horses with complete indifference
and had even endured the spectacle longer than anybody else
in her party.

I felt myself tried and condemned, not only by this
disgusting experience but by the entire moral situation which it revealed. It was suddenly made quite
clear to me that I was lulling my conscience by a
dreamer's scheme, that a mere paper reform had
become a defense for continued idleness, and that
I was making it a raison d'être for going on indefinitely with study and travel.... Nothing less
than the moral reaction following the experience at
a bull-fight had been able to reveal to me that so
far from following in the wake of a chariot of
philanthropic fire, I had been tied to the tail of
the veriest ox-cart of self-seeking.

Curiously, her letters at this time did not mention such a reaction, and it has been suggested that this account, written
for her autobiographical Twenty Years at Hull-House, may
have embellished the bullfight incident.

        With "stumbling and uncertainty" she told Ellen Starr
about her plan and just five years after first seeing the sear-
ing poverty of the East End went back to London to get suggestions from such prototypes as Toynbee Hall and the People's Palace. Toynbee Hall was a unique community of university men, who had settled in among the poor to bring
them recreation and clubs; and the People's Palace, a large
philanthropic institute for working people, had been inspired
by Walter Besant's novels, which Jane read. She was already
molded by the philosophies of John Ruskin and Leo Tolstoy.

        Influenced now by the social gospel movement, the
"mission side of London, " as she called it, she decided to
join a church so that her decision to found a settlement in
an immigrant section of Chicago would actually be a religious
commitment. Having already struggled with doctrinal difficulties and doubts, she found now that a religion of social
action demanded not professions of faith, but rather the wish
"to serve. " Soon after her return from Europe she was baptized at the Presbyterian Church in Cedarville, and 11 months
later she was a member in full standing.

        In September, 1889, Jane Addams and Ellen Starr
rented an old mansion at the corner of Halsted and Polk
streets in Chicago, the former home of a real estate millionaire, Charles Hull. Almost like brides they furnished
it with new pieces, "the photographs and other impedimenta
we had collected in Europe and with a few bits of family

mahogany. " Their goal was to provide a social center for
the impoverished immigrants who lived in crowded tenement
houses--Italians, Bohemians, Greeks, Poles, Irish, Germans,
Jews.   As the first settlement house in the city, and as one
of the first anywhere, Hull-House prospered immediately.
In time, despite some setbacks, it spread out in old English
buildings and grew to include a nursery, labor museum,
boys' club, working-girls' home, little theater, and discussion groups and classes in music and pottery.

A remarkable band of men and women gathered there
as residents, but Jane Addams was always top fiddle. She
was benevolent, saintly, conciliatory, but she kept herself a
rather formal and reserved figure, always "Miss Addams"
to the many, "Jane" to only a few.   There was another unusual side to her--that of shrewd businesswoman, expert
fundraiser and organizer, and public relations genius.   Without it Hull-House could never have prospered.

Almost from the beginning the innovative Jane Addams
concerned herself with social legislation and action.   During
her first 20 years in Chicago she led the movement to get
the first eight-hour law for working women, the first state
child labor law, housing reform, the first juvenile court,
and the Immigrants' Protection League, all landmarks of
social progress in the United States.   For a time she even
accepted an official post as garbage inspector for the Nineteenth Ward.

With the help of spirited colleagues like Julia Lathrop
and Florence Kelly, she also attacked the political corruption
and evils of city life and began speaking to many civic groups.
She was described as a "smallish, dark-faced women, gentle
of manner and soft of voice....   She is slightly stooped as
she stands with her hands clasped behind her in a way touch-
ingly childish, looking out at her audience....   Her face is
sad though the eyes are luminous and the lips adapt themselves readily to smiles. "   Then, trying to reach an even
larger audience, she rewrote her lectures and published
them in popular magazines.

In 1895, Hull-House Maps and Papers described the
conditions under which 19 nationalities lived in the Nineteenth
Ward.   A series of Jane Addams' articles came out in 1902
as Democracy and Social Ethics.   In 1909, in The Spirit of
Youth and the City Streets, she dwelt on juvenile delinquency.
A year later she wrote Twenty Years at Hull-House, the

record of her great social experiment in the slums. It became an American classic. Next in A New Conscience and an Ancient Evil Jane Addams developed her thesis that economic needs drove girls to prostitution. Some of her followers were shocked that she would even write about the subject.

All this time Hull-House was making her internationally minded and concerned with peace. As a child she had seen her father, who had vague Quaker leanings, recruit a regiment to fight in the Civil War. At college she had never been troubled by thoughts of war. Even on her trips to Europe as a young woman she was excited by military pomp and display. Suddenly several experiences turned her into a confirmed pacifist. Deploring the talk about American imperialism, she sickened at the Spanish-American War. She read William James and caught up his remarks on sublimating and redirecting human drives. By 1904 she was ready to give three formal speeches at the Peace Conference in Boston. She visited Leo Tolstoy at Yasnaya Polyana in 1906 and listened to his talk against war. In 1907 she published New Ideals of Peace, giving credit to James for suggesting a moral equivalent to war and the military spirit. Here she idealistically assumed that the new individualism and growth of democracy and woman suffrage would make war impossible. Chiding her for her basic idea that there must be a substitute for war, Theodore Roosevelt called her "foolish Jane Addams."

In spite of those remarks she was ready in 1912 to second his nomination as the Progressive Party candidate for president and to campaign for the program of social reform he promised. But when as a convention delegate she voted for a platform that advocated building two warships a year, she "found it very difficult to swallow two battleships." Roosevelt, though the recipient of a Nobel Peace Prize in 1906, had offended many pacifists with his militarism. The Baroness Bertha von Suttner for one accused Jane Addams of joining an anti-peace organization, which favored "the ancient and barbaric system of justice called war." Perhaps the Baroness did not know that at the very same time she was campaigning for the Progressive Party, Jane Addams was lecturing about peace under the auspices of the Carnegie Foundation.

By 1914 Jane Addams was the best known and most influential woman in America. The first news of the war,

she wrote, brought "a basic sense of desolation, of suicide,
of anachronism ... to thousands of men and women who had
come to consider war a throwback in a scientific sense."
Now she was pushed into even more decisive action by the
arrival of two militant peace agitators and suffragettes,
Rosika Schwimmer of Hungary and Emmeline Pethick-Lawrence
from England. After Mrs. Pethick-Lawrence visited Chicago,
the Emergency Federation of Peace Forces was founded with
Jane Addams as chairman. The new group tried to enlist
all peace forces to exert pressure on the belligerents.

But soon there were greater things to come. Carrie
Chapman Catt, president of the International Suffrage Alliance,
asked Jane Addams to join her in calling for a peace conference of women in Washington, D. C., on January 10, 1915.
With her formidable national reputation and prestige, Miss
Addams was a natural choice for chairperson. From this
peace conference came the Women's Peace Party, which put
out a platform of planks foreshadowing many of President
Woodrow Wilson's international programs. The various resolutions and amendments, which Jane Addams managed with
her usual parliamentary skills, called for liberal peace terms,
the establisnment of a permanent international court, a permanent international conference, and the representation of
women in national and international life. It also prohibited
the transfer of territory without a people's consent. The
most notable plank contained a plea for "continuous mediation," first suggested by the volatile Mme. Schwimmer and
worked out by Dr. Julia Grace Wales.

In spite of its chairperson's fame, the conference was
given little publicity. But within a few weeks the women
popped into the headlines. Dr. Aletta Jacobs, a noted suffragette and one of the first women physicians in Holland,
asked the Women's Peace Party to send delegates to an international congress of women to be held at The Hague. This
congress was the offspring of the International Suffrage Alliance, which had a strong pacifist bias in its leadersnip.
After the German branch of the ISA had withdrawn its invitation for an international congress in Berlin in June, 1915,
and Mrs. Catt canceled the international meeting altogether,
Dr. Jacobs jumped into action.

On her party's behalf Jane Addams accepted the invitation to come to The Hague. With her on the Noordam
sailed Emily Balch and 40 other women. Altogether, 1500
women from 12 countries made the journey. It was, Jane

Addams said, "little short of an act of heroism." Because
of her enormous prestige, Jane Addams, motherly and conciliatory, was chosen chairperson. The "continuous mediation"
plan formed the focus of the Women's Congress, which resolved to ask the neutral countries to create a conference of
neutral nations to offer continuous mediation while fighting
raged on the Western front.

Rosika Schwimmer succeeded in getting the group to
pass a resolution that the conference resolutions be carried
to the belligerent and neutral nations. Doubtful at first, Jane
Addams finally decided to participate and with Dr. Jacobs
and Rosa Genoni of Italy went the rounds of war capitals
of London, Berlin, Vienna, Rome, and Paris. On the whole,
the little group met with much friendliness, the warmest reception occurring in Vienna. Meanwhile a second delegation
left for the Scandinavian countries and Russia. In October
the envoys reported that many statesmen had welcomed their
mission. Most importantly, within diplomatic circles the
calling of a neutral conference for mediation was being seriously discussed.

To carry on the work of the new international women's
peace movement the conference at The Hague set up an International Committee of Women for Permanent Peace with Jane
Addams as president and Dr. Jacobs and Mme. Schwimmer
as vice-presidents. The central office was set up in Amsterdam with Dr. Jacobs taking on the additional job of secretary. The International Committee also included members
from the several national committees that delegates to the
Hague Congress had gone back to establish in their own countries. The Women's Peace Party became the American National Committee.

When Jane Addams came home, she immediately
dropped a bombshell. At the end of a speech in Carnegie
Hall she remarked that to the soldiers war "was much more
anachronistic than to the elderly statesmen who were primarily responsible for [their] presence in the trenches...."
Writing about the incident six years later, she said, "It was
the latter statement which was my undoing, for in illustration
... I said that in practically every country we had visited, we
had heard a certain type of young soldier say that it had been
difficult for him to make the bayonet charge (enter into actual
hand to hand fighting) unless he had been stimulated; that the
English soldiers had been given rum before such a charge,
the Germans ether and that the French were said to use
absinthe."

Although American soldiers had not yet gone to war,
her statements enraged editorial writers around the country,
who believed that Jane Addams had challenged the invincible
American myth that war was glorious and patriotic. The
vehement attacks had something to do with the fact that she
was an important national symbol.

The transformation from saint to villain was a trau-
matic experience for Jane Addams in her fifty-fifth year.
Accustomed to praise and adoration, she did her best work
when surrounded by disciples like her lifelong friend, Mary
Rozet Smith. But now even Mary gave her little support.
In August, Jane Addams spoke with President Wilson to
little avail. Then, to add to her troubles, she fell ill with
a kidney and bladder infection.

Even as she was being reviled in the American papers,
the national committees of the International Committee of
Women for Permanent Peace began enlisting popular support
for a conference of neutrals to press for continuous mediation.
They saw President Wilson as its presiding officer. Meanwhile Rosika Schwimmer, once more in the United States, was
ready with an alternative proposal that the neutral conference
consist of lay experts rather than government representatives.

Having failed with Wilson, she enlisted the support of
Henry Ford for the alternative plan, and he chartered the
Oscar II to sail for Europe. Somehow the real purpose became lost in his vow to get the boys out of the trenches by
Christmas. Though somewhat distrustful of the mission,
Jane Addams felt it might be a necessary symbolic action
and decided to sail with Ford and his party. Then a sudden
illness changed her plans. When the Germans resumed unrestricted submarine warfare, Ford withdrew and canceled
his financial backing for a neutral conference. Nonetheless,
such a conference, composed of lawyers, parliamentarians,
economists, and civic officials was organized in Stockholm
and did much useful work. Even though she did not sail on
the Peace Ship, Jane Addams' name was linked with its mis-
adventures, and she was ridiculed like Ford. Still in poor
health, she saw Wilson again in January, 1916, and noted
that he had read the resolutions she had given to him six
months earlier.

She took new hope in December when he asked the
belligerents to state their peace terms. In January, 1917,
he made his famous "peace without victory" speech, calling

for an end to the war before any side had achieved victory
and for the formation of an international organization to keep
the peace. Jane Addams was pridefully aware that his speech
repeated many of the proposals of the Hague conference.

Three months later, however, the United States was
at war. Jane Addams saw many of her pacifist friends bow
to the inevitable. She herself was now forced to make the
most agonizing decision of her life. Because she was known
for her spirit of compromise and mediation, she might have
been expected to join her friends in accepting the war declaration. But she chose to remain a pacifist. "My temperament
and habit had always kept me rather in the middle of the
road," she wrote five years later, "in politics as well as in
social reform. But now I was pushed far toward the left on
the subject of war." Boldly she declared, "That the U. S.
has entered the war has not changed my view of the invalidity
of war as a method of settlement of social problems a particle,
and I can see no reason why one should not say what one believes in time of war as in time of peace."

Her stand left her lonely and terribly depressed. Hate
letters poured in, newspapers reviled her, she was even kept
under the surveillance of the Department of Justice. Invitations to speak, of course, fell off. Nobody wanted to hear a
pacifist. But by early 1918 she was on the platform again.
Under the auspices of Herbert Hoover's Department of Food
Administration, she began asking Americans to conserve and
produce more food. She fully approved of the program.
This time though Rosika Schwimmer and other committed
pacifists criticized her for supporting the American government's war effort.

After the Armistice, Jane Addams started putting the
women's peace movement together again. The delegates to
The Hague in 1915 had agreed to hold their next conference
at the same time as the peace conference of the warring nations. With Versailles in mind, they met in Zürich in May,
1919. On the way Jane Addams stopped in France to look for
the grave of her nephew, killed in the Argonne.

In Zürich the women formed themselves into a permanent body called the Women's International League for
Peace and Freedom. As one of the delegates remarked,
"Only in freedom is permanent peace possible." The creed
perfectly exemplified Jane Addams' own philosophy: "To
unite women in all countries who are opposed to any kind of

war, exploitation and oppression, and who work for universal disarmament and for the solution of conflicts by the recognition of human solidarity, by conciliation and arbitration, by world cooperation, and by the establishment of social, political, and economic justice for all without distinction of sex, race, class, or creeds."

Jane Addams was elected international president with Emily Balch as secretary-treasurer. Almost immediately the Zürich conference sent formal envoys with recommendations to the statesmen conferring at Versailles. Among the selected delegates was Jane Addams, who tried to see President Wilson again. But she managed to get only as far as the inscrutable Col. Edward House and left him with the resolutions passed by the Zürich conference. In Paris, however, Herbert Hoover helped her organize a trip to Germany to bring food to starving children. Some time later the new League issued an overwhelming indictment of the Treaty of Versailles.

When Jane Addams came home, she continued urging audiences to send more food to European children. But when she mentioned German children, she was accused of being pro-German and unpatriotic. Within the ranks of the American Legion, the Daughters of the American Revolution, and the Ku Klux Klan she was considered a dangerous woman. Frightened by the excesses of the Russian Revolution, the United States was entrapped in a giant Red scare, and all who had opposed the war suddenly found themselves labeled Bolsheviks.

In 1919 Archibald Stevenson of the Military Intelligence Bureau produced a list of 62 names of persons who he claimed held dangerous, destructive, and anarchic sentiments and who were connected with pro-German pacifist movements before April, 1917. Heading the list was Jane Addams. Stevenson subsequently convinced the New York Legislature to investigate "radicalism" full-scale, and the Lusk Report, mostly written by Stevenson, was the result. Again Jane Addams' name figured prominently in a welter of half-truths and whole falsehoods. The vicious attacks continued when she spoke out against the United States Justice Department's raids, arrests, and deportation of aliens and radicals, and her name was frequently included in the infamous spider-web charts, a network of lines linking various prominent Americans with the Communists.

Fortunately, the flourishing Hull-House and the Wom-
en's League could console her and keep her busy. On behalf
of Hull-House she continued to be a shrewd fund-raiser and
propagandist.   She was too far away from the international
headquarters in Geneva to run the League's daily operations
and did her best work at the international conferences in
Vienna, Washington, Dublin, and Prague, where she was
hailed as their "guiding spirit." As one of its first acts,
the Women's League issued a constructive criticism of the
League of Nations Covenant.   Afterwards it lobbied constantly
to influence League of Nations policies.

Philosophically, the Women's League wanted to remove the causes of war rather than to allay the sufferings
caused by war.   Actually, it helped children and refugees
and set up many rescue missions.   And throughout the years
of Jane Addams' presidency the League worked to build a
more rational society by pushing nonviolent methods to change
the economic order.   Meanwhile there were constructive proposals in times of international crisis, campaigns for disarmament, and programs of reconciliation.   Unfortunately it
had only limited resources to carry on its political and economic studies and policy formulations.   So Jane Addams generously guaranteed a sum of $500 every month.

In the beginning the Women's League was rather solidly
upper-middle class.   Its members were some of the most
brilliant and talented women in the United States and Europe.
Most were professionals--doctors, lawyers, professors, journalists, social workers, reformers, and public officials.
Many were daring social innovators.   Jane Addams' harmo-
nizing genius worked constantly as divergences sprang up
among national sections and among strong personalities; the
members professed different faiths, for example, and some,
no faith at all.   But under their gentle and soft-spoken international president they seemed drawn together in a spiritual
fellowship.

After a heart attack in 1926, Jane Addams had recur-
ring problems.   Because of poor health she resigned as president in 1929, but was immediately named honorary international president.   From then on, unable to attend international
conferences, she contented herself with raising money through
her busy correspondence.   During the fast-changing 1920s,
while keeping her home at Hull-House, she went on writing
books.   An account of women's work for peace, Peace and
Bread in Time of War, came out in 1922.   She also finished

The Second Twenty Years at Hull-House, which covered her
life from 1909 to 1929. In 1909 Yale had given her the first
honorary degree it had ever awarded a woman, and other
degrees had followed in 1914. Now they streamed in on her
again.

On the heels of the American tributes came the Nobel
Prize on December 10, 1931. As she lay in a Baltimore
hospital, Halvdan Koht was saying in Oslo, "... Jane Addams
combines all the best feminine qualities which will help us
to develop peace on earth." A bit earlier he had commented,
"To an American an ideal is not just a beautiful mirage but
a practical reality the implementation of which is every man's
duty."

Just the year before the "Bread-giver" had written,
"In my long advocacy of peace I had consistently used one
line of appeal, contending that peace is no longer an abstract
dogma; that a dynamic peace is found in the internationalism
promoted by the men of all nations who are determined upon
the abolition of degrading poverty, disease and ignorance,
with their resulting inefficiency and tragedy. I believed that
peace was not merely an absence of war, but the nurture of
human life and that in time this nurture would do away with
war as a natural process."

In 1932 she gave a very specific recipe: "... peaceful methods substituted for war in the settlement of international disputes should be increased and strengthened....
[T]hese peaceful methods should be given a fair chance invariably to succeed, even in grave crises, by the final abolition of armaments."

Like Julia Lathrop and Florence Kelly, many of her
close circle of settlement pioneers were now dying. The
death of Mary Rozet Smith, her closest companion for over
forty years, was a tremendous blow. In 1935, Jane Addams
and Grace Abbott wrote a biography of Julia Lathrop, who
became the head of the Children's Bureau at its formation in
1912.

In the spring of 1935 Jane Addams attended the
League's twentieth anniversary celebration. Actually it
turned out to be in her honor, and Eleanor Roosevelt, the
First Lady, sat among those applauding her. Ten days later
the honoree was taken ill. She underwent surgery, but died
of cancer on May 21.

At the funeral service held in the Hull-House court-
yard, the Dean of the Chicago Chapel said, "If you would see
her monuments, look around you." She was buried in the
family plot at Cedarville.

Perhaps Emily Balch paid the most moving tribute of
all in a personal recollection some eight years later: "She
was so utterly unlike anyone else that I ever knew--so utterly
real and first-hand; so subtle, so simple and direct, so free
from any preoccupation with self, as free from asceticism as
from self-indulgence; full of compassion without weakness or
sentimentality (though she grew up in a sentimental generation), loving merriment while carrying the world's woes in
her heart--both the many which pressed upon her in immediate
personal shape at Hull-House and those of the nameless, un-
seen millions whose fates are part of our own personal fates.
A great statesman, a great writer, one of the world's rarest
spirits, how can I or anyone evoke her?"

Holy Fire Within
EMILY GREENE BALCH

On December 10, 1946, one of Oslo's leading newspapers carried the headline, SHE HAS WITHIN HER THE
HOLY FIRE. It was echoing what Gunnar Jahn, chairman of
the Nobel Committee, had said that afternoon about Emily
Greene Balch: "She has taught us that the reality we seek
must be earned by hard and unrelenting toil in the world in
which we live, but she has taught us more: that exhaustion
is unknown and defeat only gives fresh courage to the man
whose soul is fired by the sacred flame."

The Prize was the crown for 33 years of pioneering
for peace. Unfortunately, like Bertha von Suttner and Jane
Addams, this third Peace lady laureate was too ill to attend
the Nobel ceremony. On hand, however, was her co-laureate,
81-year-old John Raleigh Mott, an international Christian
leader and chairman of the International Missionary Council.

At 81 herself, Emily came to the Norwegian capital
in 1948 to deliver her Nobel lecture, "Toward Human Unity
or Beyond Nationalism," the theme of her life work. It was
a woman of immensely youthful and courageous spirit who
told her distinguished audience, "We must remember that
nothing can be woven out of threads that all run the same
way.... An unchallenged belief or idea is on the way to
death and meaninglessness."

This pioneer pacifist, who was to be filled with holy
fire, was born January 8, 1867, in Jamaica Plain, a Boston
suburb. Her mother's sister, Catherine Porter Noyes, made
the following notation for that day: "Little Emily was born
at about seven in the evening. Nice dark hair and a tolerable
face." A third child, she was named at once for Emily
Greene, one of Mrs. Balch's bridesmaids. Of old New England stock on both sides, Emily grew up in a close-knit family
with four sisters--Annie, Elizabeth, Alice, Maidie--and a

Emily G. Balch

brother, Francis. Two sisters died in infancy, Catie at ten
months and Ellie, at three.

Their father, Francis Vergnies Balch, a man of delicate health, was a forceful and distinguished lawyer. A
friend was to comment later that from him Emily inherited
her two most salient traits, intellectual penetration and exquisite courtesy. He had married his first cousin, Ellen
Maria Noyes, lovingly described by Emily: "Quick-tempered,
deeply loving, a fascinating personality. No wonder my father
loved her as he did.... She was the center of my life and
its chief influence as long as she lived."

The household included several lively Irish maids and
Catherine Porter Noyes. "Auntie," who had once gone south
to teach children of the liberated Negroes to read, also
taught Emily. Eventually the nearsighted, plain-looking little
girl fell in love with books. During her childhood the family
moved to progressively larger and more pleasant houses,
from Lowder's Lane to Burroughs Street to Prince Street.
"Mine was a simple, happy suburban home," Emily wrote
long afterward. "Grass underfoot and a sky overhead were
part of my birthright."

She attended private schools in Jamaica Plain and in
Boston. Then at 13 she was enrolled in another Boston
school run by the remarkable Miss Ireland, who infected her
pupils with various enthusiasms. Emily was still a pupil
there in 1884 when her mother died. "I think I had no jealousy," Emily once remarked, "but I always wanted more of
her than I could have as one of a nursery full of children."
She always remembered as one of the happiest periods of
her life those weeks when she was quarantined with her
mother for scarlet fever. She was only ten, and she had
Nelly Balch's undivided attention.

While family and friends mourned deeply, one of Mrs.
Balch's friends urged the 17-year-old Emily to enjoy her
youth, go to parties, meet young men. "This," Emily commented later, "was beyond me." A year later, to soften his
daughter's intense grief, Francis Balch sent her with friends
on her first trip abroad, to Sicily, Italy, Switzerland, Belgium, Holland, England, and Scotland.

Always considered brilliant, Emily entered the newly
founded Bryn Mawr College in 1886. There she joined a
circle of gifted girls that included Alys Pearsall Smith and

Alice Gould. On her twenty-first birthday she noted, "I
should like to be ... much more careful in personal habits
and manners, including buttons of all sorts. " In 1889 she
was an outstanding member of the first graduating class.

For a time she had concentrated on literature. Then
in her senior year she took up economics. At this point
she was more influenced by books than by people. Literary
revelations of bad labor conditions distressed her, especially
Walter Besant's novel, All Sorts and Conditions of Men, an
account of London's seamy East End.

After graduation the calm young intellectual with her
"noble brow" was awarded the first Bryn Mawr European
Fellowship for a year of study abroad. The faculty had recommended her to the trustees as "a woman of unusual ability,
of extraordinary beauty of moral character, of great discre-
tion and balance of judgment, very gifted. " Accompanied by
a lively and pretty school friend, Lena Fabens, she settled
in Paris. As a child the novelist, Dorothy Canfield Fisher,
saw her there. Long afterwards she wrote down her memory
of "Mees Balshe": "She was a tall, slim girl in her early
twenties, comely with youth, with a magnificent smooth forehead, and gleaming young hair, which she wore in classic
simplicity, not tortured into the frizzes, then fashionable.
Her great eyes were clear, intelligent, calm as few young
eyes ever are. She dressed simply and unobtrusively. "

By the time Emily left for home she had become dissatisfied with her research on public assistance to the poor
in France. She complained it had been done with secondary
sources. She had never visited a slum or even a pawn shop.
Her perplexity lasted only until she decided to do social work.
Ultimately it was to lead her to mingle with prisoners, prostitutes, paupers, and strikers, all "less privileged" than she.
"At least I had the sense to be dissatisfied and seek actual
contact with the problems I had read of in books, " she said.
She wanted to be "of use"--a fundamental yearning that came
to motivate her life.

Her first job came as an apprentice to Charles Birt-
well, a zealous social pioneer and shaper of the Boston Children's Aid Society. Remembering the "comfort, plenty, and
essential security" of her childhood, Emily realized with a
shock that "these things were not universal. " In 1892 she
first met up with Jane Addams at the Summer School of Applied Ethics at Plymouth, Massachusetts. That winter she

was part of a little group that organized Denison House, a
Boston settlement, trying to improve the sweatshop conditions
in which underpaid girls worked. She also served as its temporary headworker. About this time she joined the Federal
Labor Union under the American Federation of Labor. Already Emily was dressing "in such a style as would be free
from any differentiation of social class. A sister complained
that I said I wanted to dress so that anyone might suppose I
was the cook. "

     Before long, however, Emily decided on a different
career--college teaching. As she put it, "I gradually became
dissatisfied with my philanthropic efforts and decided that
the point of leverage was in teaching social-economic subjects. "
To prepare herself she spent a semester at the Harvard An-
nex (later Radcliffe College) and one quarter at the University
of Chicago. Next she stayed for a happy and fruitful year at
the University of Berlin, where she became fast friends with
the beautiful Mary Kingsbury. On spring mornings the two
young women liked to sit in the Tiergarten reading Kant and
"tiring the sun with talking. " They came home by way of
London, and waving press passes primly walked into the Internationalist Socialist Workers and Trade Union Congress, the
last of the huge international social and labor congresses.
Emily also visited Toynbee Hall and was shocked at the gin-
soaked squalor of the East End.

     Sailing to New York, she met a Wellesley professor,
Katherine Coman, who offered her a half-time job in the economics department, mostly reading student papers. Emily
jumped at the offer. "I saw that after being supported by
my father till nearly thirty it was time that I ceased to be
an expense to him. " Still she continued to live at home as
Francis Balch wished.

     By the second semester she was teaching a class. In
1900 she was asked to set up a sociology course. Said Emily
long afterwards, "I think I felt that if I did not know what a
course in sociology should cover neither did anyone else. "
Thirteen years later she was named head of the department
of economics and sociology. Also on the Wellesley faculty
was Katharine Lee Bates, the author of "America the Beautiful, " who became Emily's close friend.

     Meanwhile in 1898 Francis Balch had died, leaving
Emily to write to one of his friends: "I feel as if I were

missing him now so much in the whole tone of my life; it was having the standard pitch (or a human approximation to it) constantly struck so that one kept regaining what one had lost. I constantly find myself below this, and it is harder to get right again."

In the classroom this crisp and angular spinster was a remarkably lucid teacher. But sometimes she appeared absent-minded and unsystematic. She was one of a new breed of college teachers, who participated in what they tried to teach. The strong-minded Miss Balch always insisted that her students could make individual judgments only by combining on-the-spot investigation with library research.

During her Wellesley years she also worked for women's suffrage and against racial prejudice. Frequently she left the campus to serve on arbitration panels or on state and municipal commissions dealing with industrial relations and immigration. For relaxation from all these duties Emily liked to go on long country walks. In spite of her myopia she was always watching for wild flowers and birds. She had learned from her father, "a passionate lover of botany" and a student of Asa Gray. And she had a gift for the unexpected. Students and faculty would remember that sometimes the spare Professor Balch sent them into fits of laughter by dancing a spirited Highland fling.

In 1903 she helped found the Women's Labor Union League to organize women wageearners into trade unions agitating for decent working conditions and fair pay. Here, as at Denison House, Emily Balch worked closely with Mary Morton Kehew, a wealthy member of the "Boston aristocracy of goodness and public spirit," who pioneered in worker education and social reform that spread from Massachusetts across the country. Emily called her the "greatest social statesman I have ever known." In 1913 she and Mrs. Kehew served on the Massachusetts Minimum Wage Commission, which under Emily Balch's chairmanship drafted the first minimum wage law in the country.

To the Wellesley curriculum Emily Balch had added a course on immigration. It came to be her special field. By 1904 she decided to use a sabbatical leave for a comprehensive study of Slavic immigration to the United States. She wanted to base it on firsthand inquiries. First she visited Slavic colonies in Pennsylvania, New York, Michigan, Nebraska, and Texas. During a brief stay at a Colorado mining camp

near the Oklahoma border she had her first and only proposal.
A lonely miner, not Slavic, invited her for a long walk.   At
one point they sat down to admire the view.   Suddenly he
slipped his arm around her waist and asked her to marry
him.   Quietly and gently Emily told him she was a Wellesley
professor.   Then she mentioned her salary.   He had nothing
more to say.

Emily spent most of 1905 in Austria-Hungary.   "The
study of the Slavic world is full of fascination," she wrote.
She brought back a fine collection of brightly embroidered
textiles in which she took great pride.   In Prague she became
friends with Thomas Masaryk, then a college professor, and
his American-born wife, Charlotte.   When Masaryk came to
the United States in 1917 to plead the cause of Czech independence, he and his daughter Olga were guests in Emily's
home in Jamaica Plain.

In Prague, too, she saw a starving man fumbling with
bare fingers in an icy ash barrel.   It was one of many inci-
dents that led her to become a Socialist.   She accepted her
reappointment at Wellesley "only on condition of the president's knowing this."   She added, "It will lead to some misunderstanding, of course, but I hope to some better understanding too."   After World War I, however, she stopped
calling herself a Socialist because the word had too many
Marxist connotations.   Besides, she felt that labels "are terribly obliterative of vital shades of difference and in general
suit only simple situations."

Our Slavic Fellow Citizens appeared in 1910.   As
Emily's biographer, Mercedes M. Randall, says, "it interpreted with rare insight, sympathy, and humility the much
depreciated Slavic immigration.   It served to refute the pre-
vailing assumption that an undiluted old English stock was
indispensable to the American experiment in democracy."
Among other things, it inspired Willa Cather, who was interested in Bohemian immigrant farmers, to invite Emily to
lunch.

The busy life of this Wellesley professor and civic
worker gave promise of going on indefinitely.   But World
War I broke out and pushed Emily Balch toward a third career,
working for peace.   Actually, all along she had been sympathetic toward peace movements and had closely followed the
two big peace conferences at The Hague.   In fact, her social
work and international outlook could not make her anything

but a pacifist. In January, 1915, she attended the Washington, D. C., conference that led to the founding of the Women's Peace Party. Then in April she boarded the Noordam as a member of the intrepid delegation sailing over a mine-strewn Atlantic to The Hague. This trip changed her life.

Emily Balch acted as the chairperson of different committees and subcommittees. Still she played a rather unobtrusive role at the International Congress of Women. Like the other delegates she advocated in her quiet way a permanent international court and a permanent international conference to solve international quarrels. She was important enough, however, to be chosen a member of the second of two delegations calling on European statesmen with their plan of continuous mediation for attaining an early peace. Like Jane Addams, Emily Balch had some doubts about the mission, but in the end decided to go along. Her delegation included Rosika Schwimmer, the formidable Hungarian suffragette, and Chrystal Macmillan, a Scottish lawyer and suffragette. Under dangerous war conditions they traveled to the Scandinavian countries and Russia. Later Emily wrote, "For a brief accidental period of my life I consorted with men in the seats of power. We talked with Prime Ministers and Foreign Ministers in Saint Petersburg and Copenhagen and Christiania and Stockholm and The Hague and London, and King Haakon chatted with us familiarly."

After her return Emily Balch worked with Jane Addams and Dr. Alice Hamilton preparing Women at The Hague. She also went to the White House for unsuccessful interviews with President Wilson, Col. Edward House, and Secretary of State Robert Lansing. She did not sail on Henry Ford's Peace Ship, but did become an alternate for the ailing Jane Addams. Thus she served as one of two American delegates to the neutral Conference for Continuous Mediation, set up in Stockholm as a sequel to the Ford voyage. She stayed on the Mediation Committee until July, submitting a proposal for international colonial administration, which in many ways resembled the mandate system initiated by the League of Nations.

Emily Balch returned from Stockholm to find she was due for another sabbatical from Wellesley. She spent it in New York, a 50-year-old spinster with pince-nez, still lean and precise of speech, working with various peace groups. Friends thought she looked a little out of place among the young radicals and bohemians. Eagerly she joined the

American Union against Militarism, the New York branch of
the Women's Peace Party, and the American Neutral Conference Committee, later to be called the Emergency Peace
Foundation. In May, 1917, a month after the United States
entered the war, the Federation became the core of the
People's Council of America. The Council denounced war
profiteering and opposed conscription and the suppression of
civil liberties.

Together with other ardent pacifists, Emily Balch stood
in the gallery of the House of Representatives on Good Friday,
1917. After the long debate on the war resolution she waited
anxiously for the roll call. Finally it came--373 for war,
50 against. In spite of the rebuff she noted that the nay-
sayers included Jeanette Rankin of Montana, the first woman
member of Congress.

Emily Balch was still head of the department of economics and sociology at Wellesley. But because of her pacifist connections she felt her return might be embarrassing to
the college. So she asked for and received a year's leave of
absence without pay. She was well aware that by the end
of the year her existing appointment would expire and have
to be renewed.

All this time she was writing various articles on the
settlement of the war. With Norman Angell, the English
journalist, she gave a series of 11 lectures on "Current De-
velopments in World Politics." Little did the audience realize
that they were listening to two future Nobel laureates--Sir
Norman Angell was to win the Peace Prize in 1933. In 1918
Emily Balch published Approaches to the Great Settlement, a
thoroughgoing account of different peace proposals, parties,
issues, and methods. Angell wrote the introduction. Not
long after came the moaning sirens of the armistice.

At the close of the year Emily's Wellesley appointment had expired and no decision had been made about her
reappointment. So she welcomed an invitation from Oswald
Garrison Villard to join the staff of The Nation. Within a
few months, however, she found even greater use for her
talents. Women at The Hague in 1915 had agreed to meet
again as soon as the war was over. They wanted to meet
in conjunction with the peace conference. Again Emily Balch
sailed on the Noordam with old friends, including the inspiring
Jane Addams. During the voyage one delegate complimented
Emily for having a disposition "fit for the kingdom of Heaven."

At Zürich in May, 1919, the nature-loving Miss Balch delighted in a landscape of lake, mountains, and flowering apple trees. She found it a moving experience to come face to face with "the enemy." Years later she wrote, "Those who came to Zürich from the countries which had been spared the least ravages of war were aghast at the bodily suffering from famine and cold in the faces of their friends."

In her usual self-effacing but confident way, Emily Balch helped plan the agenda, decide on resolutions, and translate materials. Not one of the main speakers at the congress, she remained the quiet, efficient, behind-the-scenes worker. Still, the delegates recognized her worth. After the new organization had been given the name of Women's International League for Peace and Freedom, Emily Balch was elected secretary-treasurer, to serve with Jane Addams, the international president.

Only two Frenchwomen were present. On the final morning of the conference a third French delegate from the devastated region of the Ardennes arrived. At once a gaunt German woman, Lida Gustava Heymann, welcomed her with roses saying, "We hope we women can build a bridge from Germany to France and from France to Germany, and that in the future we may be able to make good the wrongdoing of war." Jeanne Melin, the sad-faced French delegate, replied passionately, repudiating the statesmen at Versailles and urging the women of the world to unite.

Then Emily Balch sprang to her feet and with upraised hand solemnly pledged, "I will do everything in my power to work for permanent peace." All the women present accepted her invitation to rise and join in the pledge. Said one delegate, "I have never witnessed or imagined so remarkable an affirmation."

While in Zürich Emily received a cable telling her that the Wellesley trustees had decided not to reappoint her to her professorship. Since smoking was strictly taboo on that campus, she celebrated by puffing on a cigarette. But she found she did not like it and "did not continue the habit." Several of her friends urged her to appeal the Wellesley decision as a breach of academic freedom. But, perhaps remembering Thomas Masaryk's academic trials, Emily never wanted it to be a cause célèbre. Never expressing any bitterness, she admitted she might have overstrained "the well-known liberality of Wellesley College." Still, at 52 she was

left with her professional life cut short and without a pension.
A few weeks earlier her name with that of Jane Addams had
appeared on Archibald Stevenson's list of so-called subver-
sives.

Fortunately, as secretary-treasurer of the Women's
League, she had some new prospects. Quickly the League
leased a lovely eighteenth-century house in Geneva for its
international headquarters. It contained offices, library,
dining room, and bedrooms and a small walled garden, complete with fountain, where Emily liked to seat her guests for
lunch. Named the Maison Internationale, the charming house
was only a short distance from the meeting place chosen for
the Assembly of the League of Nations. Among the leaders
there she met Fridtjof Nansen, whom she admired deeply.

As one of her first jobs she prepared the proceedings
of the Zürich congress in three languages. It was not a difficult task for a linguist, fluent in German, French, and
Italian. She had also studied Latin and Greek and knew some
Dutch, Czech, Polish, and Russian. Later she tried to co-
operate with the League of Nations and drafted letters and
memoranda, covering such pressing issues as limitation of
armaments, mandates, and blockades.

About this time Emily Balch, born into a Unitarian
family, decided to join the unified English Society of Friends
rather than the divided American Quakers. Writing to Jane
Addams, she commented that she was "as frankly untrini-
tarian, as remote from orthodox Christian theology as ever."
But, she added, "what is central to the Friends is central
to me--the wish to listen as it were, to understand and receive as much as we can and to try to live out, as far as
we can, all that one has of enlightenment--no creed, no pretending to honor what we don't know."

Because of her background of Slavic studies, Emily
Balch was also asked to be responsible for the third International Congress of the W. I. L. P. F. in Vienna in 1921.
The next year she set up the League's summer school in Lu-
gano, Switzerland. Among its speakers were Bertrand Russell and Romain Rolland.

After three long years in Geneva she began to suffer
from nervous fatigue and strain and took a four months'
leave of absence from the Maison Internationale. Finally
she sent in her resignation. The next two winters she spent

recuperating in Egypt and California. Settled in Washington,
D. C. by 1924, she helped organize the fourth W. I. L. P. F.
congress and edit its voluminous proceedings. The next year,
on behalf of the Women's League, she traveled to North
Africa, the Middle East, and the Balkans.

On her return to Massachusetts, she moved into the
little two-story wing of a new house built by some colleagues
in Wellesley. She called her home Domichek, Bohemian for
"little house." Always a flower lover, she was happy about
the tulips and lilies-of-the-valley at her doorstep and the
little plot of land she cultivated behind the house.

Emily Balch had scarcely settled there when she left
on a mission to Haiti in February, 1926. The American
Marines had occupied the island since 1915, and ten years
later some Haitian members of the W. I. L. P. F. asked the
International Executive Committee to look into conditions
there. As head of the mission, Emily could pick her assistants. Among them was Paul Douglas, then a young university professor at the University of Chicago. The group arrived in the rainy season, and at one point a bridge went
out so that Emily had to be carried over the stream on a
lame man's back.

The mission found the Haitians with an angry sense
of hurt and frustration. The American occupation had indeed
built roads and bridges and hospitals. But the clearsighted
Emily thought that the average Haitian needed a title to his
land most of all. In addition to investigating social and economic conditions, Emily Balch's group decided to recommend
a future American policy for the island. This included with-
drawal of the American occupation and the restoration of self-
government. The policy was clearly explained in Occupied
Haiti, edited and mostly written by Emily Balch. Some time
later President Herbert Hoover sent an official commission
to Port-au-Prince. The American policy it recommended
was much like that sketched by the unofficial group.

Emily Balch was keenly aware that the goals of the
Women's League were harshly challenged between 1929 and
1939. That decade saw a world-wide depression, a failed
disarmament conference, Mussolini's conquest of Ethiopia,
the Japanese invasion of China, and Hitler's conquest of Austria and Czechoslovakia. At the very beginning of those
troubling years Jane Addams resigned as international president, and Emily Balch, Gertrude Baer of Germany, and

Clara Ragaz of Switzerland were named as joint international
chairmen.   Then in 1934, when the Women's League found it
could not continue the salary of its international secretary,
Emily offered her services without pay for half a year.   Actually, she stayed in Geneva a year and a half.

Jane Addams' death in May, 1935, was a tremendous
blow.   "Help me not to dwell on my loss, " Emily wrote in
her diary: "Help me to enjoy her still.   To learn from her
and be glad of her and to do what is in me to do, as she did,
living to the full her great soul. "   The end of that year brought
a deep satisfaction, an invitation from Wellesley College to
give the formal Armistice Day address there.   Emily Balch
responded with a masterly speech, "What of Peace Today?"

Because she was caring for her invalid sister Annie,
she could not attend the ninth congress in Luhacovice, Czechoslovakia, in July, 1937.   Here, she heard to her surprise,
she had been elected honorary international president to succeed her beloved Jane.   Compared to Miss Addams, Emily
Balch seemed austere.   But all who met her remarked on
her friendly handclasp and the kindness that radiated from
her gray-blue eyes.   She continued to dress unobtrusively
and once was chided by a chic French friend for wearing a
dark blue hat with a black dress.   She simply was not interested in hats and sometimes put them on backwards.

During the 1930s Emily wrote and circulated proposals
on Manchuria, economic reconstruction, disarmament, and
the internationalization of aviation.   Again and again she returned to her favorite theme: supranational authorities should
be set up to settle international differences.   The League of
Nations sent her paper, "An Economic Conference, " to all
governments.   Meanwhile she worked hard to get the necessary
affidavits for European refugees to enter this country.

In 1939 Emily began to shift her pacifist position somewhat.   "When the war broke in its full fury ... and especially
when, after the disaster at Pearl Harbor, the U. S. A. became
a belligerent, I went through a long and painful mental struggle,
and never felt that I had reached a clear and consistent conclusion.   'How can you reach inner unity, ' I said, 'when in
your own mind an irresistible force has collided with an im-
movable obstacle?' "

After the Japanese attack Emily said, "Any government would have found it impossible to refuse to fight, im-

possible, that is, given the existing degree of development of mankind and its failure to have ready any effective and generally understood technique for constructive non-violent <u>action</u>, such as Gandhi had aimed at. On the one hand, I refused to buy war bonds; on the other, I contributed, however modestly, to the so-called Community War Funds, a large part of which was devoted to wholly peaceful social aid-- which typifies my mixed reaction." The allusion to Gandhi was significant, for Emily, who had met him at Geneva, gave him first place in her gallery of heroes. Like him she was horrified by the atomic bomb.

Throughout her life she kept diaries and journals and wrote a number of autobiographical fragments. She also habitually jotted down her spontaneous thoughts on little scraps of paper. The Miracle of Living, a small book of poems written through the years, was published just before Pearl Harbor. It was not a great literary success. But her friends treasured lines such as

> Dear to me, beyond words dear to me
> Is the Earth:
> Wherever I pass, I am at home.

Or these, written "Beside an Egyptian Mummy,"

> All, all that speaks of change,
> Of Life's sacred communion, of process.

Those friends thought her poetry resembled the delicate aquarelles of New England and European landscapes that she habitually dashed off and sent to them.

Nine years after the meeting in Luhacovice, the W. I. L. P. F. held its tenth congress in Luxembourg. At the age of 79, Emily Balch made her first air flight, across the Atlantic. It proved to be a most worthwhile trip, for by acclamation she was reelected honorary international president.

Three months later came what she herself called "the amazing event of the Oslo award of the Nobel Prize." When the radio announced one mid-November afternoon in 1946 that she had won it together with Dr. Mott, she was lying ill of viral bronchitis in the Wellesley-Newton hospital. Later she was to learn that John Dewey had been one of her sponsors. She had never been nominated before. Her admirers pointed

xt2n

48The Lady Laureates

out that she was actually the only one of all the peace laureates, male and female, to completely fulfill the three requirements Alfred Nobel had laid down: "to have done the
most or the best work for fraternity among nations, for the
abolition or reduction of standing armies, and for the holding
and promotion of peace conferences."

The chairperson of the Nobel Committee, speaking in
the Assembly Hall of the University of Oslo on December 10,
paid special tribute to the Women's International League for
Peace and Freedom: "Time does not permit me to review
the resolutions which were passed as a result of this [W. I.
L. P. F.] study. What I can and will say is that it would
have been judicious to have heeded the women's counsel."

Following Jane Addams' example, Emily turned over
most of her prize money to the W. I. L. P. F. She gave
$10,000 to be used by the League without restriction, de-
posited $5000 in a bank for a European co-worker, and kept
$2000 for the voyage to Oslo and secretarial help for future
peace work.

Accompanied by her niece, Ellen Stone, Emily Balch
sailed for Norway in March, 1948, one year later than expected. The day before her lecture, angular and fragile,
she turned her direct, quizzical gaze on King Haakon, who
greeted her as an old acquaintance, more than 30 years after
she had had a wartime conference with him. With renewed
energy and customary crispness, Emily spoke elsewhere in
Oslo and also in Stockholm, Helsinki, Copenhagen, and
Odense, Denmark. Then she and Ellen traveled to Germany
and England. In London she was honored at a gala dinner.

Even past 80, she continued to travel, write, work
hard for peace. She was not lonely because she had two
friends, Agnes Perkins and Mabel Cummings, living with
her at the Domichek and three sisters and her brother staying close by. She still painted her little aquarelles, still
read widely, and still jotted down her random thoughts on
little scraps of paper. On her eighty-fifth birthday in 1952,
she met another Nobel laureate, Pearl Buck, the principal
speaker at the jubilee dinner given Emily Balch by the Wom-
en's League.

The last four years of her long life she spent, somewhat enfeebled, in a nursing home in Cambridge. While admitting to a friend that her days there could sometimes be

as "dull as ditch water," she assured herself that she was
"never lonely, never unoccupied, never bored." At 92 she
could write: "I have had a long and happy and I should like
to think not wholly useless life to look back on. I think few
people can have gone through nine decades with so little suffering, physical or non-physical. I dare say one ought to
choose, if one has the choice, an experience richer in contrasts. But one is not given the choice. This is the way
my life has worked out, and I should be ungrateful indeed if
I was not thankful for it."

At 34 she had been more acutely aware of those missing contrasts: "I am happy as an unmarried woman (not only
unmarried but virgin in my emotions, never having loved or
been loved) but I know that I have only a small part of life.
The passion, whether of mother or of wife, whether joy or
tragedy, is not for me. From the deepest sympathy even I
am excluded. Family affection I have, friends I have, objects in life, work and deepest of satisfactions, religion, but
the most simply primitively human gift, the deepest reach
of life, I have not."

Quietly and gracefully Emily Balch lived out her time
until January 9, 1962, one day after her ninety-fourth birthday. Her friend, the Harvard philosopher W. Ernest Hocking, once commented that no other life known to him had been
so consistently and almost exclusively devoted to the cause of
peace. "It will be long before the sum of her labors can be
gathered, but when it is done, the achievement will be recognized as the more remarkable because its methods have been
so much the ways of friendly reason."

Another root of that achievement was Emily Balch's
own basic philosophy, "Deeply and happily, I feel myself a
citizen of the world."

Pipers of Peace
BETTY WILLIAMS and MAIREAD CORRIGAN

Betty Williams and Mairead Corrigan, two homey young "women next door," came to Oslo on December 10, 1977, to receive the delayed Peace Prize for 1976. For 16 months they had worked to try to stop the violence in Northern Ireland.

It was, in fact, their second trip to the Norwegian capital. One year earlier they had arrived at the red brick, twin-towered city hall to be handed the Norwegian People's Peace Prize, a gift of $340,000 sponsored by Norwegian newspapers and civic groups. No 1976 Peace Prize had been awarded by the Nobel Committee, which found no acceptable candidate by the February 1 deadline for nominations, six months before the Williams-Corrigan peace movement had even begun. That December evening in Oslo thousands of Norwegian sympathizers massed with flaming torches before the city hall, and more than a thousand jammed the auditorium. The remarkable thing, many noted at the time, was that in just four months Betty and Mairead had captured the imagination of Ulster and the world. And they had set their own lives on edge.

In the late summer of 1976, Betty Williams and Mairead Corrigan launched their peace crusade in a place long marked by bitterness and blood. Belfast, capital of Northern Ireland and a world center of shipbuilding and manufacturing, had become a bleak city of bombed-out buildings and barricades, charred walls, armored trucks in the streets, and armed soldiers on the sidewalks. Here Protestants and Catholics lived completely apart, separated by barbed wire and a burning, centuries-old hatred. Here as nowhere else, except perhaps in Londonderry, the "Irish problem" showed its deep historical, political, and religious roots.

Simple, ordinary women, Betty and Mairead dared to

Betty Williams and Mairead Corrigan

defy the complexities of Irish history.   Their plea was elementary and forthright.   "Forget the past," they said.   "My
God," exclaimed Betty, "how we have learned to hate!"

After a long period of English conquest, Ireland had
been made part of Great Britain in 1801.   For over a century violence erupted along sectarian lines as Catholics agitated for Irish home rule and Protestants fought against it.
In 1920 and 1921 the country was divided into two self-
governing parts of Great Britain--Northern Ireland (Ulster)
with a Protestant majority fiercely loyal to the British; and
the Irish Free State, with a Catholic majority.   In the 1920s,
certain Catholics, unhappy with that division, formed the
secret Irish Republican Army (IRA) to press for one Ireland.
Finally in 1949 the Irish Free State declared its independence
and cut all ties with Britain.

A terrible new chapter in the age-old story of hatred
broke out in Northern Ireland in 1969 when the Catholic civil
rights movement, protesting discrimination in employment
and housing, began to gather force.   The Protestants saw this
drive as a plot to reunite all Ireland and to make them the
despised minority.   In fact, on the heels of the civil rights
movement the IRA did move in to protect the Catholics.   Soon
there was civil war.   In seven years at least 1600 persons
died in bombings and assassinations, carried out by extremists
on both sides, and in battles between British troops, sent to
Ulster in 1969, and the Provisional Wing of the IRA (the
"provos").

Northern Ireland spent 1976 in a political stalemate.
Some of the Catholic demands had been met, but the chasm
had widened.   There seemed no chance that Roman Catholic
and Protestant politicians would agree on a power-sharing
government.   The British, who had instituted Direct Rule
(rule by the British Parliament) in 1972, saw no hope of isolating the terrorists or gaining a military victory over them.

During that period of stalemate Betty and Mairead's
partnership was born in a moment of horror.   On Tuesday
afternoon, August 10, petite, blonde Anne Maguire, the wife
of a Belfast mechanic, was out walking on Finaghy Road
North with her three young children.   Eight-year-old Joanne
proudly pushed six-month-old Andrew in his pram, and two
and a half-year-old John clung to his mother's hand.   Anne's
sister, Pat O'Connor, also accompanied by her children, was
a few yards behind.   Suddenly a blue Ford sped down the

road, pursued by British Army jeeps. The driver of the
Ford, a member of the IRA, had just been shot through the
heart. The car veered and slammed all the Maguires against
a school railing. Just in time Pat O'Connor yanked her own
children out of the car's path. The official version of the incident was that a few minutes earlier the occupants of the
car had fired on a British patrol. When jeeps set out in
pursuit, shots had been exchanged.

Betty Williams witnessed the accident as she was
driving home from a visit to her invalid mother in Andersonstown. She was sickened. "I kept seeing my own children lying there," she later remembered. The rest of the
day she hardly knew what to do with herself.

Placed in the intensive care ward of the Royal Vic-
toria Hospital with both her hips and her pelvis broken,
Anne Maguire eventually recovered. But Joanne and baby
Andrew had been killed instantly, and John died the next day.

That evening as Betty Williams sat in her comfortable
home and discussed the grisly scene, her anger mounted.
Suddenly she realized she had to get out "from behind the
Venetian blinds." With a notepad she set out for Andersonstown, an IRA stronghold, and soon was knocking at the doors
of Catholic women and asking them to sign a petition to stop
the violence. "I was like the Pied Piper," she remarked
afterwards. "I ended up with a hundred women doing the
same as me." Within hours she had gathered hundreds of
signatures for her peace petition and already was planning
a peace rally for the following Saturday at the spot where
the Maguire children had been killed.

Meanwhile Mairead Corrigan, a young secretary and
aunt of the Maguires, had gone on television to plead: "My
sister's children were killed because of the activities of the
IRA in our area. We don't want any more violence. I condemn all violent organizations, all men of violence. We
have taken enough. We will take no more." That afternoon
Mairead had seen her sister's neighbors moving in a small
silent march down the street. Soon she heard that a housewife named Betty Williams was organizing a peace rally for
the following Saturday. Impulsively she called Betty on the
telephone and invited her to the children's funeral. Betty
came. When the two women met again at the peace rally,
they burst into tears. Another piper had joined Betty Williams.

Ten thousand women, both Catholic and Protestant,
some wheeling prams, streamed in to that rally. Almost
all waved banners bearing the names of their streets in dis-
tricts long regarded as irreconcilable. There were no
speeches--only prayers. It turned out to be the biggest and
most impressive peace demonstration seen in Ulster in years.

Already Betty and Mairead recognized what had to be
done. "Bury all your hate with the Maguire children," they
told the people of Belfast. As Betty put it, "All I want to
do is to take a bomb out of a kid's hand and put a tennis
racket in it." Another time she said, "The greatest single
task in Northern Ireland is to take the stone out of the
child's hand and give him a playground ball."

Violence had touched her life too often. Her 18-year-
old cousin had been shot by a Protestant paramilitary outfit
when he was returning home from work. One of her second
cousins was killed as he passed an exploding car, booby-
trapped by the Catholics. Once in a department store Betty
and her little daughter Deborah were terrorized by bombs
blasting off about them. "I literally ran into walls, not
knowing where to go; we were black and blue all over,"
Betty recalled. Another time her father, a butcher, had
told her about cleaning up a restaurant after a bombing.
"Hands and fingers and eyes and pieces of flesh" were splat-
tered all over.

Both peace pipers grew up in Belfast, where they
were born in wartime, Betty on May 22, 1943, and Mairead
on January 27, 1944. Betty Smyth assumed responsibilities
early. She was only 13 when her mother suffered a stroke.
After that Betty had to take care of her eight-year-old sister,
Margaret. Betty went to St. Theresa's School and then enrolled in a commercial course. She was just 18 when on
June 14, 1961, she was married to Ralph Williams, a Protestant merchant seaman. Thus she became a member of a
smaller and more despised minority in Northern Ireland,
where mixed marriages are considered almost treasonous.
Some three years later Betty moved away to Bermuda with her
husband and their infant son, Paul (born in 1963), but because
Ralph Williams was at sea much of the time, Betty went
to work. When she and Mairead began their peace movement, she was a night waitress at an inn ("fired fourteen
times by the maître d'," she joked) and also a "girl Friday"
in an office of technical consultants. At the same time she
was known as a careful mother (Deborah was born in 1970)

and a spotless housekeeper.   Her special interests were
dressmaking and gardening.   For a while, in a way, she believed in what the IRA was doing.   Then she began to per-
ceive that violence only caused more violence.

The beautiful name Mairead is Gaelic for Margaret.
The daughter of a window cleaner, Mairead Corrigan left
St. Vincent's School at 14 to take a business course.   At 16
she was hired as an assistant bookkeeper in a textile factory,
and at 21 she became a secretary at the Guinness brewery, a
job she kept for 11 years.   She was deeply attached to her
family, which included two brothers and four sisters.   She
was also deeply religious, a staunch member of the Catholic
Legion of Mary, an organization somewhat similar to the
Salvation Army, that operated in Belfast's Catholic ghettos.
Between 1972 and 1974 the Legion was the only lay organization allowed to visit prisoners in the Long Kesh internment
camp for Catholics and Protestants accused of acts of ter-
rorism.   There Mairead reminded them that violence was
not the way of Christ.   In 1972 she attended the World Council of Churches in Bangkok.   The next year she went to the
Soviet Union to make a film on Russian believers.   She
showed this film and gave lectures in Catholic schools.
Despite her busy schedule, pretty green-eyed Mairead had
her share of boyfriends to take her to dances, movies, and
restaurants.   Swimming was her favorite sport.

These two different personalities and backgrounds complemented each other.   Soon Betty and Mairead had a staunch
ally in Ciaran McKeown, a gaunt, bearded young Belfast
journalist.   Within a month he left his job on The Irish Press
to work with them full-time.   The 33-year-old Ciaran, a
family man, natty dresser, and inveterate pipe smoker, became the driving intellectual force of the movement.   He was
the one who decided which towns would next have marches
and rallies.   For every march in Ulster there was to be a
corresponding one in Great Britain.   Ciaran scheduled Betty
and Mairead to take turns attending the smaller marches but
to appear together at the big ones.

Already on August 18, the new comrades-in-arms
picked the name "Community of the Peace People."   Ciaran
also wrote a "Declaration of Peace," which boldly stated,
"We reject the use of the bomb and the bullet and all the
techniques of violence."   Many of the rallies opened with
somebody reading it aloud.

So began the headline-grabbing marches and rallies, with Ciaran at first remaining quietly in the background. Invariably they inspired taunts, scuffles, and stone throwing. Television crews were always on hand to record the altercations. A march on August 28 began in Falls Road, a fiercely Catholic district, and crossed over into Shankill Road, the Protestant heartland, where a welcoming committee was waiting. Pridefully, the Andersonstown delegation headed the line of march. By now husbands were coming along with their wives. The invaders carried banners with the names of their groups, placards with drawings of doves, and songbooks. In a procedure followed in all the rallies, a stage was erected in the bed of a truck, and a loudspeaker system was installed. After prayers and speeches, hymns and nostalgic Irish airs floated out over the gray city. In the tense, emotional atmosphere tears streamed down many faces. "It was the first time I had been there in seven years," Mairead said. By now she considered her work for the peace movement to be an extension of her work for the Legion of Mary.

On September 4, thousands of women poured into Londonderry, the second-largest city in Ulster, with its own black history of violence. The Catholics gathered on the west bank of the Foyle River, the Protestants on the east. Singing "Abide with Me," the groups marched toward Craigavon Bridge, which divides the city's Protestant and Catholic sections. It was in the Catholic ghetto of the Bogside in August, 1968, that Catholic civil rights activists marched for the first time to protest Protestant domination. It was for fighting in the Bogside one year later that Bernadette Devlin, the fiery girl-politician, was later sent to prison.

In Derry (as the Catholics always refer to the city), a young woman named Fiona Malloy stepped up to the microphone and began singing a song dedicated to the Peace People by its composers. Danny Feeney had written the words in 1974 after his 14-year-old sister was killed in crossfire between the British army and the "provos."

> Say Peace, Think Peace,
> And walk with Peace in your heart.
> Pray Peace, Dream for Peace,
> Let's all make a start....

The movement now had an anthem.

Predictably, the marches and rallies brought ominous

threats to the organizers.   On a brick wall in Andersonstown,
IRA supporters carefully daubed the words, BETTY WIL-
LIAMS IS A TRAITOR.   A slogan scrawled in a roadway
close to her home read, DEATH TO BETTY WILLIAMS.   To
newsmen Betty admitted she had "a cold sweat of fear" running down her back.   When a youthful gang tried to set fire
to the Williamses' modest brick and frame semidetached
house in Orchardville Gardens, Betty sent six-year-old
Debbie and 12-year-old Paul into temporary hiding with
friends.   Her husband, an engineer on an oil tanker, was
on duty in Canada, but he wired her, "Am with you with all
my heart.   Keep going."   When tall, redhaired and redbearded
Ralph Williams returned home, he continued to give her his
full support.   Betty once said of him, "He really is 'somebody.'   It is because of him that I can live at home without
pressure.   He has never complained.   He is the quiet
strength in the background, and he pays a high personal
price for this."

     The Rev. Ian Paisley's fanatically loyalist newspaper
denounced the peace movement as "spurious" and "priest inspired."   There were priests and nuns in the ranks, but
most of the marchers were housewives.   Betty and Mairead
were overwhelmed with obscene letters, many branding them
"touts" (IRA parlance for informers).   Garbage was pushed
through their mail slots.   Both vowed not to give in.   In
Betty's words, "We will not be intimidated by these thugs."
According to her, the thugs were equally the IRA terrorists
and the Protestant murder gangs ("bully boys" all of them)
stalking the streets.   As Georgie Ann Geyer has pointed out,
Betty and Mairead had embarked "on a demythologizing of
the gunmen who have ruled Northern Ireland society for so
long and so disastrously."

     Appearing on the platform together, the two pipers
of peace made an oddly contrasting pair--Betty, tall, talkative, outgoing, emotional, aggressive, and Mairead, almost
a head shorter, fragile looking, quiet, reserved.   Betty was
blunt, blasting the hecklers with earthy humor.   Mairead was
gentle, soothing, and spiritual.   "They call us the saint and
the sinner," Betty could joke.   She exhorted, Mairead inspired.   Still Betty would insist that her little partner had
"the guts of a lion."

     On October 22, in a freezing rain, men, women, and
children moved out under black umbrellas from Shankill Road
to Falls Road to hold a prayer gathering.   Their procession

was designed to be the reverse of the August march which
had ended in Shankill Road. A crowd of IRA supporters
pelted the marchers with anything they could find. Several
heads were cracked, and Ciaran McKeown was among those
injured. In spite of the attacks many felt that the Shankill
march was the most moving and memorable of all the
marches.

By this time Ciaran had written a pamphlet, "The
Price of Peace," which summed up the movement's philosophy of peace, nonviolence, and community politics. In it
he argued that the most urgent need in Northern Ireland was
to create a new consciousness--a respect for persons as
human beings, not primarily as Protestants and Catholics--
and then develop appropriate neighborhood structures to help
break down the old divisions. Peace committees would create
centers of social activity that would disseminate the philosophy
of nonviolence and a new concept of the political game. Community politics would be developed to the maximum extent.

As Ciaran steered the Peace People into politics, his
intensity frightened some followers. "We do not want any
more attempts to solve our problems from the top down,"
he said, "we want to do it from the bottom up. What we
have is the opportunity to create an ideal democracy." Although Betty and Mairead denied any political ambitions,
Ciaran declared, "This is an intensely political movement.
We are out to unite the community, and if we do there will
be no place for politicians who rely on sectarian division to
keep them in power." He called his concept "community
democracy."

On November 27, the Ulster peace ladies found themselves in London's Trafalgar Square, flanked by celebrities
like Joan Baez, the American folk singer and civil rights
activist, and Jane Ewart-Briggs, the widow of the British
ambassador to Northern Ireland, assassinated earlier in the
year. Heavily guarded, they had marched the three miles
from Hyde Park. Many supporters came from West Germany,
Norway, Denmark, and the Netherlands. Many carried white
carnations, the flowers of peace. "We have lived with violence," Mairead said, "and not one single life was worth it.
We now say to the people outside Northern Ireland, to the
people of the world we say, look to Northern Ireland and
never make our mistakes."

Red policemen's whistles also became symbols of the

campaign. Four thousand arrived from admirers in West Germany. Anybody seeing an act of violence or a man with a
gun was supposed to blow the whistle. But then the "provos"
began using whistles too, and the Peace People had to abandon
theirs.

One October day in 1976 Betty and Mairead were
scheduled to address a Catholic meeting. When they arrived,
a mob of angry women attacked them, punching, kicking, and
pulling their hair. Walking with her husband, Betty was
knocked unconscious for a few minutes. Already in September one of the peace leaders, Bridget McKenna, had been
hit in the face with a shotgun blast. At that time Mairead
said she was ready to die for peace.

Just a week before they left for Oslo to receive the
Norwegian People's Peace Prize, Betty and Mairead, again
joined by Joan Baez, staged a climactic rally on the banks
of the river Boyne near the city of Drogheda in Eire. It
was the place where the Protestant English king, William III
(William of Orange), defeated his Catholic predecessor,
James II, in 1690. Neither side has ever forgotten the Battle
of the Boyne, for afterwards the ruling Protestant minority
in Ireland took away all political rights from the Catholics
and seized much of their land. With history much in their
minds, the marchers from Ulster reached the Bridge of
Peace in the center of Drogheda and were met by several
thousand delegates from Eire. Suddenly the fog lifted, and
the sun shone brilliantly. Mairead declared it was the happiest day of her life.

By the time of the first Oslo ceremony, money was
pouring in from all parts of the world, especially from Norway and West Germany. The Peace People, who had already
started over a hundred activist groups, used the donations to
invest in some small community center buildings, to buy
equipment for youth clubs, and to sponsor cottage industries,
notably in Strabane, where there was high unemployment.
But the "foreign influence" invited criticism.

Even more criticism was heaped on Betty and Mairead's
globe-trotting activities. A leading Ulster politician growled,
"They don't exist except as a figment of media imagination.
These two lassies with no record of working or caring for
peace took off round the world, and no one has seen them
since." Actually, during some of their long periods abroad,
Mairead and Betty had the very real task of arranging escape

routes for about 150 Protestants and Catholics whose names
had appeared on terrorist death lists. On a trip to the United
States in October, 1976, they pleaded with Americans to stop
sending money to organizations that claimed to be engaged in
relief but that really were running arms.

In April, 1977, the Peace People bought a fine three-
story house on Lisburn Road in Belfast for their headquarters
and named it Peace House (now rendered as the Norwegian
Fredheim). The founders still put in hours from early morning till after midnight. "Flying squads" of the Youth for
Peace organization sold the movement's newspaper on the
streets. It was a way, one of the Peace People exclaimed,
of keeping hundreds of youthful recruits out of the paramilitary.

One of the appeals fell on stony ground. Betty and
Mairead asked their supporters to divulge the whereabouts
of arms or--even better--to hand them in to authorities. No
guns were turned in.

Because Mairead, Betty, and Ciaran arranged no emotional marches or rallies in 1977, there was much less cov-
erage by the news media. One Protestant clergyman declared, "The rallies were a miracle, but they aroused false
hopes of peace." The women were so often abroad that they
had less time for organizational duties, and membership in
the Peace People fell off. To be sure, some committees
were achieving remarkable results in social actions. Still,
for much of the year the movement seemed to be searching
for new directions beyond what Ciaran gave it. He offended
some with his attacks on the churches, which he thought remained too aloof from the civil conflict. Critics pointed out
that the Peace People, refusing to come to grips with the
questions of politics and power, had never been clear enough
about how exactly peace was to be achieved. Gunmen on both
sides thoroughly detested Betty and Mairead and their sym-
pathizers.

For these reasons the Nobel Peace Prize astonished
many. The citation read: "Alfred Nobel's wish was that the
Peace Prize should be given to those who most actively worked
for peace and brotherhood. Mairead Corrigan and Betty Williams acted from a profound conviction that the individual
can make a meaningful contribution for peace through constructive reconciliation."

Betty was sitting at a luncheon at London's Savoy Hotel when she heard the news. Tearfully, excitedly, she put a call through to Mairead in Belfast. Then with her usual exuberance she told reporters, "I'm completely shattered. Today it's the Nobel Peace Prize, but tomorrow it's back to the Shankill Road." Later she reflected, "We've only been going fourteen months, but I know how hard we've worked and perhaps we deserved it." Against guerrilla warfare, as she once remarked, they had been waging guerrilla peace.

Mairead also was moved to tears. "I feel very humble. I accept on behalf of everyone throughout the world who works and longs for peace and the many people who have suffered and been jailed in the interests of promoting peace."

Picking up their delayed Prize at an emotion-filled ceremony in Oslo University's Aula Hall, Betty and Mairead shared the spotlight with Thomas Hammarberg, who accepted the 1977 Peace Prize for Amnesty International, a London-based human rights organization with member groups in more than 30 countries. It had proclaimed 1977 "Prisoner of Conscience Year."

In her speech Mairead said, "Our world is rushing towards disaster. But it's not too late to prove the power of love.... We've got to prove that nonviolence can bring social change."

Meanwhile she and Betty remained somewhat controversial figures in their own country. There was endless debate about how effective they had been in making the streets safer. They themselves were cautious about taking credit. On first learning they were to become Nobel laureates, Betty made this assessment: "In the fourteen months since we started, violent deaths in Northern Ireland have dropped by fifty per cent. We hope that this has something to do with our movement. We have not yet brought peace to Northern Ireland."

Then, after a pause, she put her finger on what she and Mairead and Ciaran had done: "We have created a climate for peace to become respectable."

Even before Mairead and Betty received the Nobel Prize, Mairead's grief-stricken sister Anne Maguire, her husband Jackie, and their surviving son, Mark, left Belfast

for New Zealand to begin what they hoped would be a new life.
There, in the summer of 1977, Anne gave birth to a daughter,
Joanne, named for the little girl whose murder had helped
spark the peace movement.

Betty and Mairead were criticized for not giving their
prize money to the Community of the Peace People. Instead
they made donations to community projects--some in the
Third World--and placed the balance in trust funds. Mairead
explained that she had given up a top, pensionable job and
drew only a small salary at Fredheim.

Early on, vigorous debate broke out there. To en-
courage new members to chart the way, Betty, Mairead, and
Ciaran resigned from the executive committee in 1978. That
same year the homesick Maguires returned to Belfast, and
Mairead was often called on to help her increasingly despond-
ent sister.

For Mairead and Betty there were more international
trips, which their critics called ego-tripping. In a 1981
newspaper article Ciaran sprang to their defense:

> The overseas stuff was part of the same conscious
> strategy of getting people to look outward from the
> trenches, see the world through new eyes, feel
> friendship from places where only the sovereign
> British or Irish might expect to have respect while
> the North Irish were to be viewed as a quaint tribe
> of bigots imprisoned in the seventeenth century.

He went on,

> To have some 'ordinary folk' from here received
> and feted throughout the world was probably a psy-
> chological treatment for the besieged mind, and
> organized ego trip for the entire community, if
> you like, a community where self-hatred is part
> of the disease.

Home or abroad, the peace pipers remained idealistic. In
Ciaran's words, they assumed "that the outpouring of senti-
ment ... was an inarticulate recognition that a new consensus
must and could be built and that it was only a question of
steady work to make it articulate."

By October, 1979, the founding trio was reelected to

the executive committee. Betty told an interviewer: "Mairead
and I have cried many times in the last few years--we have
even been criticized for doing that. But no matter how many
times we cry, we know that tears are not enough and we are
as angry as we are sad at the waste of life and suffering
that go on. "

Anne Maguire committed suicide in January, 1980.
Mairead, who had begun a full-time course in political science,
moved into the home of her brother-in-law, Jackie Maguire,
to help care for his three children. Another girl, Mary
Louise, had been born in 1978.

Anne's death strained nerves at Fredheim, and there
was open wrangling between Ciaran and Betty, who admitted,
"My own worst enemy is my tongue. " With the ouster of
Peter McLachlan as chairperson, Betty's temper flared again.
She resigned and left for a lecture tour in the United States.
Mairead, who had taken over as mother to the Maguires, was
confirmed as chairperson of the executive, but Ciaran resigned the following October. Later he reflected, "... trying
to get too many ideas going at once can jam the transmission,
which was probably my major fault in the last few years. "

In 1979 Mairead had explained to a reporter: "I am
always asked, why are you not married? My answer is if I
met the right man, and I would know immediately, I would
love to get married, but if not, I am quite happy to continue
my work for peace. " The right man, in fact, proved to be
her brother-in-law, Jackie Maguire. In 1981, when their engagement was announced, Mairead said, "I am delighted that
God has blessed our relationship with love. " They were
married in a quiet ceremony in Rome on September 8, 1981,
and honeymooned in Assisi. The next month Mairead did
not seek reelection to the executive, but remained a member
of the organization. In the spring of 1982 she gave birth to
a son, John Francis.

That fall Betty was deep in domestic problems. Her
marriage broke down completely, and in 1982 she obtained a
divorce from Ralph Williams. To escape from her troubles
she made another lecture tour of the United States. A few
days after Christmas came the announcement that she had
married James Perkins, an electrical engineer, whom she
had met while on holiday in Florida. The romance had begun
through the friendship of their children, Debbie Williams and
Hollis and Jason Perkins.

Neither she nor Ciaran, who had become a free-lance
journalist and typesetter, returned to Fredheim. Only Mairead
stayed on. In 1983 at the annual assembly she was reelected
to the executive committee. Betty worked for peace in other
ways. In the summer of 1984 she sailed to Nicaragua with
four other Nobel laureates to deliver supplies donated by
Sweden and Norway. In July, Mairead gave birth to a second
son, Luke.

At Fredheim, with Ann McCann, former secretary to
Betty Williams, as administrator, peace work proceeded
quietly. In 1984 the Peace People numbered 100. Their
youth group, 100-strong, scheduled sports events and open
discussions. Inspired by Mairead, Peace People were still
taking mingled groups of Catholic and Protestant children to
summer camps in Norway. Also in the cause of "reconciliation and understanding," they gave advice and support to political prisoners and their families. The brochure of the Peace
People described them as still "putting into practice their belief that a just and peaceful society can only be built from the
bottom up, through the efforts of ordinary people."

In 1981, Ciaran had expanded on their ideal:

Yes, sometimes we feel like spitting in the wind,
but there's always plenty to be doing in the Irish
peace movement, by which it should be obvious
that I mean the establishment of a just, non-violent
democracy in which individuals have a sense of
their own power enshrined in a constitution and
felt in their daily lives and in which the idea of
bearing arms, or preparing to kill anyone, becomes
the major taboo of our culture.

In the Steps of St. Francis

MOTHER TERESA

In Calcutta, Mother Teresa always restricted her
wardrobe to three white cotton saris edged in blue--"one for
wearing, one for washing, one for mending." When she came
to Oslo in December, 1979, to receive the Peace Prize, she
was still sari-clad, but made a concession to the Norwegian
winter by donning a simple knitted jacket. Her feet remained
in open sandals.

Before the elegantly attired audience of royalty and
diplomats in the Aula, John Sanness, the chairman of the
Norwegian Nobel Committee explained its choice: "There
are many paths we can and must pursue to reach our goals--
brotherhood and peace.

"In awarding Nobel's Peace Prize for 1979 to Mother
Teresa the Committee has posed a focal question that we encounter all along these paths: Can any political, social, or
intellectual feat of engineering, on the international or on the
national plane, however effective and rational, however idealistic and principled its protagonists may be, give us anything
but a house built on a foundation of sand, unless the spirit
of Mother Teresa inspires the builders and takes its dwelling
in their building?"

As he pointed out, "The hallmark of her work has
been the respect for the individual and the individual's worth
and dignity. The loneliest and the most wretched, the dying
destitute, the abandoned lepers, have been received by her
and her Sisters with warm compassion devoid of condescen-
sion, based on their reverence for Christ in man."

The tiny nun with sparkling gray eyes in her heavily
creased, nut-brown face used no notes for her acceptance
speech. She had spoken and written the words many times:
"Our poor people are great people, a very lovable people.

God bless you
M. Teresa mc

Mother Teresa

They don't need our pity and sympathy. They need our understanding love and they need our respect. We need to tell
the poor that they are somebody to us, that they too have
been created by the same loving hand of God, to love and be
loved."

Then she asked the distinguished guests to join her in
the prayer attributed to St. Francis of Assisi: "Lord, make
me a channel of thy peace; that where there is hatred, I
may bring love; that where there is wrong, I may bring the
spirit of forgiveness; that where there is discord, I may bring
harmony; that where there is error, I may bring truth; that
where there is doubt, I may bring faith; that where there is
despair, I may bring hope; that where there are shadows, I
may bring light; that where there is sadness, I may bring joy.
Lord, grant that I may seek rather to comfort than to be
comforted; to understand rather than to be understood; to love
rather than to be loved; for it is by forgetting self that one
finds; it is by forgiving that one is forgiven; it is by dying
that one awakens to eternal life." (Aftenposten in Oslo reported, "It is likely the first time that a gathering in the Aula
has prayed out loud together.") In the spirit of St. Francis,
Mother Teresa accepted her award "unworthily but gratefully
in the name of the poor, the hungry, the sick and the lonely."

The next day during her Nobel lecture she again asked
her audience to repeat the famous prayer. Her lecture, simple and direct, followed the same lines as her acceptance
speech. Nineteen hundred seventy-nine had been designated
the International Year of the Child, and in both speeches
Mother Teresa attacked abortion. "The greatest destroyer
of peace today," she said on December 10, "is the crime of
the innocent, unborn child. If a mother can murder her own
child, in her own womb, what is left for you and me but to
kill each other? ... To me, the nations which have legalized
abortion, they are the poorest nations. They are afraid of
little ones, they are afraid of the unborn child. And the
child must die because they don't want to feed one more child,
to educate one more child. So the child must die."

On December 11 she repeated her theme: "The greatest destroyer of peace today is abortion, because it is a direct
war, a direct killing--direct murder by the mother herself."
Mother Teresa offered only one weapon. "We are fighting
abortion by adoption."

Her words set off strong protests around the world.

Some critics noted that by opposing abortion, birth control, and sterilization in a country where such measures were urgently needed, she was increasing the misery to which she ministered.

Mother Teresa had already surprised Norwegian officials when she asked them to cancel the Nobel banquet for 135 at the Hotel Continental and to give to the hungry in Calcutta the $6,000 it would cost. By her reckoning, 400 persons would be able to receive one meal every day for a year. Impressed Oslo journalists called her the most modest person who had ever received the Peace Prize. The $192,000 she earmarked for building homes and hospitals for the poor throughout the world. To that sum she added the Norwegian People's Prize of $70,000, collected from private citizens throughout the country.

At the invitation of the Norwegian government, two members of her family, her brother Lazar and his daughter Agija from Palermo, Sicily, had flown with her from Rome. Two members of her religious family, Sisters Agnes and Gertrude, her first postulants, had accompanied her all the way from Calcutta. Still another special guest at the Nobel ceremony was the Archbishop of Skopje, Yugoslavia, Mother Teresa's birthplace.

Skopje, which lies on the Vardar River, is now the capital of Yugoslavian Macedonia. A tourist brochure describes the region as one of "myths and legends, lakes, valleys and mountains, sunshine and grapes, wine, dance and song." Rebecca West once wrote of Skopje's "domes and minarets and russet roofs; green hills surrounding the town with the white toothpicks of nameless Moslem graves ... the bare blue mountains beyond," a place holding "the essences of Christianity and Islam."

At the time of Mother Teresa's birth the entire area called Macedonia belonged to the Turks, but after the Balkan Wars of 1912-1913 it was divided among Greece, Serbia, and Bulgaria. The Serbs won Skopje and surrounding territory. But following the assassination of Archduke Franz Ferdinand at Sarajevo, Austria declared war on Serbia in July 1914. The Central Powers crushed Serbian armies and occupied the country until the armistice. In December, 1918 Serbia helped form the new kingdom of the Serbs, Croats, and Slovenes. Eleven years later this kingdom became Yugoslavia.

Of sturdy Albanian peasant stock, Agnes Gouxha Bojaxhiu was born on August 27, 1910, to Koli Bojaxhiu, a phar-
macy assistant, and his wife Dronda. The Bojaxhius lived in
the old family home, built in the Turkish style in the center
of Skopje. (It was destroyed in the devastating earthquake of
1963.) Besides Lazar and Agnes they had a daughter Agija.
After acquiring some property, Koli opened a little general
store near Skopje Fortress.

Mother Teresa has characterized her home life as exceptionally happy. In Oslo in 1979 Lazar described his famous sister as a mischievous tomboy in her childhood. She
loved nature and with her schoolmates, who always carried
musical instruments, went on Sunday outings to the nearby
mountains. Agnes had a fine soprano.

She attended local schools, learning her lessons in
Serbian. At the age of 12, she later said, she first knew
that she had "a vocation to help the poor." She was active
in her church, where she became a member of the Sodality
of Mary, a Roman Catholic association for children with a
special interest in foreign missions. Some local Jesuits had
gone to do missionary work in Bengal, and the enthusiastic
letters one of them sent home were regularly read aloud at
the Sodality meetings, further inspiring young Agnes to do
mission work. Lazar was aghast when he heard that she had
decided to become a nun. "You are throwing your life away,"
he protested. He had become head of the household, for
Koli had died, leaving the family in somewhat difficult straits.

In spite of family opposition, 18-year-old Agnes applied
for admission into the Congregation of Loreto nuns working
in Bengal. She was accepted, but as she prepared to leave,
she fell ill. Nevertheless she pushed on. "If I die here, you
will lose me," she told her mother. "If I leave, maybe I'll
survive. I won't be close to you, but I'll be alive and useful. God calls me." First she was sent to Ireland to learn
English at the Loreto Abbey at Rathfarnham, Dublin.

Then she left for India to begin her novitiate in the
genteel hill station of Darjeeling at the foot of the Himalayas,
where the Loreto sisters had a school for the daughters of
European tea planters and Westernized Indians. Here Agnes
Bojaxhiu became a teacher, and here she took her vows with
the Loreto order in 1931.

For her new name she chose Teresa, in honor of the

patron saint of missionaries, St. Térèse of Lisieux (1873-
1897), a French Carmelite nun who had been canonized in 1925.
Recognized for her piety, simplicity, and patience in struggling
with consumption, the "Little Flower of Jesus" was credited
with many miracles. But she was best known for her advocacy
of "the little way, " the joyful undertaking of the most humble
duties. Many of Mother Teresa's admirers believe that much
as she resembles "the little Térèse, " she seems also like St.
Teresa of Avila (1515-1582), a Spanish nun of great organizational abilities and practical wisdom who introduced reforms
into the Carmelite order. In their opinion, Mother Teresa
combines the best qualities of both saints. (Another Mother
Teresa was Frances Ball, who founded the Loreto order in
Ireland.) Sister Teresa took her final vows in Darjeeling in
1937.

After completing her novitiate, the young nun became
a teacher of history and geography at St. Mary's, an exclusive
school for Bengali girls, taught in their own language. St.
Mary's shared grounds with an English high school for girls
run by the Loreto Sisters at Entally, Calcutta. Sister Teresa
was popular as a teacher, and later she became the principal.
She also took charge of the Daughters of St. Anne, an Indian
religious order affiliated with the Loreto sisters. For almost
20 years she led a well-protected, somewhat secluded life at
the convent. Its well-manicured lawns, however, were set in
the midst of one of Calcutta's worst "bustees" or slums, and
Sister Teresa's rooms looked out on scenes of squalor. Members of a Sodality at the Entally complex helped the poor and
regularly visited patients in the nearby hospital. The tragic
stories they told shocked Sister Teresa.

Rudyard Kipling's description of Calcutta as the "City
of Dreadful Night" has never been challenged. Though it is
full of palaces, its slums are among the world's worst.
Shortly before the partition of India, the Muslim and Hindu
communities were at sword's point and essential services
began to break down. One day in August, 1946, when food
supplies did not arrive at the school, Sister Teresa went out
to buy provisions from street vendors. Dust and blistering
heat, the stink of decaying offal, and the din of auto horns,
clanging trams, and angry crows almost overpowered her.
But she trudged on, feeling great love for the unfortunates
she saw, especially the naked urchins and the hungry and ill,
mere skeletons, who lay in the alleys.

One month later, on September 10, as she traveled by

train to a retreat in Darjeeling, she received what she refers
to as her second summons from God: "I heard the call to
give up all and to follow him into the slums and to serve
among the poorest of the poor." After the retreat she set
out to acquire release from the Loreto sisters so that under
the Archbishop of Calcutta she could lead the life of a religious
person among the poor. Papal permission soon came.

When she took off her black-and-white Loreto habit,
she donned a new uniform, a white cotton sari to blend with
the street people. To her shoulder she pinned a gold cross.
She had already determined to found a congregation whose
members would live like the poor. To acquire some training
in nursing and dispensary work, Sister Teresa spent three
months in Patna, India, with the Medical Missionary Sisters.
That same year she became an Indian citizen.

On her return in December, she found Calcutta in increasing turmoil. With Indian independence, Pakistan had
been set up as a separate Muslim state. Bengal had been
divided into West Bengal, which became a state in the new
Indian republic, and East Bengal, the eastern portion of Pakistan. Calcutta was named capital of West Bengal. Religious
hostility caused millions of Hindus to flee into Calcutta,
streaming into already overcrowded "bustees."

For a short while Sister Teresa lived with the Little
Sisters of the Poor. Then a kind man named Michael Gomes
offered her a private flat in his family home. Her first task
was to start an open-air school in a family compound in
Motijhil, the big slums near Loreto, Entally. Her pupils
were homeless older children she found in the streets. The
curriculum was simple. She taught them some personal hygiene and the Bengali alphabet which she scratched in the mud
with a stick. About this time a young girl named Subhasini
Das, who had been a pupil of Sister Teresa at St. Mary's,
arrived as the first recruit. Magdalene Gomes, later to take
the name of Sister Gertrude, soon followed. As voluntary contributions began to come in and as other former pupils joined
her mission, Sister Teresa expanded her work, going out into
the streets and bringing rice, powdered milk, and simple medicine into the shabby homes. She had by now formulated her
philosophy: love of the poor is the adoration of Christ.

Her own order, the new diocesan Congregation of the
Missionaries of Charity, was approved by the Pope and instituted in Calcutta in 1950. Sister Teresa dedicated her con-

gregation to the Immaculate Heart of Mary because she believed that it arose through the Virgin's intercession. A Mother House was opened at 54A Lower Circular Road and, as its head, Sister Teresa assumed the title of Mother Teresa. Subhasini Das, adopting her mentor's baptismal name, became Sister Agnes, the chief assistant. The Sisters of the Missionaries of Charity, who in the beginning numbered 12, took vows of poverty, chastity, obedience, and charity. The poverty vow ran, "To give wholehearted free service to the poorest of the poor. " As Kathryn Spink has explained, Mother Teresa's concept of the new congregation "was based on the fundamental aim 'to quench the thirst of Jesus Christ on the Cross'--the thirst which is the physical, symbolic expression of the spiritual cry for love and acceptance. The suffering Christ, himself the ultimate expression of sacrificial love, cries out for a response, a response which the Missionaries of Charity strive to provide in the observance of four vows. "

Their days began at 4:30 with prayer, and their schedule was rigorous, ending almost 16 hours later, again with prayer. In the streets they were everywhere exposed to dirt, disease, and misery, but because they had seen Mother Teresa's chapped hands picking maggots from a derelict's wounds or tenderly touching a leper's stumps, they did not spare themselves. Gradually doctors and nurses volunteered to work with the Missionaries.

One day in 1952, Mother Teresa picked up from the streets a dying woman, half eaten by rats and ants. When no hospital would admit her, Mother Teresa went to the municipal authorities and asked for a shelter. She was offered two former dormashalas or pilgrims' rest places adjacent to the temple dedicated to Kali, the goddess of death and fertility and the wife of Siva. The next day Mother Teresa moved several destitute and hopelessly ill persons into the rooms to allow them to die with dignity, in a clean place and in an atmosphere of love. For her it became an article of faith that the dying should know that they were loved. As she later said, "I still think that the greatest suffering is being lonely, feeling unloved, just having no one. I have come more and more to realize that it is being unwanted that is the worst disaster any human being can ever experience. "

The new home was called Nirmal Hriday, Place of the Pure Heart. From the beginning it was meant only for street cases, for people who would not be accepted by the hospitals, and for those who had no one else to take care of them.

Mother Teresa taught her missionaries to see the suffering
Christ in every derelict on a stretcher. Some visitors criticized the inadequate medicine practiced at Nirmal Hriday on
those suffering from terminal tuberculosis, dysentery, malnutrition, and various infectious diseases, but went away impressed with the aura of peace that rested over the home despite its long rows of steel cots, heavy smell of disinfectant,
and feel of death.

Though the dying were given the rites of their faith,
she met opposition. One day 400 Brahmin priests staged a
noisy protest outside the building. She addressed them: "If
you want to kill me, kill me. Let them [the inmates] die in
peace." Her courage won the priests to her side.

Next Mother Teresa began to help unwanted children.
In 1955 she opened a home called Shishu Bhavan in a non-
descript two-story building, which also became a work center
and a medical dispensary. Each postulant was required to
spend her first day here. Shishu Bhavan was the first of a
whole series of homes for children.

Mother Teresa's work with another class of unfortunates
began in 1957 when five lepers, who had been thrown out of
work and lacked shelter, came to the Mother House. In 1959
she founded several leprosariums and put out on the road mobile leprosy clinics (ambulances carrying sulfone drugs). The
same year she started a hospital and rehabilitation center at
Titagarh in the industrial suburbs of Calcutta, where horribly
disfigured lepers, some from upper-caste homes, were taught
to weave cloth and bandages and to make paper bags for their
medicines. Later a leper colony was built at Shanti Nagar,
the Place of Peace.

Though still depending on voluntary contributions,
Mother Teresa had her own shrewd ways of raising money.
When Pope Paul VI came to Bombay in 1964, to attend the
Eucharistic Congress, he gave her the Lincoln Continental he
used. She never rode in it. Instead she raffled it off.

Canon law required the Congregation of the Missionaries
of Charity to undergo ten years of probation before it could ex-
pand. By 1960 Mother Teresa was invited to establish centers
in Ranchi, New Delhi, Jhansi, and Bombay.

To extend her work she was granted permission to
start a new branch, the Missionary Brothers of Charity.

Official approbation came from Rome one year later.   Unlike
the sari-clad Sisters, the Brothers, who had been trained as
doctors, nurses, and social workers, wore no distinctive habit.
Their only distinguishing mark was a cross pinned to their
coats or shirts.   A small number were non-Indian.

Since Sisters and Brothers came from many parts of
India, Mother Teresa realized that the variety of languages
could make training difficult.   Besides there were not enough
spiritual books in the Indian languages.   So members of her
community spoke and read English.

In 1965, after 15 years, the Congregation of the Missionaries of Charity became a society of pontifical right directly under papal jurisdiction.   Customarily, congregations
are raised to the pontifical order only after 30 or 40 years.
Mother Teresa rejoiced, "This shows the great love and appreciation the Holy Father has for our congregation."

As the numbers of missionaries and volunteers increased, so did their services.   Besides elementary and
secondary schools, clinics, dispensaries, homes for the dying
and destitute, homes for abandoned children, leprosy villages
and clinics, commercial schools were added, even classes in
carpentry, metalwork, embroidery, child care, and home
management.   The Missionaries of Charity also gave help in
emergencies and disasters.

With a center that opened in Corocote, Venezuela in
1965, Mother Teresa began spreading her work to many parts
of the world: to Colombo, Ceylon in 1967 (the center closed
in 1971), to Tabora, Tanzania and Rome in 1968, and to
Bourke, Australia (a center for aborigines) in 1969.

Also in 1969 the Pope received the Institutes of the
International Association of Co-Workers of Mother Teresa,
committed to assisting the Missionaries of Charity. The first
article of its constitution states that the association "consists
of men, women, young people and children of all religions
and denominations throughout the world, who seek to love God
in their fellow men, through wholehearted free service to the
poorest of the poor of all castes and creeds, and who wish
to unite themselves in a spirit of prayer and sacrifice with
the work of Mother Teresa and the Missionaries of Charity."
Branches of the association were established in several countries.

In the 1970's, Mother Teresa established an astonishing 57 foundations on five continents. In 1971 she opened a house in the heart of the South Bronx area of New York. It was the first of 14 American centers. Meanwhile the Brothers opened centers in South Vietnam and in Phnom Penh, Cambodia. But Calcutta and its never-ending problems remained the base of operations. Monsoon floods in 1972 caused the sewers to overflow, and Mother Teresa and her workers waded in muck to their knees to rescue slum dwellers.

She asked a French priest named Father Georges Gorreé, who was also the chairman of the French Co-workers, to promote a link between her houses and various contemplative communities of other orders throughout the world. Soon 400 convents agreed to remember the Missionaries of Charity in their daily prayers. Two years later the indefatigable "angel of mercy" established a second group of Sisters in New York, a contemplative branch. In Kathryn Spink's words, "[It] provided a role for those whose vocation was to the contemplative life, in a pattern of prayer, which nevertheless included several hours in the afternoon for active apostolic work among the poorest of the poor."

She remained a tireless bundle of energy and love. As Malcolm Muggeridge wrote in 1971, "[D]oing something beautiful for God is, for Mother Teresa, what life is about ... I see [Mother Teresa and the Missionaries of Charity] diligently and cheerfully constructing something beautiful for God out of the human misery and affliction that lies around them. One of their leper settlements is near a slaughterhouse whose stench in the ordinary way might make me retch. There, with Mother Teresa, I scarcely noticed that another fragrance had swallowed it up."

Desmond Doig has described her after he saw her at Howrah Station, "burdened with homeless, hungry people who slept everywhere, on the platforms, the parapets, the busy road ... Here in one place was a shattering glimpse of what Mother Teresa is all about; a simple frail woman in a white sari reaching out to a multitude of hopeless and bewildered, nameless and destitute, diseased and dying people."

The Indian government deeply appreciated her. In 1972 it gave her the Jawaharlal Nehru Award for 1969 for International Understanding. As Prime Minister, Nehru's daughter, Indira Gandhi, was a devoted friend, praising her: "Who else in this wide world reaches out to the friendless and the needy so naturally, so simply, so effectively? Tagore wrote: 'There

rest Thy feet where live the poorest, and lowliest, and lost. '
That is where Mother Teresa is to be found--with no thought
of, or slightest discrimination between colour or creed, language or country. " The Nehru Prize was only one of a flood
of prizes. The Pope John XXIII Peace Prize in 1971 foreshadowed the Nobel Peace Prize eight years later.

October 16, 1979 had been a typical day for Mother
Teresa. Early in the morning she had visited Shishu Bhavan,
where the children had flocked around Mataji (Mother) and
touched her feet and hugged her. She had also watched some
of the 7, 000 who would be fed there. Then she had gone on
to one of the hospitals. Accompanied by a sick nun, she arrived back at her tiny office in the Mother House to find reporters and television cameramen waiting for her. In Oslo,
John Sanness, the chairman of the Norwegian Nobel Committee,
had just said, "This year the world has turned its attention
to the plight of children and refugees, and these are precisely
the categories for which Mother Teresa has for many years
worked so selflessly. It is not the first time that the Norwegian Nobel Committee has awarded the Peace Prize for
work undertaken in the struggle to overcome poverty and distress in the world, which also constitute a threat to peace. "

Reporters at the Mother House clamored for a state--
ment. "I am unworthy, " she protested. "Personally I feel
I am not worthy to receive it. But I feel that this gift has
been given to me because in this way people will become more
aware of the poor. "

Two months later in the Aula, Sanness quoted an Indian
journalist to point up a special link: "The Sisters, with their
serene ways, their saris, their knowledge of local languages
... have come to symbolize not only the best of Christian
charity, but also the best in Indian culture and civilization,
from Buddha to Gandhi, the great saints, the seers, the
great lovers of humanity with boundless compassion and consideration for the underprivileged; what Shakespeare called
'the quality of mercy. '" Sanness ended by quoting Robert
McNamara, president of the World Bank: "Mother Teresa
deserves Nobel's Peace Prize because she promotes peace in
the most fundamental manner, by her confirmation of the in-
violability of human dignity. "

In 1979, the statistics were impressive. The Missionaries of Charity had 158 branches in more than 25 countries.
Eighteen hundred Sisters belonged to the order, considered

by many to be the most flourishing in Christendom.   There
were 120,000 Co-workers.

After Oslo, despite a touch of angina, Mother Teresa
did not slow down one bit.   By 1984, 238 houses in 63 countries held 2,000 Sisters.   That year she went to famine-struck
Ethiopia and then to Bhopal, the scene of a terrible industrial
accident.

Her program was unchanged.   "Love cannot remain by
itself--it has no meaning," she had once written.   "Love has
to be put into action and that action is service ... All works
of love are works of peace."

Constant Crusader

ALVA MYRDAL

Special interest centered on the 1982 Peace Prize given to antiwar activist Alva Myrdal, still an elegant figure at 80. It was the second Nobel award in the family. Her husband, Gunnar, had shared the 1974 Prize in Economic Sciences with Friedrich von Hayek for "a penetrating analysis of the inter-dependence of economic, social, and institutional phenomena." Thus after long lives of extraordinary achievement, the Myrdals became the first husband and wife to earn Nobel honors in separate fields. Gunnar, who often had described Alva as "fantastic," looked on proudly and applauded as she too entered the ranks of laureates.

She shared her prize with Alfonso Garcia Robles, a Mexican career diplomat for over 40 years. Both had served in the United Nations and worked for the Disarmament Com-mission in Geneva, Switzerland. Both had strongly criticized the United States and the Soviet Union for threatening the world with thermonuclear disaster.

Alva Myrdal, Swedish sociologist, diplomat, and former cabinet minister, had been active in disarmament movements for two decades; Garcia Robles, for twice as long. A former foreign minister, he had been the moving force behind the 1967 Treaty of Tlatelolco, which declares Latin America to be a nuclear-free zone. He was also co-author of the Nuclear Nonproliferation Treaty, which 115 nations had signed by 1982. To the Norwegian Nobel Committee, these two pio-neers best represented the spirit of the nuclear-freeze move-ment as it gained ground in Western Europe and the United States in 1982.

When the joint award was announced in October, the Nobel panel mentioned two roads to disarmament: "the patient and meticulous work undertaken in international negotiations on mutual disarmament" and "the work of numerous peace

Alva Myrdal

movements with the greater emphasis on influencing the climate of public opinion and appeal to the emotions. " The
prizewinners had traveled both roads.   They had played a
central role in United Nations disarmament negotiations and
had influenced international opinion by their writings and
speeches.

Alva Myrdal's career had been studded with other
achievements. Before she became a peace activist, she had
devoted three decades to special spheres of interest--the
1930s to population control, family welfare, and women's rights;
the 1940s to educational reform; and the 1950s to large-scale
developmental aid to impoverished countries.

As Hammond Innes has written: "A driving energy seems
to be a characteristic possessed by almost all Swedes.   There
is a sense of thrust and concentration manifested in the way
they work, in the intensity of their lives, even in the way
they handle their cars.   Yet they are conformists, both to
the regulations of law and to the formalities of social life. "

From early years Alva Myrdal was shaped by that
driving energy.   The eldest of five children of Gustaf Albert
and Lowa Reimer, she was born on January 31, 1902, in the
university town of Uppsala.   She had two sisters, Rut and
Maj, and a brother, Folke, fairly close to her in age.   She
was 15 when her younger brother, Stig, arrived.   Maj died
young, but Rut proved a close and reliable companion.

Alva spent her first years in Stockholm.   The family
moved to Alvsjö where Albert Reimer, temperance man and
atheist, became active in organizing and directing coopera-
tives.   Young Alva liked to sit under his desk and listen to
his business dealings.   World War I brought an abrupt halt to
such enterprise.   The Reimers settled in Eskilstuna, about
60 miles from Stockholm, where Albert became a farmer,
contractor, and later a city councilman.   He and his wife belonged to opposing political parties, Social Democratic and
Liberal, and their children constantly heard political discussions and read the party newspapers.

Unfortunately Lowa Reimer, who never put her considerable talents as a dressmaker to professional use, felt burdened by her many children.   Her situation contributed to her
eldest daughter's eventual feminist drive.   Alva shrank from
the idea of being just a housewife.

She corresponded with a girl in Norway, and after they had exchanged textbooks, she was surprised to discover how differently Swedish and Norwegian writers treated the union crisis that resulted in Norwegian independence in 1905. Along with the political discussions in her home, this discovery sparked her interest in people worldwide. At 14 Alva received a diploma from Eskilstuna folk high school and the next year one from a trade school in Eskilstuna. Girls still were not allowed to enter the public Gymnasium, which prepared students for the university. Only private schools would admit them. Alva had ambitious horizons, but Lowa Reimer failed to understand her bookish daughter's craving for higher education and frowned on her leaving home. So for two years Alva worked as a clerk in the city audit department. Then her father, sympathetic to her goals, took the initiative in forming a little study group which followed the curriculum of the Gymnasium, and Alva was on her way.

One June day in 1919 at the Reimer farm, the hired man complained that three male cyclists had trespassed and spent the night in a haystack. The three turned out to be personable young university students, and they were invited to breakfast. Pretty blonde Alva served them coffee and began talking eagerly with the ruddy, good-looking law student, Gunnar Myrdal. The attraction was immediate and mutual.

They met again at the University of Stockholm. Alva, who had once considered becoming a physician, studied religious and literary history and Nordic languages. During long philosophical dialogues, she and Gunnar experienced a deepening of their intellectual interests. They were intrigued by the philosophers of eighteenth-century France, Britain, and Germany. "Fornuftet måste segra" (reason must win) became their life-long credo. In later years Gunnar declared, "We have stayed loyal to the ideas of the Enlightenment." Alva and Gunnar also shared goals of working hard and making something of their lives. Above all, they were never to waste time.

On October 8, 1924, one month before Alva finished her studies for the final examination, they were married. Their tiny apartment quickly became a weekly salon for a circle of young intellectual friends and achievers. Lively, intense Gunnar would rather talk than listen and liked to dominate the conversation. Often Alva, taciturn but sharply observant, would gently lay a hand on his arm to remind him

to let others speak. From the beginning Gunnar gave his remarkable wife the freedom to develop in her own way. "Alva
is my hobby, " he frequently said. He also shared the household chores. He fully supported her decision to continue
classes at Stockholm University until 1926. They always
operated as equal partners.

From 1924 until 1932, with some interruptions for
further study abroad, she led study circles within the Workers
Education Association in Stockholm. In 1927 she was off to
London and Leipzig for classes in psychology and pedagogy,
in which she had become intensely interested. Gunnar accompanied her, the trips increasing his contacts in academic and
political circles. That same year the Myrdals' first child,
a son, Jan, was born. It was also the year that Gunnar, who
had briefly practiced law, received his doctorate in economics,
published a book on price theory, and obtained a position as
a docent in political economy at Stockholm University.

In 1929, leaving Jan with Gunnar's parents, husband
and wife traveled through the United States as Rockefeller
Fellows. Having arrived the day before the Wall Street crash,
they were able to observe the beginnings of the Great Depression. Alva also continued her psychological studies. For
both Myrdals the fellowship year resulted in a strong tie to
the United States and a better understanding of Sweden when
seen from afar. But as Alva later told an interviewer, she
felt "a fury at free enterprise, which was more enterprise
than free. " And so, she said, "I returned to Sweden
radicalized--glad we had state-owned railroads and hospitals,
which I had never thought about till I saw the other option.
And I knew that I could work [in Sweden] in an organized way
to get something accomplished. And yet we ... were tremendously backward in many ways. Our teaching system was
backward, psychology was sorely lacking in the academic cur-
ricula, and women were less emancipated. " Her peace work
would not begin for another 20 years.

Next, with Jan in tow, the handsome young couple
spent a year in Switzerland, where Gunnar served as associate professor of national economy at the Post-Graduate Institute of International Studies and Alva studied social psychology and social pedagogy with the famous Jean Piaget at
the University of Geneva.

After Gunnar returned to Stockholm University as acting professor, his wife became a psychological assistant at

the Central Prison in Stockholm. At the same time she
studied theoretical philosophy and pedagogy at the University
of Uppsala and began a successful journalistic career, serving
on various editorial boards and contributing articles on social
and educational problems to newspapers and periodicals. Now
the Myrdals joined the Social Democratic party to which Alva's
father and grandfather had belonged. Meanwhile Gunnar's
academic star was rising, and in 1933 he succeeded his former
professor in the Lars Hierta Chair of Political Economy and
Financial Science.

By their tenth wedding anniversary, in 1934, the Myrdals had authored a book, <u>Kris i Befolkningsfrågan</u> (Crisis
in the Population Question), inspired by Sweden's low birth-
rate. It shocked and shook up the country for daringly they
championed voluntary parenthood, sex education, contracep-
tion, abortion, generous maternity benefits, free school
lunches, and rent subsidies for large families. They were
widely suspected, even disliked, but eventually their suggestions shaped much of Sweden's new social policy.

That year of 1934 was filled with other important happenings. Alva gave birth to a daughter, Sissela, and received
her master's degree from Uppsala University. A second
daughter, Kai, was born in 1936, completing the family.
Gunnar always stood by to help, but a maid was now necessary. As Alva combined child rearing with her expanding
career she found that there were problems with Jan, a stout,
gifted, eccentric boy. Years later, Jan wrote a bitter memoir
of his childhood, complaining that he had often been shunted
off to relatives and that his parents had never understood
him.

Always the dedicated feminist, Alva served as secretary of the Government Commission on Women's Rights from
1935 to 1938 and wrote its official report, a profeminist document. In it she suggested that Swedish marriage laws be
made more flexible and that unmarried couples be free of
legal discrimination. She often observed that in marriage,
payment was not made in relation to the value of women's
work but decided by the good will and financial capacity of the
husband.

Dominating all her activities was the conviction that
there must be equality between the sexes, among generations,
among social classes, and among countries. Her detractors,
however, carped that for a champion of equality, Alva's
clothes always looked too fashionable.

Intensely concerned with the welfare of Sweden's children, she founded the Training College for Pre-School Teachers in Stockholm in 1936, and held the post of Director for
12 years.   She inaugurated many reforms reported in books
and articles.   One of her popular ideas was the establishment
of adventure playgrounds.

Caught up in a whirlwind of activity, she also served
as president of the Swedish Federation of Business Women
from 1936 to 1938 and from 1940 to 1942.   In the meantime
Gunnar, who had been elected to the nation's Senate, served
on the new housing and population commission.

Taking leaves of absences in 1938, the Myrdals sailed
with their family and two baby sitters to the United States,
where Gunnar began research for the Carnegie Corporation
on race relations, and Alva studied statistics at Teachers
College, Columbia University.   The final result of Gunnar's
work was An American Dilemma, The Negro Problem and
Modern Democracy (1944), which has been credited with inspiring the civil rights legislation of the 1950s and 1960s.

At the beginning of 1940, Herbert Hoover asked Alva
to join a Norwegian architect and a Norwegian journalist in
a six-week lecture tour of the United States to win support
for Finland in its winter war with the Soviet Union.   Alva
reached large audiences with her topic of Scandinavian democracy.

After the Nazis invaded Norway and Denmark in April,
1940, the Myrdals returned with Jan, Sissela, and Kai to
Sweden.   Here they collaborated on another book, Kontakt
med Amerika (Contact with America), 1941.   A best-seller,
it was a description of democratic institutions.   The next
year, Alva's Nation and Family, chronicling "the Swedish experiment in democratic family and population policy," was
issued.

But soon Gunnar decided that he must return to the
United States and his work on race relations.   Alva wanted to
join him.   Leaving the children in the care of her mother-in-
law, she set out by air in the summer of 1941.   Because
long stopovers in England and Portugal were necessary, she
did not reach New York until October.   In London she had
sat up several nights and screamed when the bombs rained
down.   One year later the Myrdals flew on a secret plane
back to Stockholm, and Gunnar resumed his teaching post.

But he returned to the United States again in 1943 and 1944 as economic advisor to the Swedish legation in Washington, D. C.

Following a long tradition, Sweden remained neutral during World War II. Nonetheless the war years were politically active for the Myrdals, who, when they were home, were closely associated with an international group of Social Democrats, refugees from Fascist Europe living in Sweden. Among the hundred or so intellectuals, who called themselves the "Little International," were Willy Brandt, later chancellor of West Germany, and Bruno Kreisky, a future chancellor of Austria. In numerous sessions held in the living room of the Myrdals' villa in Åppelviken, the group worked out plans for the postwar economic and cultural reconstruction of Europe. Their studies and discussions bore fruit when the ideologists returned to their countries to help establish free democratic societies.

After war's end, from 1945 to 1947, Gunnar Myrdal was named commerce minister, but drew fire for being too "socialistic." His resignation cleared the way for a United Nations assignment, his appointment as secretary general of the Economic Commission of Europe with an office in Geneva.

Soon the United Nations beckoned Alva as well. She had already served on three important Swedish government commissions--Training the Handicapped (1943-1947), International Postwar Aid and Reconstruction (1944-1948) and Educational Reform (1946-1948). She had also acted as chairperson of the World Council on Pre-School Education, and vice-chairperson of the International Federation of Business and Professional Women and of the Swedish Organization for Cultural Relief in Europe. So she was an excellent choice in 1949 for the job of principal director of the Department of Social Affairs at the United Nations at Lake Success, New York. It made her the highest ranking woman in the United Nations. But the new challenge meant leaving her family again.

Two years later she moved to Paris, where she brought her customary energy and organizing skills to the post of director of the Department of Social Sciences of the United Nations Educational, Social, and Cultural Organization (UNESCO). The International Political Science Organization was one among several social science programs she established. At the same time careful reports on integration and racism came from her busy office.

In 1953, at the height of the McCarthy period, an immigration officer denied her entry to the United States, but refused to spell out the charge. Alva, who was scheduled to make a speech at the General Assembly in a few hours, pointed out that the United States and the United Nations had agreed that all United Nations personnel be allowed unrestricted entry to this country. Finally, the officer was persuaded to give her a temporary visa.

Gunnar's judicial training was evident in the bulky document the Myrdals sent in protest to Secretary General Dag Hammarskjöld. They did not know if she had been stopped because she was a member of the Swedish Social Democratic party or because American authorities were alarmed about Jan. At 26, he had gone his independent way and was already known as a radical writer, who always commented disparagingly about his parents' social and economic beliefs. At the time the immigration authorities detained Alva, Jan was in Bucharest, Rumania helping to organize a youth festival.

The Myrdal defense considered both possible reasons for entry denial. The Social Democratic party, Alva pointed out, had always fought Communism within Sweden. As for Jan, she declared that for the last ten years he had been living his own life. She wrote, "During different periods of his independent existence--though not now--he has had some financial support from his parents, as his income as an author has been very meagre. My husband and I have also held it as a principle that our home should always stand open for him as for our other children.... We have also recognized his right to have his own opinions, even if we continuously have criticized them. Our relationship was characterized by Jan himself--in a way which makes me proud to be his mother--when he was called up over the telephone in Bucharest by a Swedish journalist and told that I had had trouble because of him in entering the United States. In his answer ... he expressed astonishment and regret...: 'I am very sorry that my mother has been maltreated for my sake. My parents are golden honest people, straightforward and incorruptible in their opinions and actions. I esteem and respect them and, in spite of the contradiction of our opinions, I know that they also respect my opinion.'"

The Myrdals had always encouraged independent thinking in their children. When Jan was only six, Alva had written, "When authoritarian obedience beats its breast, then we have to understand better than ever how to raise the next generation

to be critical, oppositional, and with a healthy sense of self-
assertion. "

   After much argument, the case of Alva's entry was resolved, and America's United Nations ambassador, Henry
Cabot Lodge, officially welcomed her to the United States.
That same year, Alva Myrdal, international civil servant,
switched to diplomacy, becoming Sweden's first woman ambassador. From 1955 to 1961 she was ambassador to India
and minister to Ceylon; from 1955 to 1958, also minister to
Burma; and from 1960 to 1961, ambassador to Nepal as well.
Flying to her assignment in 1955, she had written Gunnar in
a burst of enthusiasm, "Here I am on my way to India, to
what was a girl's dream of pearls and turbans, of rajahs, of
Mogul history and Gandhi and Tagore and Buddha. " Stationed
in New Delhi, she made numerous trips to Rangoon, Colombo,
and Katmandu.

   The Myrdals were again separated for long periods,
but they dealt with such problems naturally, seeing them as
"something that had to be faced. " They were deeply interested
in each other's work, and together or apart remained the intellectual team they had always been. "We never found anybody else so interesting to talk to, " they explained.

   In 1953 Gunnar had toured South Asia for six weeks and
became intensely aware of the problems in countries emerging
from colonialism. When his work in Geneva was finished in
1957, his wife welcomed him to New Delhi, where he began a
huge technical investigation, financed in part by Stockholm
University's Institute for International Economic Studies. His
three-volume study, Asian Drama: An Inquiry into the Poverty
of Nations, was completed in 1968. Like An American Dilemma, it commanded world attention although it did not present any detailed action plan.

   Presiding graciously over the Swedish Embassy in New
Delhi, Alva Myrdal achieved an instant rapport with Prime
Minister Jawaharlal Nehru, who sparked her interest in the
social development of underprivileged nations. With his en-
couragement she campaigned through speeches and articles
for large-scale financial aid. She was in fact on good terms
with Indians at all levels. Her detailed reports showed a
firm grasp of Indian affairs, and under her leadership, the
Swedish Embassy acquired a reputation for great effectiveness
in matters of trade. During this period Alva Myrdal, ever
the feminist, collaborated with Viola Klein on Women's Two

Roles. Home and Work (1956). The authors declared: "Attitudes and ideologies are gradually being brought into line
with technical and social development and tend toward greater
participation of married women in the economic, political, administrative, and cultural activities of the community. "

        Alva's sociological and educational work, her interna-
tional service, and her diplomacy were now capped by her
work for peace and disarmament. In 1961, Östen Undén, the
Swedish foreign minister, asked her to prepare a major statement on disarmament for his farewell speech at the United
Nations. Alva asked for a delayed announcement of her assignment while she explored the possibilities. Quickly she grew
positive. "Once I had begun, I was never able to stop the
search for the why's and how's of something so senseless as
the arms race. " Then she set out to become an expert. She
carried out her task so well that she was appointed a member
of the Swedish delegation to the United Nations General Assembly, then a member of the Swedish delegation to the United
Nations disarmament conferences in Geneva from 1962 to 1973.
For years she was the chief delegate. Under differing names,
first the Eighteen-Nation Disarmament Conference (END) and
then, as members were added, the Committee of the Conference of Disarmament (CCD), the ongoing assemblies discussed
general and complete disarmament, a ban on nuclear testing,
nonnuclear measures including the questions of chemical and
biological weapons, and an arms race in the sea.

        Alva received help from Swedish experts. But it was
her own profound commitment to the goals of disarmament and
her intensive study of the science and technology of the arms
race that made her a leader in the nonaligned nations. Through
discussions and proposals they tried to bring pressure on the
two superpowers, the United States and the Soviet Union.

        She had hoped to find compromises between the two ad-
versaries and had urged more emphasis on reason, analysis,
and constructivity than on hollow words. But she and her colleagues came to realize that the United States and the Soviet
Union "had been playing games with us, and often with their
own delegates, pretending those years at the negotiating table
were important, when all it was was a kind of occupational
therapy. It was the two superpowers who were on the same
side, working behind our backs, while the rest of us who believed in disarmament were cruelly deceived. " Since she and
the members of her group had presented many concrete and
elaborate proposals, they felt great frustration. In 1972 she

lamented, "We can see hardly any tangible results of our work, and the underlying major cause must be that the superpowers have not seriously tried to achieve disarmament."

To celebrate Sweden's 150 years of unbroken peace, Alva Myrdal founded the Stockholm International Peace Research Institute (SIPRI) in 1964 and became its first chairperson. Scientists from all over the world come to SIPRI to explore questions of armament, military technology, and disarmament. The Swedish government appointed her to chair its Commission on Studies of the Future (1971-1972) and its delegation for Expanding International Laws Against Brutality in War (1972-1973). Alva also succeeded in getting the government to set up the seismological Hagförs station, which independently monitors even the smallest subterranean nuclear tests and publishes the results internationally.

No woman has been more active in Swedish government than Alva Myrdal. In 1962, giving every appearance of youthful vigor, she was elected to the Swedish Parliament. From 1961 to 1966, she served as ambassador at large in the Swedish Foreign Office. In 1966, still a senator and still attending the disarmament conference in Geneva, she was named minister in charge of disarmament, a post she held for seven years. Her enormous influence on foreign policy helped lead to Sweden's formal and unilateral renunciation of nuclear, chemical, and biological weapons. From 1969 to 1973 she was a cabinet minister in charge of church affairs. Here, however, she failed in her effort to bring about a separation of church and state.

At 71 Alva Myrdal quietly retired from government service. But her writing and lecturing continued the crusade for disarmament. Characteristically she asked, "If you have a chance to reform things, don't you think you should?"

Taxing schedules had given her little leisure. But through the years she had made time for reunions with old classmates. They appreciated her tinkling laugh and the warm, spontaneous side of her personality, far different from her public image of crisp, cool reserve. One of these friends admitted, though, that sometimes Alva seemed to be "off on her own thoughts somewhere." Lars Lindskog has written: "Is there not, however, a breath of coldness and distance about Alva? Yes, perhaps--the distance one always feels when one meets a very intellectual person and maybe there is also something in her own explanation, 'When I have the

opportunity to talk about something that absorbs me, I can
talk for a long time.   Before then maybe I am a little reserved and shy.   It is possible that this is what the outside
world interprets as a certain coldness and distance. ' "

     With retirement from the government there were a few
more opportunities to attend the theater she loved.   The Myrdals had long enjoyed a generous income.   They owned a
beautifully furnished and book-lined town house in the heart of
Stockholm and holiday homes in Mariefred and on the Baltic
island of Gotland.

     But they disdained any household heip.   "Able-bodied
citizens should manage for themselves, " Alva said firmly.
She considered cooking one of her chief recreations.   The
Myrdals' lively discussions always began at the breakfast
table.

     She and Gunnar, who had become professor emeritus
in 1972, now began to collect honorary doctorates in the
United States and Britain.   In 1970 they were jointly awarded
the prestigious Peace Prize of the West German Booksellers'
Association in Frankfurt am Main.   Two years later they accepted appointments as visiting fellows at the Center for the
Study of Democratic Institutions in Santa Barbara, California.
Alva used this period to do research for her best-known book,
The Game of Disarmament (1977), in which she carefully docu-
mented 25 years of failed disarmament talks.   In her eyes
the United States and the Soviet Union were clearly the villains.
She decried the "military competition between the two superpowers irrationally and immorally proceeding on their own
courses, disregarding the insidious harm done to our whole
civilization. ...   Their building of arms has continued way
beyond an already achieved multiple overkill capacity, so
clearly unsatisfactory for any conceivable use they could have
in mind. "   The superpowers' arms race brings costs ruinous
to the world economy and wastes resources better devoted to
education, health, housing, and other social challenges.   So
the book argued for defusing the bipolar model and engaging
the world's policymakers in multilateral discussions toward
a sane arms policy with provisions for international verifica-
tion and the sharing of scientific knowledge.   Alva Myrdal
did not call for total disarmament, but rather for a complete
ban on nuclear testing and strict limitation of the deterrent
capacities of nuclear weapons.   Reflecting on her days in
Geneva, she also pleaded for internationally outlawing chemical and biological weapons.

After two years in Santa Barbara, the Myrdals were
off to new academic pursuits and more honorary doctorates.
Their durability and continued capacity to work amazed the
campuses. While he taught at City College of New York, she
taught at the Massachusetts Institute of Technology. In 1977
both were at the University of Wisconsin and in 1978 at the
University of Texas. Then, at the invitation of the Swedish
Government Commission on Defense Policy, Alva wrote about
the reorganization and reduction of the nation's defense system. She called for substituting civic training for military
service--"a new ethical tradition in the name of human
rights. "

In 1980 Alva Myrdal became the first recipient of the
Albert Einstein Peace Prize. Accepting it in Chicago, she
said, "There is a climate of despair that is being forced on
the youth of today by the ever-present threat of nuclear war. "
But despair did not stop her: "I have never, never allowed
myself to give up. " She was on crutches and still in great
pain because she had broken her thigh bone in a fall two months
earlier. Her daughter Sissela, a lecturer on medical ethics
and the wife of Harvard President Derek Bok, proudly watched
as the Boks' 11-year-old son assisted Paul Warnke, the
American disarmament negotiator, in presenting the check to
his grandmother. Thomas Bok represented the younger generation to whom Alva Myrdal has always chosen to appeal.

The other Myrdal children had also known success.
Jan had written numerous books, principally on China and
Indochina. Kai, married to a professor, was a union welfare
official in Göttingen, West Germany. The Myrdals had eight
grandchildren in all and one great-grandchild.

Alva Myrdal, like many laureates, was nominated many
times for a Nobel Prize. After the Peace Prize for 1981 went
to the Office of the High Commissioner for Refugees, Alva
received the compensatory Norwegian People's Peace Prize.
In October 1982 when the Norwegian Nobel Committee notified
her, her reaction was genuine surprise. "I did not believe
there was a thousandth of a chance that I could be awarded the
prize. " A bit later she reflected, "Millions of people are
joining the fight against nuclear weapons. I hope that after
we have received the Peace Prize, even greater numbers will
stand up in the fight.... The Prize money will come in handy
to support a peace campaign. "

When she attended the award ceremony and when she

gave her Nobel Lecture the next day, she was still lame and had to be helped to the podium. But her spirit was as strong as ever as she repeated her theme from The Game of Disarmament: "The longing for peace is rooted in the hearts of all men. But the striving, which at present has become so insistent, cannot lay claim to such an ambition as leading the way to eternal peace, or solving all disputes among nations. The economic and political roots of the conflict are too strong. Nor can it pretend to create a lasting state of harmonious understanding between men. Our immediate goal must be more aimed at preventing what, in the present situation, is the greatest threat to the very survival of mankind, the threat of nuclear weapons."

Understandably she felt a sense of urgency. In The Game of Disarmament, she had pointed out that when the Geneva disarmament conferences began in 1962, the world had a total of 500 intercontinental ballistic missile launchers. In 1982, when she accepted the Peace Prize, the total was almost 5000. But Alva Myrdal remained undaunted. "It is not worthy of mankind to give up. We win nothing by doing only wishful thinking. There is always something one can do!"

The Literature Prize

Mistress of Mårbacka
SELMA LAGERLÖF

Halt och ful--lame and ugly. Selma Lagerlöf had long
used these bitter adjectives about herself. But they faded
away that afternoon of December 10, 1909, in the Royal Academy of Music when she became the first woman and the first
Swede to receive the Nobel Prize in Literature. With her
proud carriage, this gray-haired woman of 51 was beautiful
at last. Nobody noticed that she limped slightly. The love of
a nation enveloped her.

Significantly, the family name means laurel leaf.
Selma Lagerlöf's Nobel laurel marked an important turning
point in the history of the Swedish Academy. For some years
Carl David af Wirsén, its powerful permanent secretary, had
stoutly opposed her selection. But finally, after the death of
his candidate, Algernon Swinburne, her popularity was so
overwhelming that he gave in, if reluctantly, to his fellow
academicians, who were her champions. But his humiliation
struck deep, and he never regained his authority. To cap her
triumph Selma Lagerlöf was elected the first woman member
of the Academy in 1914, one of the "eighteen immortals. "
Thus for a whole generation she participated in helping determine the Nobel awards in literature.

At the ceremonies she joined another famous laureate,
Guglielmo Marconi, the inventor of wireless telegraphy. The
diploma presented to the author of Gösta Berlings Saga and
Jerusalem carried the glowing citation, "in appreciation of
the lofty idealism, vivid imagination, and spiritual perception
that characterize her writings. "

At the Nobel banquet she spun another of her famous
fairy tales. With a twinkle in her mystical, steel-gray eyes,
she spoke of daydreaming on the train bound from her country
home for Stockholm. "Just think, if I were going to meet
Father in Paradise! ... [He] will certainly be sitting in a

Selma Lagerlöf

rocking chair on a veranda, with a garden full of sunshine
and flowers and birds in front of him." She would ask him,
she imagined, how she could pay her debts to all those who
had inspired her writing career and to those who had decided
to give her the Nobel Prize. But the old man would have no
real answer. Drying his tears of joy, he would bang his fist
and say, "I will not rack my brain about problems that no
one in Heaven or on earth can solve. I am too happy that
you have been given the Nobel Prize to worry about anything!"

The earthly Lt. Erik Gustav Lagerlöf had been jovial,
talkative, and so popular that the entire countryside came
every August 17 to his birthday party in the family garden although he could ill afford the expense. His family adored
him, especially Selma, who inherited his story-telling ability
his mother had passed on to him. He was the life and soul
of Mårbacka, the old family homestead, which lay in the
beautiful wooded province of Värmland, bordered to the west
by mountains and to the south by Vänern, Sweden's largest
lake.

Erik Gustav often talked about rebuilding Mårbacka,
but words were about as far as he got. He was an imprac-
tical farmer, often out of money, but never worried in front
of others. His good humor spilled out everywhere. "In a
facetious moment," Selma recalled, Erik Gustav even "named
his workmen's cottages after the principal cities of Europe--
thus Lars of London, Magnus of Vienna, Johan of Prague,
Per of Berlin." He had, in addition, a soft heart. No one,
said Selma, dared fish in the pond "because it was father's
wish that the carp should be left in peace." He had flocks
of doves, and "if one ever mentioned the killing of a dove, it
put him in bad humor."

Here at Mårbacka, Selma Ottiliana Lovisa was born
November 20, 1858. It was to give her an extraordinary
sense of place. Already the Lagerlöfs had two sons, Daniel
and Johan, and a daughter, Anna. A third daughter, Gerda,
arrived a few years after Selma. Lovisa Lagerlöf, born
Walroth, was more practical than her husband, quiet, and
more introspective and intuitive. Selma was to mirror something of each parent's nature.

When she was three-and-a-half years old, Selma woke
from a nap one afternoon to find she could not walk. Remembering years later, she wrote of herself: "Her legs did not
seem to belong to her; she had lost all control of them. The

child was terror-stricken. The feeling of utter helplessness
which came over her when the body refused to obey was something so dreadful she remembered it long, long afterwards ...
all her life. " The problem, the doctors discovered, was a
congenital hipbone malformation, which made one leg shorter
than the other. By clinging to the back of the huge, stern
nursery maid, Back-Kaisa, the determined little girl was able
to get around. A couple of years later at the seaside resort
of Stromstad she learned to walk again. But she was left
with a limp, which plagued her all her life.

Erik Gustav's sister, another Lovisa, and his mother
also lived at Mårbacka. Lisa Maja, the tiny old grandmother,
was the center of the children's life. Every day they nestled
happily around her as she sat "on the corner sofa of the bed-
room, " telling them marvelous stories about her romantic
youth. But it was Erik Gustav, who introduced them to Karl
Mikael Bellman's romantic late eighteenth-century ballads,
pounding out the accompaniments on the piano. "What delighted
the children above everything else, " wrote Selma, "was that
they might sing as loud as they needed. " She was learning
to love "fairy tales and sagas of heroes. "

Almost 40 years later in Nils Holgerssons Underbara
Resa gennom Sverige (translated as The Wonderful Adventures
of Nils) she lovingly described her childhood home:

> Life had been beautiful in this place. They had had
> weeks of work broken by many holiday festivities.
> They had toiled hard all day, but at evening they
> had gathered around the lamp and read Tegnér and
> Runeberg, 'Fru' Lenngren, and 'Mamsell' Bremer.
> They had cultivated grain, but also roses and jas-
> mine. They had spun flax but had sung folksongs
> as they spun. They had worked hard at their history
> and grammar, but they had also played theatre and
> written verses. They had stood at the kitchen stove
> and prepared food, but had learned, also, to play
> the flute and guitar, the violin and piano. They had
> planted cabbages and turnips, peas and beans in
> one garden, and they had another full of apples and
> pears and all kinds of berries. They had lived by
> themselves, and this was why so many stories and
> legends were stored away in their memories. They
> had worn homespun clothes, but they had also been
> able to lead carefree and independent lives.

A year after the cure at Stromstad, Lisa Maja died.
To Selma it seemed as if "the stories and songs were borne
away, shut up in a long black box, never to come again."
But they had left such an indelible impression she turned to
them constantly when she began to write. Fortunately, another
of Erik Gustav's sisters, Tante Ottiliana, knew all of Lisa
Maja's stories and could spin them again and again when she
visited Mårbacka every summer. She also had stories of her
own.

At seven, the crippled child "in short skirts with a
long flaxen braid" was convinced she was an eyesore. Halt
och ful, she told herself, halt och ful. (Actually, her face
was more plain than ugly.) But then she happened to read
Mayme Reid's Indian novel, Osceola, which excited and inspired her. Suddenly she realized that to be a writer one
did not have to be pretty.

In 1868 the little country girl went to Stockholm for
medical treatment, awed by this Venice of the North with
its many waterways, magnificent churches and palaces, and
sparkling, busy streets. Relatives took her to the theater,
where her fantasies sprang to life. In Stockholm she discovered Sir Walter Scott's romantic novels. She already
knew all of Hans Christian Andersen's fairy tales.

When she returned to Mårbacka, various governesses
tutored her, and Erik Gustav filled her life with stories and
music--he could play the violin as well as the piano. One
day when she was 13 an invitation arrived for a ball at nearby
Sunne. Knowing she would not be asked to dance, Selma
cried when the family insisted that she attend. And it happened as predicted. She sat the entire evening beside a lonely
spinster. Halt och ful.

After this ball she spent another winter in Stockholm
with her Onkel Oriel and Tante Georgina so that she could go
to the Orthopedic Institute and take gymnastic exercises. Her
diary from this period complains, "I know ... that my home-
made shoes were clumsy." But she forgot herself when her
Cousins Elin and Allan snuggled up to her on the nursery sofa
and begged her to tell old stories. She knew wonderful tales
of "water-sprites and trolls and enchanted maidens lured into
the mountains." Her new role made her feel like Lisa Maja.
But when the storyteller went home, she started scribbling
poetry.

The daybook from 1873 also tells about Selma's student.
On the train going to Stockholm with her brother Daniel, she
met one of his acquaintances from the University of Uppsala.
"He is so good looking!" she wrote. "And he is also friendly
and sympathetic. I wonder if he saw that I was sad when he
came in and if that was why he spoke to me?" She continued,
"My student and I became the best of friends, and before long
he spoke only to me."

During her first week in Stockholm Selma dreamed of
catching a glimpse of him. "Not that I am in love ... oh no!
But he was so pleasant, so good-looking, and so kind that it
would be a comfort to me just to see him once more."

Her uncle's apartment was close to the railroad station,
and one day Selma looked out the window and saw the student.
"I tapped on the windowpane very lightly and nodded.... He
doffed his hat in greeting, and then ... he threw me a kiss!
When he did that, no words can describe how blissfully happy
I was."

Quickly this "insignificant, little lame girl" built up
a dream of romantic feeling about him, imagining him the son
of a "tall, handsome prince." Then at the home of Baroness
H., her English teacher, she learned that he was engaged to
one of the baroness's young friends.

A few days later, in the street, Selma came upon "a
tall, hideous creature in a white tulle dress and white summer
hat trimmed with a garland of big red roses ... [all] turned
gray from grime and dirt--they, like the woman, and the
veils and ribbons that dangled about her, all looked as though
they had been lying in a clay pit." Selma knew at once that
this was Ragtag-Fröken. She had heard the sad story--" ...
poor thing, who had gone mad and now went about summer
and winter in some kind of bridal array because she had been
forsaken by her betrothed." Suddenly the young girl heard
the woman cry out--"one continuous savage cry." When the
Baroness H. heard about this pitiable creature, she said,
"Yes, love is terrible. There is nothing more cruel than
love."

Later that day Selma wrote in her diary: "I am beginning to think it is well that the student is betrothed. If
I were married to him I would never have time to write
stories, and that is what I have always longed to do. Besides,
I've been afraid of love ever since I saw Ragtag-Fröken."

Some weeks later Daniel arrived in Stockholm. When
he said, "I bring you greetings from the student you met on
the train last winter ...," Tante Georgina asked which student
he was speaking of. Daniel laughed. "He is one of Selma's
admirers. He said to me ... that she was one of the most
interesting girls he had ever met."

"Well, I never!" cried Tante Georgina. Selma smiled
mysteriously.

In the spring she went to visit Daniel in Uppsala. There
she heard that her student's engagement had been broken. The
appearance of his commonplace parents, who were there to
try to reconcile him with his fiancée, jolted Selma out of her
dreams. For the first time she saw that her student was "an
ordinary human being."

For the next seven years she was caught up in the
warm, loving, busy routine of her country home. In Stockholm she had realized that "we who sat around the lamp at
Mårbacka had just as good a time as the gods on Olympus."
But at 21 she felt vaguely dissatisfied. Deciding she must
make something more of her life, she returned to Stockholm
to enter a normal school. Just as she was graduated from
the Royal Women's Superior Training Academy, Erik Gustav
died. It was a devastating hurt, but fortunately she was pre-
occupied and had no time to brood.

She had found a job teaching at a girls' secondary
school in Landskrona in southern Sweden. As a teacher she
was a cut above the ordinary. She dramatized history and
literature in the most vivid manner. In good weather she
took her pupils outdoors for classes. She was, besides, the
only teacher in Landskrona who was writing a novel. Her
flash of inspiration had come at the normal school when she
had listened to a lecture about Bellman and other Swedish
balladeers. Suddenly she wanted to write about the legends
and folklore of her beloved Värmland, string the stories she
remembered into a long novel. "The faintest tune from the
Bellman lute," she noted, "called up memories of the never-
failing love and tenderness that had made our childhood such
a happy one!"

But how should she present her stories? They did
not seem suited to the sober, naturalistic, and often brutally
frank literary style of her day. She and August Strindberg
were poles apart. Then Thomas Carlyle's <u>Heroes and Hero</u>

<u>Worship</u> encouraged her to take her own inspiration as her
guide and write freely the way she wanted. After the first
three chapters of <u>Gösta Berlings Saga</u> won first prize in the
magazine <u>Idun</u> in 1890, she was encouraged to write more.
A titled lady named Sophie Adelsparre gave her money to take
a year off from teaching and finish the book. It was to become Selma Lagerlöf's most famous and characteristic work.

Her hero, Gösta Berling, is a renegade, unfrocked
priest. A Byronic figure of irresistible charm and striking
beauty, he strides into a splendidly romantic setting of "the
long lake, the rich plains, and the blue mountain." Quickly
he joins an eccentric band of cavaliers living off the bounty
of the Major's lady, the mighty ruler of Ekeby Manor. When
the evil ironmaster Sintram slanders her, she flees, and the
slightly foolish knights-errant seize power. Meanwhile the
moody Gösta gets entangled with beautiful women like Anna
Stjärnhök, Marianne Sinclair, and Countess Elizabeth Dohna.
After many misfortunes Countess Elizabeth marries him.
Then a sudden uprising routs the cavaliers, the Major's lady
returns--only to die, and a repentant Gösta begins anew as a
carpenter.

In <u>Gösta Berlings Saga</u> Selma Lagerlöf portrayed a
magic, mystical world of fairy tales, legends, and forgotten
pieces of Swedish country life. But she made it all seem con-
vincingly factual. As her friend Sophie Elkan once noted,
"Although Selma's head may have been in the clouds, she herself stood solidly with her two feet on the ground." She was
like her grandmother, Lisa Maja, who had said with the utmost conviction, "All this is as true as that I see you and
you see me."

Generally Selma Lagerlöf's style is romantic and rhap-
sodic. Sometimes she spoils it with digressions and apos-
trophes in Carlyle's most extravagant manner:

War-horse! war horse! Old friend, who now
stands tethered in the pasture, do you remember
your youth?

Do you remember the day of the battle? You
sprang forward, as if you had been borne on wings,
your mane fluttered about you like waving flames,
on your black haunches shone drops of blood and
foam. In your harness of gold you bounded forward;
the ground shuddered under you. You trembled with
joy. Ah, how beautiful you were!

When she leaves Carlyle behind, however, she achieves pure lyricism:

> Then he rose and went round the house. There lay
> the garden, so wonderfully beautiful that he had to
> stop and draw a long breath. The appletrees were
> in bloom. Yes, of course, he knew that. He had
> seen it on all the other farms; but in no other place
> did they bloom as they did in that garden, where he
> had seen them blossom since he was a child. He
> walked with clasped hands, very carefully up and
> down the gravel paths. The ground was white, and
> the trees were white, here and there with a touch
> of pink. He had never seen anything so beautiful.
> He knew every tree, as one knows one's brothers
> and sisters and playmates. The astrachan trees
> and the winter fruit-trees were quite white and the
> blossoms of the russets were pink, and those of the
> crab-apple were almost red. The most beautiful
> was the old wild apple-tree, whose little, bitter
> apples nobody could eat. It was not stingy with its
> blossoms; it looked like a great snow-drift in the
> morning light.

Here Selma is describing the garden at Märbacka.

In later years she would say that the period when she wrote Gösta Berlings Saga was the happiest of her life. She had so much to tell:

> We young people have often had to wonder at the
> old people's tales. 'Was there a ball every night,
> as long as your radiant youth lasted?' we asked
> them. 'Was life then one long adventure?'

> 'Were all young women beautiful and lovely in those
> days, and did every feast end by Gösta Berling
> carrying off one of them?'

> Then the old people shook their worthy heads, and
> began to tell of the whirring of the spinning-wheel
> and the clatter of the loom, of work in the kitchen,
> of the thud of the flail and the clearings made in
> the forest; but it was not long before they harked
> back to the old theme. Then sledges drove up to
> the door, horses speeded away through the dark
> woods with the joyous young people; then the dance
> whirled and the violin-strings snapped.

But she could not ignore a darker side:

> The wild chase for adventure rushed along the
> shores of lake Löven. The forest tottered and fell;
> all the powers of destruction were let loose. Fire
> broke out, floods laid waste the land, starving wild
> beasts roamed about the farmyards. Under the
> horses' hoofs all quiet happiness was trampled to
> death.

Involved with Strindbergian naturalism, the Swedish
public felt lukewarm toward the two volumes. Then after a
Danish translation and the praise of the famous critic, Georg
Brandes, Sweden at last took Gösta Berling to its heart. By
this time Selma Lagerlöf had launched Osynliga Länkar (Invisible Links), a collection of short stories.

In 1894 she met Sophie Elkan, a temperamental Jewish
widow and author, six years her senior. As an author,
Sophie brought history to life. She and Selma became lifelong friends although they were so different that a Danish
writer once likened them to "champagne and clobbered milk."

After Selma had been teaching for almost ten years,
King Oscar II and his artist son, Prince Eugen, arranged for
her financial support. Some help also came from the Swedish
Academy. Deciding to use the stipend for travel, she set out
with Sophie for Italy and Sicily. Selma extolled Sophie as a
"good friend and traveling companion, who not only took me
south and showed me all the glories of art but made life happier and lighter for me." The new friend also dominated
her. The travel impressions resulted in an unusual novel,
Antikrists Mirakler (The Miracles of Antichrist), in which
Selma Lagerlöf attacks socialism in a Sicilian setting.

In 1899-1900 she and Sophie took a long journey to
Palestine and Egypt. It meant another book. Jerusalem,
written in her customary fairy tale or legend form, became
her first immediate success. It is the story of a spiritual
pilgrimage. Her Dalarna peasants are a different stock from
Gösta Berling's laughing folk in Värmland. They are severe
and solidly conservative farmers, stalwart defenders of their
faith. Chief among them are the Ingmarssons of Ingmar
Farm. When a "practical mystic" arrives in Dalarna from
Chicago, he stirs such a religious revival that the family
and many of their neighbors sell their homesteads and emigrate to the Holy Land.

Certain episodes stand out starkly in the first volume of Jerusalem. One of the most moving occurs when Ingmar meets at the prison door the girl who had killed their illegitimate child and brings her back to the community. Another striking scene is the auction where Ingmar's son renounces his beloved Gertrud and becomes engaged to another girl to keep the ancestral estate in the family's hands. And finally in a vivid reconciliation episode the dead Ingmar's battered watch is handed to the man he had wronged.

The second volume of Jerusalem begins in a highly unusual manner. One stifling August night a sleepless Mrs. Gordon, founder of the American colony in Jerusalem, goes out in the direction of the city:

> Though still fighting her fears and apprehensions, she could not but notice the solemn beauties of the night. The pale-green moonlight of Palestine shed its weird lustre over the landscape, and gave to everything an air of awesome mystery. Suddenly the thought came to her: Just as in the old castles of Europe there are haunted rooms, where ghosts are said to abide, so this ancient city and the desolate hills surrounding it might perchance be the Old World's haunted chamber, a place where one would expect to see vanished grandeur descending from the mountains and the ghosts of bygone ages roaming about in the darkness of the night.

Then the Dome of the Holy Rock and the Church of the Holy Sepulchre hold a remarkable dialogue that continues for several pages. "It seemed ... as if the two old voices had taken this occasion to give vent to their pride and humiliation." Critics agreed that probably only Selma Lagerlöf could have carried off this tour de force successfully.

As the story goes on, the Dalarna peasants yearn for their old homes, but decide to stay in Jerusalem. Although young Ingmar searches a long time for Gertrud, the girl he jilted, he returns in the end to his wife, Barbro.

After Jerusalem, Selma Lagerlöf found she had enough impressions of Italy and Palestine left over to write another book, Kristuslegender (Christ Legends), a treasure she had borrowed, she said, from "pale, hollow-cheeked monks and nuns in their dark cloisters, the visions they saw and the voices they heard." Understandably, it was visionary and

mystical. By now her own faith had become highly personal,
nondenominational, and tied to great ethical strength. The
life of man, she wrote, "is a thread on God's loom."

Soon after Erik Gustav's death Mårbacka had been sold.
But in 1904 Selma Lagerlöf bought it back. In the 1890s she
had already used some of her literary earnings to buy a small
house in Falun in Dalarna, where she lived with her mother
and her aunt. Dalarna, the most typically Swedish of all the
provinces, a pastoral land filled with picturesque red farm-
houses and birch-lined roads, provided her with part of the
background for Jerusalem. And yet within its boundaries
lay the country's largest iron works and paper mill, the second largest iron ore deposits, and--close to Selma's home--
a world famous copper mine, Kopparberget.

In 1906, after three years of research and nature study,
Selma Lagerlöf published Nils Holgerssons Underbara Resa
gennom Sverige (The Wonderful Adventures of Nils), which
became a children's classic, treasured all over the world.
It was another fairy tale in pure, simple style, with cherished
old legends and stories striking fire in her memory. She gave
her story an unusual perspective. An elf transforms the 14-
year-old hero, "long and loose-jointed and tow-headed," into
a "little, little creature." As an elf Nils sails all over
Sweden on the back of a gander in company with the wild
geese. A characteristically magic passage tells of the cranes'
dance:

> And then came the gray, dusk-clad birds with plumes
> in their wings, and red feather-ornaments in their
> necks. The big birds with their tall legs, their
> slender throats, their small heads, came gliding
> down the knoll with an abandon that was full of mys-
> tery. As they glided forward, they swung round--
> half flying, half dancing. With wings gracefully
> lifted, they moved with an inconceivable rapidity.
> There was something marvelous and strange about
> their dance. It was as though gray shadows had
> played a game which the eye could scarcely follow.
> It was as if they had learned it from the mists that
> hover over desolate morasses. There was witch-
> craft in it. All those who had never before been
> on Kullaberg understood why the whole meeting took
> its name from the cranes' dance. There was wild-
> ness in it, but yet the feeling which it awakened was
> a delicious longing. No one thought any more about

struggling. Instead, both the winged and those who
had no wings, all wanted to raise themselves eternally, lift themselves above the clouds, seek that
which was hidden beyond them, leave the oppressive
body that dragged them down to earth and soar away
toward the infinite--

Such longing after the unattainable, after the hidden
mysteries back of this life, the animals felt only
once a year, and this was on the day when they
beheld the great crane dance.

Two years later Selma Lagerlöf wrote Tösen från
Stormyrtorpet (The Girl from the Marsh Croft), another peasant story with a theme of unselfish love. Seeing the young
girl's sacrificial love, the stern judge is moved to say, "That
is my people. I shall not be angry with them since there is
so much love and fear of God in one of those humble crea-
tures. " It is Selma Lagerlöf's own heart speaking.

In 1907 Uppsala University, which "her student" had
attended, gave her an honorary degree, and other academic
honors followed. In 1904, despite Wirsén's opposition, she
had been given the Gold Medal of the Swedish Academy "because of the imaginative wealth, idealism, and narrative
talent that are evidenced in her works, which are beloved inside and outside the borders of Sweden. "

Then on December 10, 1909, came the great moment
of the Nobel Prize. When Claes Annerstedt, president of
the Swedish Academy, made the presentation he pointed out
that Selma Lagerlöf's works were full of the idealism Nobel
required. He continued, "It should not be thought that this
decision was inspired by excessive national self-esteem, especially since many important foreign opinions have supported
her candidacy. Nor would anybody consider it a lack of modesty if the Nobel Prize, which is now being awarded for the
ninth time, remains in the country of its founder; on the contrary, such modesty could be interpreted as a lack of national
self-confidence. "

Annerstedt spoke of the "marvellous bloom of artistic
genius" that rested over Gösta Berlings Saga, of Selma
Lagerlöf's visionary quality, and her original depiction of
peasant life. Her style, he said, sprang from "the rich heritage of her mother tongue; from this source come the purity
of diction, the clarity of expression, and the musical beauty

that are characteristic of all her works. " And he added, "It
is easy to understand why the mystical, nostalgic, and miracu-
lous dusk that is peculiar to the Nordic nature is reflected in
all her works. The greatness of her art consists precisely
in her ability to use her heart as well as her genius to give
to the original peculiar character and attitudes of the people
a shape in which we recognize ourselves. "

After the Nobel Prize, Selma Lagerlöf's next book was
Liljecronas Hem (Lilliecrona's Home), a novel about the
violin-playing cavalier from Gösta Berlings Saga. Actually
the central character is his beautiful and faithful wife, Maja
Lisa, modeled on Selma's unforgettable grandmother, Lisa
Maja. And the setting is pure Mårbacka.

Philosophically, she had become a feminist who spoke
boldly at an international women's suffrage convention in 1911.
She was also a lifelong pacifist, and World War I distressed
her so much she stopped writing for a while. Just one novel,
Bannlyst (The Outcasts), came out in this period, and it
strongly denounced war. Hoping that the United States might
lead the world to peace, she paid her one and only visit to
America in 1924 as a delegate to the Women's Congress.

She had used the Nobel Prize money to buy up the
lands surrounding Mårbacka so that the estate grew to 140
acres. One of its grains was even made into a breakfast
food and marketed under the name "Mårbacka. " Selma and
her mother lived there every summer until Fru Lagerlöf's
death in 1915. A few years later Selma rebuilt the two-
story, red frame house into a Swedish manor with cream
stucco walls, a gabled black metal roof, and four sets of
double Doric columns across the front veranda. It was a
style, she thought, to which Erik Gustav might have aspired.
In the back garden bloomed her huge cherry tree, the pride
of the countryside in summer. By contrast, not far away
lay Bofors, the internationally famous munitions works, whose
great days began in 1890, when Alfred Nobel gained control
of the enterprise.

Except for a secretary and the necessary servants,
Selma Lagerlöf stayed alone at Mårbacka. Sometimes there
were guests. She lived simply, but wrote under ornate crystal chandeliers in her spacious study. If she was lonely, she
did not show it. She had become the grande dame of Swedish
letters. She was by now a confirmed old maid. Romance
was in her writing, not in her life. She recorded no other

personal episode like the one about the student on the train.
Still, as an old lady she was once on the verge of confiding
to Elin Wägner, one of her biographers, that she had had
some romantic inclinations. But in the midst of their conversation the telephone rang, and her mood was broken. She
never resumed the story. At an early age it was clear to
her, she once intimated, that she had very little chance of
getting married. She was halt och ful and she was not wealthy.
All her life she had money problems.

The simple lady loved the limelight nonetheless and
was not above appearing in public in fine dresses and feath-
ered hats. She became keenly interested in seeing her books
turned into films. The finest was Gösta Berlings Saga with
an exquisite young Greta Garbo playing her first important
role as Countess Elizabeth Dohna.

By the 1920s the lady of the manor was supremely
confident of her place in Swedish literature. Although she
was never arrogant and wore her success gracefully, she
did crave admiration and adulation. And she required many
services from friends like the deeply devoted Valborg Olander.
After her sixtieth birthday she decided it was time to look
backward. Several books of childhood memories from Mårbacka came out.

As Selma Lagerlöf grew old at her estate, her naturally plain face under her upswept white hair impressed others
with its beauty, distinction, and dignity. Her American translator, Velma Swanston Howard, described her as "a woman of
medium height, with a fine, fair face, splendid head, superbly
set on neck and shoulders.... Her sense of humor was keen.
There was a twinkle in her eye, a twist about the mouth, and
a certain sly humor that preceded her speech, while her
chuckle was inimitable."

She was becoming more interested in the occult. Often
she spoke of communicating with her mother. But sometimes
she brooded over the wrong she had done to her longtime
friend, Ida Bäckman. The episode concerned the lyric poet,
Gustav Fröding. At the height of his career the intemperate
Fröding suffered a mental breakdown and was befriended by
Ida Bäckman, who at Selma's urging wrote a book about him
after his death. Critics pounced on it and denounced its author. People expected Selma Lagerlöf to defend Ida, but she
said nothing. Later she told Ida that someone had threatened
her with blackmail if she raised her voice in defense of the

book. In her increasingly lonely old age she felt more than
ever the shame of her silence.

In 1927-28, Selma Lagerlöf offered her public a long
trilogy, Löwensköldska Ringen (The Ring of the Löwenskölds),
which tells how a ring stolen from General Löwensköld's
grave becomes a perpetual curse. The setting is Värmland
about the time of Gösta Berling. The style is simple, almost
naive. At 70 she was still not an expert plotter or creator
of complex characters. Critics even complained that her
imagination no longer ran so warm and colorful and luxuriant.
Some said she had exhausted her Värmland theme. Still, her
reputation was intact, her popularity extraordinary. "Reading
Selma Lagerlöf," said the Swedish composer, Hugo Alfvén,
"is like sitting in the dusk of a Spanish cathedral. Afterwards
one does not know whether what he has seen was dream or
reality, but certainly he has been on holy ground." She remained a national institution. Her last book, Höst (translated
as Autumn), was published when she was 75. Her countrymen
were amazed that she could keep on writing. By the outbreak
of World War II she was an octogenarian and still a passionate
pacifist.

In the last year of her life she and Prince Eugen
helped arrange a visa for a trembling German Jewess with
whom she had long corresponded. That exile, Nelly Sachs,
would write her best poetry in Sweden and win the Nobel
Prize in Literature in 1966.

Unfortunately, Selma Lagerlöf was dead before Nelly
Sachs and her mother reached Stockholm. She had died of
peritonitis March 16, 1940, at Märbacka. That beautiful
manor house is still one of Sweden's greatest literary shrines.
For, as Claes Annerstedt had said at the Nobel ceremony in
1909, "... what makes Selma Lagerlöf's writings so lovable
is that we always seem to hear in them an echo of the most
peculiar, the strongest, and the best things that have ever
moved the soul of the Swedish people."

Today she may be a little old-fashioned. But modern
Swedes and foreigners still bring along a copy of Gösta Berlings Saga when they visit Värmland. Usually they carry two
maps of the Fryken Valley region, one with the true geographical names and one with Selma Lagerlöf's nomenclature. The
renegade priest still haunts that romantic landscape.

Sardinian Legend
GRAZIA DELEDDA

While making coffee in the kitchen of her Rome villa
one November day in 1927, Grazia Deledda received a telegram from Stockholm announcing that she had won the Nobel
Prize in Literature. Calmly she remarked to her husband,
Palmiro, "Già, it's about time." This was not conceit. She
was only referring to the fact that her name had appeared
quite regularly on the Nobel ballots since 1907.

Her award, however, was for 1926, not 1927. Occasionally, like the Peace Prize, the Literature Prize has
been put on reserve when there are not enough votes for a
winner. In 1926 no less a playwright than George Bernard
Shaw had received the 1925 award.

On December 10, 1927, Grazia's citation read, "for
her idealistically inspired writings which with plastic clarity
picture the life on her native island and with depth and sympathy deal with human problems in general." Of all the
laureates in literature, Grazia Deledda was, next to Pearl
Buck, the most prolific. But she was also one of the least
known internationally. Although she had been translated into
several other European languages, very few of her works can
be found in English.

The 56-year-old author who arrived in Stockholm was
a shy, elfin, white-haired figure. A blunt nose and luminous
brown eyes marked her perceptive face. During the Nobel
ceremony she sat quietly in her dark maroon velvet suit and
listened to praise pour over her. At the banquet the words of
Archbishop Nathan Söderblom were especially glowing: "You,
Madame, do not limit yourself to man; you reveal, first of
all, the struggle between man's bestiality and the high destiny
of his soul. For you the road is extended. You have seen
the road sign which many travellers pass by without noticing.
For you the road leads to God. For this reason you believe

Grazia Deledda

in rebirth in spite of the degradation and frailty of man. You know that it is possible to reclaim the swamp so that it becomes firm and fertile land. Therefore, a bright ray gleams in your books. Through darkness and human misery you let shine the solace of eternal light. "

Grazia Deledda's belief that good ultimately triumphs over evil came in part from her own life, filled with family tragedies during her first 25 years and replete with happiness for almost the next 40. She was born in the small town of Nuoro, one of the most picturesque places in Sardinia, on September 27, 1871. Her birthdate is often given as 1874 or 1875 because as a young writer, in the hope of deflating criticism, she subtracted a few years from her age.

In a letter she once confided, "Destiny caused me to be born in the heart of lonely Sardinia. But even if I had been born in Rome or Stockholm, I should not have been different. I should have always been what I am--a soul which becomes impassioned about life's problems and which lucidly perceives men as they are, while still believing that they could be better and that no one else but themselves prevents them from achieving God's reign on earth. Everything is hatred, blood, and pain; but, perhaps, everything will be conquered one day by means of love and good will. "

By Sardinian standards Grazia's father, Giovantonio Deledda, popularly called Totoni, was fairly well-to-do. He had gained a diploma from the university in Cagliari and was qualified to act as a notary and to negotiate contracts and deeds for those who exported timber, wood, oil, wine, and almonds to Italy. He himself added to the property he had inherited from his father, expanded the oil press, and built a winery. Three times he was elected mayor of Nuoro. He was even something of a poet. Grazia's mother, Chiscedda, née Cambosu, was 20 years younger than her husband, an artist in embroidery, but illiterate, like 95 per cent of the town population. Grazia was the middle child in a family of two boys and five girls.

In the 1870s and 1880s, Sardinia was an isolated island, and Nuoro, situated in the mountainous zone of Barbagia, was an isolated town. It had neither railroad nor telegraph, and visitors usually arrived on horseback, women mounted behind the men. Only traditional holidays and carnival time, when colorful striped costumes appeared on the streets, broke the monotony of daily life. To compensate for Nuoro's isolation,

the natural surroundings were savagely beautiful.   Scores of
nuraghe dotted the mountainous areas.   Prehistorical conical
constructions, they were thought to be places where evil spirits
lived.   Grazia herself described Nuoro as "a village of the
Bronze Age."

The Deledda household was run with a kind of biblical
simplicity.   Chiscedda's brother, Uncle Sebastiano, was a
priest who issued strict orders about his nieces' upbringing.
Although they were never allowed to go out alone, sometimes
they broke the rules and ran free in the streets.   Yet it was
not all that lonely.   Because of Totoni's prominence in town
affairs priests, farmers, and artisans came and went in his
house, and his sharp-eyed young daughter tucked them all
away in her mind.

At home the family spoke the sonorous and musical
Logudoro dialect, which of all the Italian dialects is considered the closest to Latin.   Like other middle-class children,
Grazia went to the local elementary school.   Just before her
tenth birthday she was given the Onore al Merito, a special
diploma.   Despite her keen intelligence, she was never to
enter a classroom again.   There were no other schools in
Nuoro or even nearby for her to attend.   For a time Uncle
Sebastiano tutored her in Latin.   Then the literature teacher
from the boys' school, who boarded at the house of Grazia's
Aunt Paolina, was hired to give the girl lessons in grammar
and composition.   Suddenly one day, however, he fled from
some overwhelming debts, leaving behind most of his books,
which gradually made their way into the Deledda home.   Soon
after, the elderly bishop of Nuoro willed all his library to
Totoni.   These books helped Grazia educate herself.

She delighted in folk songs, ballads, and hymns and
eagerly absorbed the legends and traditions she heard all
around her.   Many concentrated on the nuraghe or on the
mysterious bronze sculptures found by the shepherds.   A
half century before Grazia was born the Savoy government
had legislated radical land reforms that created a landowning
middle class.   Land reform, however, brought taxes, proprie-
tary laws, and money as a means of exchange, innovations
rural Sardinians were not prepared to accept.   Open rebellion
erupted, and an army of carabinieri was sent to protect the
taxpayers.   Many Sardinians became outlaws.

At eight Grazia already felt a compulsion to write.
When her studious older brother Santus came home on vaca-

tions from the university in Cagliari and talked about the
beautiful coastal city, Grazia dreamed of following him there.
She also dreamed of Rome and distant castles along the Bos-
porus, the subject of her first poem. Still another dream
was attached to Santus's friend, Antonio Pau, with whom she
fancied herself in love.

One day Santus built a gas-filled balloon, which made
a successful ascent. Another time he tried to build a pyro-
technical wheel, but in launching it was knocked to the ground
and badly burned. Given medication with a great amount of
cognac, Santus began drinking more and more to ease his
pain and soon became an alcoholic.

In the meantime Grazia's second brother, the rebellious
Andrea, began running half wild, sometimes streaking across
the countryside on horseback, sometimes ranging farther afield.
But he was always protective of his sister. Once he returned
from Rome with several issues of a fashion magazine called
Ultima Moda, which the Deledda girls devoured. Grazia felt
inspired enough to write her own story, "Sangue Sardo" (Sardinian Blood). Her young heroine Ela loves Lorenzo, but finds
out he loves her sister. In a fit of jealousy Ela pushes him
from the top of a cliff into the sea and then disappears herself. The story was accepted by the editor of Ultima Moda
and published in two parts just before Grazia's sixteenth birthday.

Other Nuorese who read Ultima Moda were shocked at
the violence, but even more at what they considered Grazia's
insolence in presenting herself as an author when she did not
even have a university diploma. Even her family, with the
exception of the understanding Totoni, criticized her. But
with steely determination Grazia now set her mind on a literary career. For the next few years, sometimes using pseudo-
nyms, she wrote a couple of novels and several more stories.
Since all were published in Roman journals, they were free of
professional reviewers' criticisms.

Early in 1892 she published Fior di Sardegne (Flower
of Sardinia), dedicated to the Contessa Elda di Montedoro,
the nom de plume of Epaminanda Provaglio, the editor of
Ultima Moda. He became her staunch friend, advisor, and
agent. Grazia wrote this book out of her own sufferings.
The beloved Totoni was slowly dying, and the fortress-like
Deledda house was already filled with a funereal gloom.
Dreamy Lara was a girl like herself in a world like her

own.   Even getting the manuscript off to the publisher had involved difficulties.   Having no money for stamps, Grazia stole
some of the coins she had received for selling olive oil from
her father's press.   After she mailed the manuscript she
went directly to confession.   When the book was accepted, she
had to sell more oil and take the profits to use for mailing
the galley sheets back.   Unfortunately, the book brought her
no royalties, and to her disappointment the only payment was
one hundred copies.

By now Grazia was corresponding with several writers,
critics, and journalists,   The most inspiring was Stanis
Manca, a Sardinian nobleman and drama critic for the Tribuna
of Rome.   Traveling to Nuoro to see her, Manca called her
"a dainty figurine" with a gentle and teasing smile.   Grazia
fell in love with him.   At the same time, to her distress, she
found herself in love with Andrea Pirodda, a schoolteacher in
Nuoro.   Caught in the dilemma of loving two men simultaneously, Grazia gradually realized she could marry neither the
poor but physically attractive Pirodda nor the rich but only
platonically appealing Manca.

About this time Totoni died, and the Deledda family
lost status in Nuoro and began to fall apart.   Chiscedda suffered from depression.   Grazia continued to be criticized
for her writings, but kept gamely on.   Santus, who had tried
to return to his studies, came home half mad.   One sister,
Enza, who was subject to epileptic seizures, endured an unhappy marriage, had a miscarriage, and died.   Then while
showing off to his friends Andrea was caught stealing chickens
and sentenced to ten years in the Cagliari prison.   What more,
Grazia wondered, could a family endure?

Such tragedies made her the head of the household and
the oil press, an important source of the family income.
Joined by the unfortunate Santus, the poor of Barbagia hud-
dled around the huge fire used for the olive press.   Watching
them closely, Grazia was moved to write two socialistic
novels, Anime Oneste (Honest Souls) and La Via del Male
(The Evil Way), both about poverty and moral vindication.
Accepted by Treves of Milan, one of the finest Italian publishers, they were immediately successful.   Soon afterwards
Grazia negotiated a pardon for Andrea, who returned home
somewhat confused and apprehensive.   Then Santus became
dangerous and was judged insane.   When the doctor recommended that he be kept away from the family, Andrea offered
to stay with his brother out near the olive press.

During this time something happened that colored the
rest of Grazia's life.   Years later she told about the incident
in Cosima.   One day she was out on the vineyard plateau during a shimmering sunset.   In fascination she watched a ladybug inch up her skirt and settle on her fingers.   To Grazia
the closed wings looked like a Japanese mask, whose eyes
were staring at her in a mysterious, wonderful manner.
When the ladybug flew off, she yearned to go with it.   As
the sun sank, she felt "the eye of God" and with her forehead
seemed "to touch the early star. "   Life was beautiful, the star
over the mountain as marvelous as the ladybug.   "She decided
not to wait for anything that would arrive from the outside,
from the agitated world of man. "   From now on she would be
consumed with her own internal mystery.

Still she knew what to do when she unexpectedly received
a rather large sum of money from the French translation of
Anime Oneste.   As a well-known author, she had been sent
many invitations from Cagliari and the mainland, but had always turned them down.   She had continued to dream of Rome,
but family circumstances kept her in Nuoro.   Feeling unusually
prosperous now, she decided to accept an invitation from Donna
Maria Manca (no relation to Stanis), a real contessa, who was
the editor of Donna Sarda (Sardinian Lady), a journal to which
Grazia frequently contributed.

In October, 1899, Grazia was staying in a luxurious
suite in Donna Maria's magnificent seaside villa in Cagliari.
Early in her visit she went to the theatre and was introduced
to the handsome ("perhaps too handsome") young Palmiro
Madesani, a government employee in the Ministry of Finance.
He was tall and slender with a slightly military bearing.   Grazia knew she was not beautiful.   She was tiny and small bos-
omed, and she thought her nose too broad.   But others saw
beauty in her almond-shaped dark eyes and the blackest of
hair.   A few days later she met Palmiro again at a small
party.   "He had not yet read anything of mine, " she wrote a
friend, "and he loved me for myself. "   Swiftly Palmiro proposed.   Two weeks after her arrival in Cagliari they were engaged.   While preparing for her wedding, Grazia completed
Il Vecchio della Montagna (Old Man of the Mountains) and
started Elias Portolu, her acknowledged masterpiece.

The wedding took place in Nuoro on January 11, 1900,
and the Madesanis honeymooned in the hills and on the beaches
of the southern coast.   It was to be a singularly happy marriage.   Grazia called their happiness "pure and serene" and

their life "rich in peace and in dreams." Palmiro, who had
no literary talent himself, appreciated his wife's gifts and
came to act as her agent and business manager.

Anticipating a transfer within the Ministry of Finance,
the young couple left in March for Naples and Venice and
Cicognara-sul-Po near Mantua to visit Palmiro's parents.
Then to their delight he was assigned to Rome, and Grazia
could finally realize her dream of living there. The huge
city thrilled her, but loyally she took Palmiro back to Sardinia that summer for a short visit. Despite so much travel,
she finished Elias Portolu toward the end of the first year of
marriage and just before the birth of her first son, Sardus,
whom she named for Sardus Pater, the legendary founder of
Sardinia. "I am happy, happy to be in Rome," she wrote a
friend. "Happy with the love that surrounds me. Happy to
have a beautiful son (he is brown, rosy with a cleft chin,
with beautiful black eyes and tiny, tiny hands and feet)." She
told a visitor, "My single passion is maternity."

The character of Elias Portolu is partially based on
that of her brother Andrea. The setting is still Sardinian.
Elias returns home after being imprisoned for a crime he
did not commit and in spite of himself falls in love with his
brother's fiancée. After the wedding he commits adultery
with her, and Maddalena bears his child. To do penance
Elias joins the priesthood, but does not take final vows.
When his brother dies, he is free to marry Maddalena, but
cannot bring himself to do so. He feels guilty and also real-
izes that everyone would consider him his son's stepfather.
After the boy becomes ill and dies, Elias feels a tremendous
sense of release.

In the next few years before the birth of her second
son, Franz, in 1904, Grazia completed Dopo il Divorzio
(After the Divorce) and Cenere (Ashes), which dramatizes
the effect on a Sardinian youth of a life in Rome. After his
mother's death Anania opens the amulet she had given him
when he was a baby. Inside he finds only ashes:

> Yes, all was ashes; life, death, man; the very
> destiny which produced her. And still in the last
> hour, as he stood before the body of the most mis-
> erable of human creatures, who after doing and
> suffering evil in all of its manifestations had died
> for someone else's good, he remembered that
> among the ashes there often lurks the spark of a

luminous and purifying flame. And he hoped. And
he still loved her.

Grazia had hoped for a daughter, but after Franz was
born she found it hard to regain her strength, and the doctor
warned her against bearing any more children. The happiness she felt with Palmiro and their sons was not reflected
in the books she wrote in the next decade. They are per-
meated by pessimism. In their elemental settings most of
her heroes are simple, strong peasants with primitive sensi-
bilities, almost always under the influence of some obsession.
More than a touch of Sardinian violence affects their destinies.

Palmiro Madesani was assigned to Naples and Turin
for brief periods and to Paris for nearly a year. Every
August the Madesanis returned to Nuoro, especially for the
Feast of the Redeemer. But after 1911, when Chiscedda came
to stay with them, Grazia never went back. Her sisters,
Beppa and Nicolina, were married and living in Rome, and
Andrea arrived on frequent visits. Santus died in 1914,
Chiscedda in 1916, and Grazia sold most of the properties
her mother had left her, except for the agricultural enter-
prises, which Andrea supervised until he died in 1922.

Satisfying Grazia's longing for a daughter, her niece,
Mirella Morelli, lived with the Madesanis for several years
while her parents were off on assignments in Sardinia. Grazia described Mirella as "all fresh and pink like a coral out
of the sea." Increasing success brought the Madesanis their
own properties in Italy. In 1912 they leased a house on the
Italian Riviera north of Pisa and some years later built a
second home called "Villino Madesani" in the fishing village
of Cervia on the Adriatic coast. As World War I broke over
Europe, Grazia was working on <u>Marianna Sirca</u>, which stresses
Sicilian banditry.

In Kipling's words, the tide of writing had set in. She
kept to a methodical, daily routine, and sitting at a small table
in her austere study wrote for at least two hours every day.
When her sons were small, they sometimes resented the silence enforced when she was busy. Sardus, however, inherited
her love of reading and showed promise of becoming a writer.
Unfortunately, he was to die at the age of 37, just one year
after his mother. Franz would become a professor of chemistry at the University of Rome.

Shy and reticent, Grazia Deledda did not feel at ease

in the Roman literary salons she had to attend.   But when out
in society she took care to look elegant.   She was admired
by the woman suffragists, and in 1908 she joined Dr. Maria
Montessori, the noted educator, in opening the first women's
congress held in Rome.   Palmiro, transferred to the Ministry
of War, stayed on as her agent.

Motion pictures intrigued Grazia Deledda.   The only
film in which her friend Eleanora Duse ever appeared was
based on Cenere.   In 1916 the aging Duse played the mother,
who gives up her illegitimate son to assure him a better life.
Poignantly, it was a role the actress had played long ago in
real life when she gave up her baby daughter to foster parents.
L'Edera (The Ivy) was made into a four-act play and was first
presented in 1909.   La Grazia, an opera with a libretto based
on one of her short stories, was performed in 1923.

Again in 1920 Grazia Deledda was high on the list for
the Nobel Prize because of La Madre (The Mother), published
that year.   The British edition carried an introduction by an
admiring D. H. Lawrence.   In a half-civilized Sardinian village the dramatic story of Maria Maddalena, the poor illiterate mother, and her son Paul, the young parish priest, takes
place within two days.   Paul falls in love with a lonely woman,
Agnes.   Toward the end Maria Maddalena begins to understand
what happiness the Church's laws deny Paul and to question
the right to impose such a denial.   Then the strain becomes
too much for her, and she dies of grief and shock.

With deep understanding Grazia Deledda penetrates her
hero's soul:

> Paul moved towards the door, then turned and be-
> gan to walk up and down the kitchen.   The moaning
> of the wind outside made an accompaniment to the
> rustle of his clothes, which was like the rustle of
> a woman's dress, for he wore a cassock made of
> silk and his cloak was of the very finest material.
> And in that moment of indecision, when he felt him-
> self caught in a whirlpool of conflicting emotions,
> even that silken rustle seemed to speak and warn
> him henceforth his life would be but a maze of
> errors and light things and vileness.   Everything
> spoke to him; the wind outside, that recalled the
> long loneliness of his youth, and inside the house
> the mournful figure of his mother, the sound of his
> own steps, the sight of his own shadow on the floor.

To and fro he walked, to and fro, treading on his
shadow as he sought to overcome and stamp down
his own self.   He thought with pride that he had no
need of any supernatural aid, such as he had in-
voked to save him, and then immediately this pride
filled him with terror.

She also goes inside Maria Maddalena:

Complete silence reigned all around.   Outside the
window the trees shone silver in the bright moon-
light, the sky was like a milky sea, and the per-
fume of the aromatic shrubs penetrated even into
the house.   And the mother herself was tranquil
now, though she hardly knew why, seeing that Paul
might yet fall again into sin; but she no longer felt
the same terror of it.   She saw again in her mind's
eye the lashes trembling on his cheeks, like those
of a child about to cry, and her mother's heart
melted with tenderness and pity.

'And why, oh, Lord, why, why?'

She dared not complete her question, but it remained at the bottom of her heart like the stone
at the bottom of a well.   Why, oh Lord, was Paul
forbidden to love a woman?   Love was lawful for
all, even for servants and herdsmen, even for the
blind and convicts in prison; so why should Paul,
her child, be the only one to whom love was forbidden?

For several years La Madre continued to be important
in Swedish Academy deliberations.   Fuga in Egitta (Flight
into Egypt) also caught the Swedes' attention.   And finally
there were enough votes for Grazia Deledda.

One unhappy note in her joy over the Nobel Prize was
the still painful memory of Luigi Pirandello's scathing attack.
Some years earlier when Grazia was nominated, the impoverished playwright showed his displeasure by writing a novel,
Suo Marito (Her Husband), that pictured a famous woman author and her agent husband in very unflattering terms.   The
two were clearly identifiable as the Madesanis.   Ironically,
Pirandello, who himself received the Nobel Prize in 1934,
seems to have regretted his book.   Before he died, in the
same year as Grazia, he was working on a more sympathetic
version.

Another discordant note was that Benito Mussolini now
chose to honor her by making her one of three women members of his Academy of Immortals.   He also invited her to
a formal reception at the Palazzo Vittoria.   Basically, Grazia
was apolitical and considered all political leaders corrupt.
She muttered "Sfarzo" (What a farce), but accepted his invitation because she felt it her duty.   And she let Il Duce
grant her one favor, to allow the owner of the old Deledda
home in Nuoro, who happened to be an ardent anti-fascist,
to return from exile.

In Stockholm the Madesanis stayed with the Italian
ambassador and his wife.   Grazia was delighted with the
whole Swedish experience and wrote to Sardus, "... you
know we are in an enchanted palace on an enchanted island
and even the princess is one of those only found in fairy
tales; young, beautiful, Grecian, and elegant."   In other letters she mentioned that she especially watched Swedish crows
because she was so lonesome for her own pet Cheecha.

In his presentation speech at the Concert Hall, Henrik
Schück, the president of the Nobel Foundation, commented:
"She does not belong to that band of writers who work on a
thesis and discuss problems.   She has always kept herself
far removed from the battles of the day.   When Ellen Key
once tried to interest her in such discussions, she answered,
'I belong to the past....'   Certainly Grazia Deledda feels
tied by strong bonds to the past, to the history of her people.
But she also knows how to live in and respond to her own
times.   Although she lacks interest in theories, she has a
great deal of interest in every aspect of human life."

He also quoted a famous Italian critic, who called
her style "... that of the great masters of the narrative; it
has the characteristic marks of all great novelists."   And
there was Schück's own assessment again, "As a painter of
nature she has few equals in European literature."   Finally
he said that the Swedish Academy was acting in conformity
with the wishes of Alfred Nobel, who "wanted the Prize in
Literature to be given to someone who, in his writings, has
given humanity that nectar which infuses the health and the
energy of a moral life."

Reading from a tiny scrap of paper, Grazia Deledda
made the shortest acceptance speech in Nobel annals: "I do
not know how to make speeches.   I would be happy to thank
the Swedish Academy for their highest honor, which, in my

modest name, it has granted to Italy, and to repeat the bless-
ing of the old shepherds of Sardinia, spoken to friends and
family on solemn occasions:

> Salute!
> Salute to the King of Sweden!
> Salute to the King of Italy!
> Salute to you all, ladies and gentlemen!
> Viva Sweden, viva Italy!"

Only a few months after she received the Nobel Prize,
a doctor found a maligant tumor in Grazia Deledda's left
breast. In spite of two operations, the cancer spread through
the lymph glands over her body. In the last months her left
arm was virtually helpless. The villa in Cervia became her
sanatorium for the summer months. Here she had as company a young Spanish nun, acting as her nurse; Franz's wife
Nanda; and her first granddaughter, Grazia, nicknamed Pitti.
Well aware that her disease was terminal, she wrote two
autobiographical novels, Il Dono di Natale (The Christmas
Gift), intended for children, and Cosima, which she hid in
her desk. Not discovered until after her death, it was published in 1937. With a title taken from her middle name,
Cosima is laced with mysticism.

In those last years she looked back on astonishing pro-
ductivity. She had written a book almost every year. Any
lapse was compensated by double production the following year.
Thirty-three novels, 18 volumes of short stories, four plays
(some in collaboration), many short philosophical poems, and
articles discussing life in Sardinia--all bore Grazia Deledda's
name. Critics had not always been kind. But she had always
taken their criticism to heart, corrected her errors, such
as a tendency to use hasty transitions, and become a better
writer as she grew older.

After receiving the last sacraments of the Catholic
Church, Grazia Deledda died in Cervia on August 16, 1936,
with Palmiro and her sisters at her bedside. Nicolina wrote
to a friend that it was a holy death to which Grazia went
with resignation and patience. She was buried in the velvet
suit she had worn to the Nobel ceremony. But, as she had
requested, no public announcement was made until after her
very private funeral.

Toward the end of her life she had written a novel,
Chiesa della Solitudine (Church of the Solitude) about a woman

dying of cancer.   She took the title from a church outside
Nuoro.   After World War II, the town, at long last proud of
its native daughter, pleaded with the Madesani family to have
her remains returned to her birthplace.   An agreement was
reached, and Grazia Deledda's tomb was placed inside that
church.   Once she had written, "Our great anguish is life's
slow death.   That is why we must try to slow life down, to
intensify it, thus giving it the richest possible meaning.   One
must try to live one's life, as a cloud above the sea. "

A Medieval Iliad

SIGRID UNDSET

"I am one who has lived two thousand years in the land,"
Sigrid Undset once said with a smile. But her playful remark
was actually profound. Remote times were her contemporary
world. The Nobel Prize for Literature in 1928 came to her
for her "powerful descriptions" of life during the Middle Ages.
Her extensive work was called "an Iliad of the North."

The dark-haired, large-boned woman with a serious
and thoughtful expression gave a surprisingly simple acceptance speech. "I write more readily than I speak and I am
especially reluctant to talk about myself. Instead, I wish
to offer a salute.... I have been asked to give regards to
Sweden, the country we think of with joy, and to Stockholm,
which we Norwegians consider the most beautiful city in the
world."

That year the French philosopher Henri Bergson received in absentia the Literature Prize for 1927. For once
the Swedish Academy had abandoned the purely literary line
and chosen him for his inspiring influence on modern literature. Bergson, however, had no influence on Sigrid Undset,
who was indisputably her own woman. If anybody was the
great inspiration of her life, it was probably her father.

Ingvald Martin Undset was a pathfinding archaeologist,
who won an international reputation with The Beginnings of
the Iron Age in Northern Europe (1881). Sigrid's mother,
Anna Charlotte Gyth, was Danish, and Sigrid was born May 20,
1882, in Kalundborg, Denmark, at the home of her maternal
grandfather, a chancery councillor. Ingvald's work called
for constant travel, and his wife set up a temporary home
with her relatives. Here, with Ingvald returning periodically
from abroad, the Undsets stayed until Sigrid was two. Then
he was appointed to a post at the Museum of Antiquities attached to the University of Kristiania.

Sigrid Undset

When past 50, Sigrid Undset wrote about her first 11 years in a charming childhood autobiography, Elleve Aar (translated as The Longest Years), 1934, in which she calls herself Ingvild, her father Seming, and her mother Anine. She was a stubborn, self-willed, independent child, but extremely precocious and highly imaginative. "One might say I was brought up on history." Ingvald Undset filled her head with archaeological lore and information about his own researches.

Almost before she could talk, the little girl babbled of "blunt-butted axe" and "shaft-hole axe" when her father showed her various implements. He also allowed her "to borrow the little terracotta horse from Troy which [Heinrich] Schliemann had given him because it amused him to think that here was his little baby patting with her damp and podgy hands a toy which perhaps some Trojan child had caressed thousands of years ago." When the museum was closed, Sigrid was allowed to run about the galleries. If she pointed at some fine things in the cabinets, they were lifted out, and she was decorated with necklaces and rings of gold and silver from the Iron Age.

In due time Sigrid and her two younger sisters, Signe and Ragnhild, went off to a coeducational school run by Fru Ragna Nielsen along liberal and progressive lines. But Sigrid developed an antipathy toward its liberalism and as a mature woman would say that the school had inspired her with "an indelible distrust of enthusiasm for such beliefs." But there she found a friend, Emma Münster, who shared her passion for botany and roamed the countryside with her.

During her "golden" childhood Sigrid heard fairy tales from three marvelous storytellers, Mrs. Winter-Hjelm, who lived below the Undset flat; the nursemaid, Caroline Thorvaldsen; and her Danish great-aunt Signe in Kalundborg. At bedtime she could tell Ragnhild and Signe stories that stretched from one night to the next.

In the summer of 1891, on a visit to her dying Grandfather Undset near Trondheim, she came upon "A Book That Was a Turning Point in My Life," as she later described it in a little essay. An Icelandic family saga called Njäls Saga, it "went straight to her head--she woke up in the morning, got into her clothes, sat at the breakfast table sick with impatience to get her fingers on the book again...." Lying on the green bleaching ground, she sometimes tried to put down the book "to swallow what she had been reading."

The most poignant chapters of <u>Elleve Aar</u> picture the
dying Seming and his harried wife, who had to act as nurse,
secretary, housekeeper, and mother.   In those last months
of her father's illness Sigrid was drawn closer to him.   Together they read the Icelandic sagas in Danish.   Sometimes
Ingvald asked her to read certain passages in Old Norse to
him.   Three weeks before Christmas, 1893, he died at the
age of forty, still hoping that Sigrid would devote herself to
science and carry on his research.   The Undsets, who had
moved to even smaller rooms as he grew weaker and could
not work,   now settled in an even tinier flat.

Charlotte Undset was hard pressed to keep her household running and, generously, Fru Nielsen offered to let the
Undset girls stay in her school free of charge.   Sigrid became enthusiastic about painting and drawing.   But at 14 she
decided she did not want to stay any longer and entered a commercial college.   At 17, a tall, slim, pretty girl with deep,
thoughtful eyes and long braided hair, she went to work in the
office of an electrical engineers' bureau, A. E. G. , and stayed
there for ten years until her sisters were self-supporting.

In her spare time she studied literature, feeling especially attracted to the Middle Ages and its ballads, songs,
sagas, and legends.   Her first long writing attempt was a
first draft of the Olav Audunsson story that later helped
make her famous.   Dressed up in a "big summer hat trimmed with a mass of flowers, " she brought the manuscript to
the prestigious Gyldendal publishers.   After a month of anxious
waiting on her part, the publishers told her, "Don't try your
hand at more historical novels.   It's not your line.   But you
might, you know, try to write something modern. "

And she tried.   "It was after I had settled down in the
office and had come to feel myself on equal terms with the
people I met there that I realized that I was at home in my
home town. "   <u>In Fru Marta Oulie</u> and <u>Den Lykkelige Alder</u>
(The Happy Age) she had the feel of Kristiania.   The first
book, in diary form, presents a heroine who feels belated re-
morse.   It opens with the words (startling for 1907), "I have
deceived my husband, " and poses the fundamental problem
Sigrid Undset would continually explore, the relationship between a married man and woman.   The second book, a collection of short stories, is a sensitive picture of Norwegian girl-
hood.   Both books depict the restless lower-middle-class world
of Kristiania early in the twentieth century and emphasize its
strangely isolated young women.   Both contain fresh and bril-

liant descriptions of Norwegian nature. Love for the mountains, first breaking through in <u>Den Lykkelige Alder</u>, would
mark all of Sigrid Undset's writing. Norwegians, she once
said, have "almost a religious feeling" about them.

With the publication of <u>Fru Marta Oulie</u>, the young
author received from her mother a copy of Steen Steensen
Blicher's <u>Traekfuglene</u> (Birds of Passage). Always loyal to
the writers of her Danish homeland, Charlotte Undset noted
on the flyleaf: "May you as an author always look up to
Blicher as your model, be as incorruptibly honest as he,
fearlessly seeing life as it is and truthfully reporting what
you see. " It was a credo Sigrid Undset respected throughout her literary career.

In 1909 she brought out <u>Viga Ljot og Vigdis</u> (translated
as Gunnar's Daughter), a frank imitation of the Icelandic sagas
she had studied with her father. That same year she finally
left the business world and went to Germany and Italy on a
traveling scholarship from the Norwegian government. Once
in Rome a patronizing lady asked her, "In what genre do you
write?" And an amused Sigrid told her, "In the immoral. "

About this time her friend, Nini Roll Anker, described
her vividly: "Everything about her stirred the imagination;
the large eyes with that extraordinary glance which seemed
as much turned inwards as outwards, but which still seized
every detail of her surroundings ... the beautiful slender
hands, which on a rare occasion, as the conversation took
her, would move most expressively; the lazy voice without
marked intonation and with the slightest trace of Danish pro-
nunciation in single words. " Nini Roll Anker added, "She was
strikingly beautiful, slim as a boy, and with a suggestion of
classical perfection about her head which she seldom moved.
She took short steps when she walked, and there was something reminiscent of a sleepwalker in her whole movement.
But from her whole physique one could sense the strength and
power of endurance which stood her in such good stead later
in life. "

In Rome Sigrid met the rather eccentric Norwegian
painter, Anders Castus Svarstad, who was married with three
children. Her senior by 13 years, he was nervous and brusque,
but keenly intelligent. No doubt her interest in painting deep-
ened the attraction. After Svarstad was divorced, he and
Sigrid were married in Antwerp, Belgium in 1912.

Meanwhile in 1911, using Norwegian and Italian settings, she had written <u>Jenny</u>, her first real success. It foreshadows the theme of <u>Kristin Lavransdatter</u>--love has its code of honor, and the cost of picking forbidden fruit is excessive. The Undset woman answers the call of love without stopping to consider the consequences and then learns she buys her happiness with heavy sacrifice. Jenny has a harrowing relationship with a young man and with his father and in the end is driven to committing suicide. With its daring erotic descriptions the novel created a sensation.

The Svarstads spent part of the first year of their marriage in London, where the bride plunged into English literature, especially Renaissance drama. They then returned to Rome for the birth of their son, Anders, in 1913. The war was threatening in Europe when the little family went back to Norway and settled in Ski. Nini Roll Anker also described the Svarstad home: "There was not much furniture, but every piece was beautiful, and most of it was old.... Her feeling for line and form is exceptionally sure and true ... [and] all her possessions have merged one by one into a harmonious whole." For a time Svarstad's three children from the earlier marriage stayed in the new home. Afterwards they always came out for Sunday visits.

In 1915 a daughter, Maren Charlotte, was born. She was pretty and well-shaped, but by the time the Svarstads moved to Sinsen, Mosse, as she was called, showed signs that she was mentally retarded. Not long after, Svarstad's youngest son began school, and teachers sent word that he too was mentally retarded. The slim Sigrid Undset had now become a heavyset housewife although her hands and feet remained slender and elegant. In spite of her weight she moved lightly. Nini Roll Anker called the Sinsen years the hardest in Sigrid's life. Still, she had an air of calm and great tranquillity.

The marriage, however, was not doing well. "So help me, I'll never feel like a real married woman no matter how much people address me as Mrs. --I think I belong to the lonely unmarried women without happiness or with an illegitimate and homeless happiness," Sigrid once wrote. She had always wanted to have the freedom to do as she wanted. Since her seventeenth year, she noted, she had always had to consider someone else's interest. Almost from the beginning she and Anders Svarstad had started drifting apart. Creative individualists, each demanded time alone. Through the next few years the rift grew deeper.

Svarstad bought a home in Kristiania, and for the time being he and his wife decided to live apart. Only now and then did he visit his family. Meanwhile Sigrid Undset moved with her children to Lillehammer, where she bought an old farm transplanted from Gudbrandsdal. To "irritate" her Danish family, she named it Bjerkebaek for "a Norse Norwegian from Norway," satirized in a song by the Danish writer, Erik Bøgh. Nini Roll Anker was to say that the house showed "one of Norway's most individual and lovely interiors." At a little distance from the town itself, it sat on a steep slope that became a beautiful garden. Sigrid's family and friends knew that a love of flowers and plants was central to her life. (Years later, when fleeing Nazi-occupied Norway, she made her first pilgrimage in Sweden to Hammersby, the home of Carl von Linné, her "lay patron saint," and kissed his writing desk.) A second son, Hans, was born in Lillehammer in 1919.

The town, some 60 miles north of Kristiania, was a summer and winter resort that attracted painters. One of its great drawing cards was Maihaugen, an astonishing open-air museum, specializing in old houses and furnishings of the Gudbrandsdal valley, collected by an itinerant dentist named Anders Sandvig. Perhaps the best-known exhibits at Maihaugen are the farm buildings from Björnstad, first built in the seventeenth century. Although her great work, Kristin Lavransdatter, is set in the fourteenth century, Sigrid Undset was able to use the Björnstad farm as a model for Jorundgaard, the farm of Kristin's parents.

In spite of frequent ill health, Sigrid Undset kept turning out novels--Vaaren (Spring), Splinten i Troldspejlet (Images in a Mirror), and De Kloge Jomfruer (The Wise Virgins)--all mirroring her earlier books in theme and style. In De Kloge Jomfruer she used a religious theme for the first time.

Meanwhile the war was confirming her doubts about the beliefs she had been brought up with--feminism, socialism, liberalism, pacifism. Already in 1912, while still in England and quite liberated herself, she had written an article, "Some Reflections on the Suffragette Movement," objecting to the drive to make the unmarried, self-sufficient woman an ideal and thus undermine woman's "fundamental position" as wife and mother. In human society, she wrote, "a woman can become nothing better than a good mother and nothing much worse than a bad one."

She was such a particular housewife, so deeply rooted
in domesticity, she could not always find time for her writing.
Often in the summer she had to withdraw to a little house
up in the _saeter_ or mountain meadow. All this while Mosse
was both a joy and a terrible trial. She was sweet and pretty,
and Sigrid had decided to keep her at home. Although she
and Mosse made frequent trips to seek medical help, these
came to nothing.

In spite of a failed marriage and the worries of rearing
a mentally retarded daughter, Sigrid Undset reached the high
point of her career in 1920 with the first volume of her medieval trilogy, Kristin Lavransdatter. In Kransen (The Bridal
Wreath) she introduces the proud, beautiful, headstrong young
Kristin, a prosperous landowner's daughter. After surren-
dering herself to the frivolous and irresponsible Erlend Niku-
lausson, she has to break her engagement to Simon Darre.
Her elopement with Erlend results in the tragic death of his
former mistress.

In Husfrue (The Mistress of Husaby) Kristin is troubled
by her sinning and makes a pilgrimage to Nidaros Cathedral
to ask forgiveness for bearing a child conceived before marriage.

> Kristin stood on Feginsbrekka and saw the city ly-
> ing before her in the golden sunlight. Beyond the
> river's broad shining curves lay brown houses with
> green turfed roofs, dark domes of leaves in the
> gardens, light-hued stone houses with pointed gables,
> churches that heaved up black shingled backs and
> churches with dully gleaming leaden roofs. But
> above the green land, above the fair city, rose
> Christ's Church, so mighty, so gloriously shin-
> ing.... With the evening sun blazing full upon its
> breast and on the shining glass of its windows, with
> towers and giddy spires and golden vanes, it stood
> pointing up into the bright summer heavens.

Kristin restores Husaby, Erlend's dilapidated estate, and has
seven sons. In time Erlend, who is always in a scrape, is
tried for treason but acquitted. He loses Husaby, however,
and he and Kristin move to Jorundgaard, inherited from her
father.

In Korset (The Cross), Kristin and Erlend become
estranged. The dying Simon Darre, who has married Kristin's

sister, begs Kristin to settle her quarrel with her husband.
Kristin joins Erlend on his farm but cannot make him return
to Jorundgaard with her. After bearing her eighth child, who
dies in infancy, she is wrongfully accused of adultery. On
the way to help her, impulsive Erlend is killed. Grief-stricken,
Kristin enters a convent. When the Black Death comes, she
acts as a sister of mercy and buries a victim. Like two of
her sons she dies from the plague.

Wisely, Sigrid Undset chose a period without any great
historical figures. Her main characters are purely fictitious.
Still, the settings and daily life of the early fourteenth century are drawn with great accuracy and almost uncanny artis-
try. Her primary sources, she noted, were old ballads and
laws. Besides this impeccable scholarship, Kristin Lavransdatter shows great psychological depth. Its strong characters
are not explained, but explain themselves. Thus Sigrid Undset blends the contemporary narrative style of a profound psy-
chologist with an ancient style of the Icelandic sagas. This
blend is grave and somewhat heavy, but well suited to the
great epic picture. Some critics called her too prolix, especially in the second volume. But they conceded that the
overall effect was sombrely majestic.

For some years Sigrid Undset had carefully been examining her beliefs. She was, she finally decided, a tradition-
alist and a conservative. And in 1924, turning her back on
the state religion of Lutheranism, she joined the Catholic
Church. Her historical studies convinced her, she wrote,
that "only the saints seemed to know the true explanation of
man's hunger for happiness, peace, justice, and goodness."
The Catholic Church was the true civilizing force. Shortly
after her conversion, her marriage to Svarstad was dissolved
since he had earlier been married to a woman still living.
Neither Svarstad nor Sigrid ever remarried.

The indefatigable Sigrid now finished another huge
medieval novel, Olav Audunsson i Hestviken and Olav Audunsson og Hans Børn (translated into English as The Master of
Hestviken in one large volume). When the first volume appeared, she burned her first draft, rejected 20 years earlier.
Olav and Ingunn are counterparts to Kristin and Erlend.
Pride estranges both Kristin and Olav from God, and pride
is the beginning of their misfortunes. But the spiritual emphasis is more pronounced in the Olav Audunsson story than
in Kristin Lavransdatter.

In one of the most gripping scenes, Olav kills Teit, a young Icelander, who is the father of Ingunn's unborn child. Olav himself intends to marry Ingunn, with whom he had had sex in their early teens.

> Olav was seized with a wild joy on seeing that Teit now grasped it all--the boy's face seemed to blacken with rage....
>
> He did not wait for Olav to attack, but dashed in at once. Olav stood still--three times he warded off the boy's strokes with the head of his axe. The lad was deft and agile, Olav saw, but not strong in the arm. When Teit cut at him the fourth time, Olav swerved unexpectedly to the right so that the sword caught him on the left arm, but the young fellow lost his head for an instant. Olav's axe struck him on the shoulder, and the sword fell out of his hand. He bent down to pick it up with his left, and then Olav planted the axe in the skull of him; the boy fell on his face.

Over the scene pass "night and wind-driven snow, the roar and soughing of the wind in the forests."

With her marriage to Olav, Ingunn miscarries and later gives birth to several dead children. All this happens, she believes, because of her sin in bearing Teit's child, Eirik, and then giving him away. In time Eirik joins the household at Hestviken, where Olav shows his jealousy. After the birth of a daughter, Ingunn wastes away. Before she dies, Olav fathers a healthy son by a servant girl. In the end he is seized by contrition:

> All the trees of the forest shall rejoice before the face of the Lord, for He comes to judge the world with righteousness, the waves shall clap their hands. --He saw that now they were waiting, the trees that grew upon the rocks of his manor, all that sprouted and grew on the land of his fathers, the waves that followed one another to the bay-- all were waiting to see judgment passed upon their faithless and unprofitable master.

Eirik dominates the last section. He falls in love with an older woman, the half-sister of the girl he cannot marry, but eventually renounces even Eldred and becomes a monk.

He dies after being exposed to a violent storm on his way to the church at Nidaros.

Critics have always favored the Kristin story over the Olav story. But both works weighed heavily in the Swedish Academy's decision to give the Nobel Prize to Sigrid Undset in 1928. "Her narrative," said Per Hallström, "is vigorous, sweeping, and at times heavy. It rolls on like a river, cease-lessly receiving new tributaries whose course the author also describes, at the risk of overtaxing the reader's memory.... [But] when the river reaches the sea, when Kristin Lavrans-datter has fought to the end the battle of her life, no one com-plains of the length of the course which accumulated so over-whelming a depth and profundity in her destiny." Hallström ended with a special accolade: "Sigrid Undset has received the Nobel Prize in Literature while still in her prime, an homage rendered to a poetic genius whose roots must be in a great and well-ordered spirit."

She gave away her prize money in three parts, one part to the authors' society in which she was long active, a second to families of retarded children so that they could keep the children at home, and a third to needy Catholic children who wished to enroll in Catholic schools.

On her return home from the ceremonies in Stockholm, Sigrid Undset was greeted at the Lillehammer station by a torchlight parade of her fellow citizens. It was one of the few times she came into contact with them because, except for the company of her children and occasional visits from close relatives, she preferred to lead a rather solitary life at Bjerkebaek.

After the Nobel award Sigrid Undset turned her back on the medieval world and began a second series of modern novels. But critics found Gymnadenia (The Wild Orchid), Den Braendende Busk (The Burning Bush), Fru Elisabeth, and Den Trofaste Hustru (The Faithful Wife) of somewhat un-even quality. During the same period she wrote some auto-biographical essays, Etapper (Stages on the Road), which met with more critical acclaim. Just before World War II came Madame Dorthea, planned as the first volume of a trilogy set around the year 1800. As things turned out, it was her last novel.

When the Nazis landed in Norway on April 9, 1940, Sigrid Undset was visiting in Oslo (named Kristiania until

1925) because she had spoken at a student society meeting just three days earlier. Stupefied, she hurried back to Bjerkebaek, where three Finnish child refugees were living with her. Late that night, hearing the drone of a plane outside, she decided to take the children down to the first floor to sleep. "In spite of everything there was something sweet and peaceful about sitting this way in the dark and hearing the three little children breathing so quietly and healthily around me. But at the same time the thought that they had come here because they were to have a refuge from bombing and suffering and death, but now violence and bombers pursued them here, was such that at times one felt one would suffocate with rage. "

Almost at once she had another refugee, a German priest, who had befriended some Jews. But Sigrid Undset's aversion to all things German was now so strong that he wore on her nerves. Quickly she arranged to have him sent over to Sweden. Soon the Germans were so close to Lillehammer that she was afraid to have the Finnish children, Elmi, Toimi, and Eira, in the house and evacuated them to a farm up in a side valley. With no refugees to look after, she telephoned the commandant at Lillehammer to ask how she could help. He gave her a job as a censor. Her sons were just as busy. Anders, trained as an engineer in England, and Hans, a student in Oslo, volunteered for service. Both Mosse and Charlotte Gyth Undset had died the year before.

By April 20 the English had given up their positions south of Lillehammer, and the Germans were expected momentarily to march into town. Because Sigrid Undset had constantly written and spoken against Nazism and had taken active part in helping refugees, the Norwegian authorities urged her to flee. With her friend, Professor Fredrik Passche, and his family she set out on a difficult journey by car, lorry, trawler, sled, and bus through Norway and then across the border.

The day after arriving in Sweden she was told that Anders had been killed on April 27 as he was bringing three machine guns into position on a river bank. Characteristically, she did not make a show of her feelings. But on Norway's Independence Day, May 17, she wrote of her hope "that one day our children will be able to live as free people in a free Norway, that the red-crossed flags will one day stream again through our towns and villages. And on that day we can go joyfully to meet our dead--the dead from olden times, our forefathers, and those who have died this spring. "

Soon Hans joined his mother and accompanied her across Russia and through Japan, across the Pacific, and on to San Francisco and New York. Sigrid Undset wrote about their journey in Tilbake til Fremtiden (Return to the Future). Almost immediately she became known as Norway's most distinguished cultural ambassador and was busy lecturing and writing for many American newspapers and magazines. Willa Cather and Marjorie Kinnan Rawlings were among the new friends she made in New York.

Settled in Brooklyn, she began reminiscing about one year of the happy life at Bjerkebaek when her children were very young and Grandmother Undset and the aunts and uncles came visiting for Christmas. In the pages of Lykkelige Dage i Norge (Happy Times in Norway), she sketched a loving portrait of Mosse (here called Tulle) and her simple pleasures.

In July, 1945, Sigrid Undset sailed back to a liberated Norway and to Bjerkebaek. The Nazi troops had rifled her extensive library, smashed her father's old desk at which she had written her great novels, and taken all her silver and linens. Fortunately, friends had saved most of her possessions, and her faithful housekeeper Thea had returned. On her sixty-fifth birthday King Haakon awarded her the Grand Cross of the Order of Saint Olav "for eminent services to literature and the nation."

By now, however, she was tired and ill. Nonetheless she began work on a biography of Catherine of Siena, a fourteenth-century Catholic saint and church reformer. It was published posthumously in 1951, for on June 10, 1949, Sigrid Undset died in a Lillehammer hospital after a stroke. Piercingly she had seen "the fleetingness of time and every event, the reality of eternity and of the spirit."

A Divided Heart

PEARL BUCK

"Pu seng" (I don't believe it). That was Pearl Buck's
reaction to her secretary's call that she had won the Nobel
Prize for Literature for 1938. Nor did she believe her husband when he telephoned her with the same announcement.
For confirmation she insisted that he must make a long distance call to Stockholm. "It's reporters' talk," she said at
first. But the report was quite true, and on December 10
she was standing in the Concert Hall shaking hands with King
Gustav V. At that moment she remembered how literary
agents and publishers had once told her she could not make
a success writing about the Chinese people because no one
wanted to read about them.

In her acceptance speech she noted: "... in my country it is important that this award has been given to a woman.
You who have already so recognized your own Selma Lagerlöf, and have long recognized women in other fields, cannot
perhaps wholly understand what it means in many countries
that it is a woman who stands here at this moment. But I
speak not only for writers and for women, but for all Americans, for we all share in this."

Her first incredulity, however, was well founded.
American literary critics hotly debated her award, the first
Nobel honor to any American woman. Her first novel had ap-
peared only eight years before. Was she really of the same
stature as her predecessors? Why had not the Prize been
given to Theodore Dreiser or possibly to Carl Sandburg or
T. S. Eliot or Ernest Hemingway? For that matter, if the
Prize were to go to an American woman, why not to Willa
Cather or Edith Wharton or Ellen Glasgow?

Pearl Buck believed that many critics were against her
because she "had been reared abroad and wrote about Asian
people." She even said that Dreiser really deserved the

136

Pearl S. Buck

Prize.   But the Swedish Academy had thought otherwise and
decided that Pearl Buck was entitled to the Literature Prize
"for her rich and truly epic descriptions of peasant life in
China and for her biographical masterpieces. " Were not five
of the 11 books she had written between 1930 and 1938 international best-sellers and was not The Good Earth an unparal-
leled success ?

        Per Hällstrom, the permanent secretary of the Swedish
Academy, who hailed her as the "interpreter to the West of
the nature and being of China, " was convinced the Academy
was right.   "By awarding this year's Prize to Pearl Buck
for the notable works which pave the way to a human sympathy
passing over widely separated racial boundaries and for the
studies of human ideals which are a great and living art of
portraiture, the Swedish Academy feels that it acts in harmony and accord with the aim of Alfred Nobel's dreams for
the future. " Certainly in selecting the lady laureates in literature, the Academy had favored those who wrote family and
peasant epics of far away and long ago.   Here Pearl Buck enjoyed a certain kinship with Selma Lagerlöf, Grazia Deledda,
and Sigrid Undset.

        On December 12 she delivered her Nobel lecture.   To
the Swedish Academy she spoke about the Chinese novel.
Tracing its origins and growth she said, "It is the Chinese
and not the American novel which has shaped my own efforts
in writing.   My earliest knowledge of story, of how to tell
and write stories, came to me in China. " The Chinese novel,
she pointed out, sprang from humble and scattered beginnings
and was forged apart from the world of art and letters.
Story and character were its chief components, especially
character, for the Chinese novelist found his true place in
the street with the people.   And here, Pearl Buck declared,
she also belonged--"a storyteller in a village tent. "

        Actually she felt both Chinese and American.   To em-
phasize her divided heart she called her 1954 autobiography
My Several Worlds.   By rights she should have been born in
China, where her father was a missionary.   But her mother,
who had lost three children to tropical diseases, decided to
come home to her father's white-pillared house in Hillsboro,
West Virginia, to bear her fifth child and third daughter.   To
Caroline Stulting Sydenstricker the baby, born June 26, 1892,
looked "like a little pearl. " Understandably, she gave her
the second name of Comfort.

When Pearl was three months old, she left with her
parents and her 12-year-old brother Edwin for China, to live
in the old river port of Chinkiang, in Kiangsu province, far
in the interior.   The family settled in a small bungalow built
on top of a hill overlooking the crowded city of red tiled roofs.
Here, young Pearl was lovingly attended by a blue-coated old
nurse named Wang Amah, "my brown mother," as she later
wrote.

Absalom Sydenstricker, Pearl's father, was a different
sort of missionary, one of the few real scholars among his
tribe, with an extraordinary grasp of classical and vernacular
Chinese.   Later he was to translate the Bible from the Greek
into Chinese vernacular.   As Pearl Buck describes him in
Fighting Angel (where he is called Andrew), he was a remote
and saintly figure of towering stature.   Often in disagreement
with the other missionaries, he could never stay long in an
established place and always had to be pushing off into the
unknown.   And yet

> Andrew was the happiest person I have ever known,
> and he never struggled.   He went his way, serene
> and confident, secure in the knowledge of his own
> rightness.   I have never seen him angry at others
> because they had obstructed that way of the Lord
> he trod so surely, but I never saw him puzzled or
> distrustful of himself.   He took his own way with
> proud tranquility.   There was a greatness in his
> clear determination.

Mrs. Sydenstricker was pretty, vivacious, musical,
and of a tragic nature, never forgetting her four lost children
--a boy, born two years after Pearl, died in China at the age
of five.   The Exile opens with an unforgettable portrait of
Carie:

> Here she stands in the American garden she has
> made in the dark heart of a Chinese city on the
> Yangtse River.   She is in the bloom of her ma-
> turity, a strong, very straight figure, of a beauti-
> ful free carriage, standing in the full, hot sunshine
> of summer.   She is not tall, nor very short, and
> she stands sturdily upon her feet.   There is a
> trowel in her hand; she has been digging in the
> garden.   It is a good strong hand that holds the
> trowel, a firm brown hand not too whitely well kept,
> and bearing evidence of many kinds of labor.   But

it is shapely in spite of this, and the fingers are
unexpectedly pointed and delicate at the tips.

Young Pearl spent many hours at a window opening on
the Yangtze River to watch its ceaseless traffic of ferries and
gunboats and painted junks and sampans. In the morning
Caroline taught her in American style, and in the afternoon
a Confucian tutor gave her lessons in Chinese reading and
writing.

Pearl felt no real physical closeness, however, to
anyone in her family although her mother exerted a strong
intellectual influence.   Pearl was a roamer and she came to
know thoroughly the smells and filth of the crowded streets
with their coolies and priests and endless streams of quaint
characters. This charming, inquisitive white child was more
than welcome in many large, noisy, and not-too-clean Chinese
households.

Since Absalom thought novel reading frivolous, Caroline hid the novels she read surreptitiously, but not so carefully that Pearl could not find them. At seven she discovered
Oliver Twist and did not stop until she had gone through all
of Dickens. About the same time, urged on by Caroline, she
began sending stories and articles to the Shanghai Mercury,
whose editor offered monthly prizes to children.

These were the dying years of the Manchu dynasty.
When Pearl was eight, the Boxer Rebellion broke out and the
Empress Dowager issued an imperial edict: "All white people are to be killed!" Absalom sent his family to safety in
Shanghai.   Then after the peace treaty, the Sydenstrickers
came to the United States to spend a year and enroll Edwin
in college. By now Pearl had a baby sister, Grace.

Within a few years of their subsequent return to China,
the country was caught up in a great famine, and the whole
family pitched in to help Absalom relieve the terrible suffering. Since Pearl was now in her teens, Caroline sent her
to Miss Jewell's boarding school in Shanghai. But when the
Sydenstrickers heard their young daughter had been dispatched
to a shelter for prostitutes to carry out some of Miss Jewell's
"good works," Pearl was not enrolled for another year.

Thanks to Caroline's excellent teaching, she was now
ready for college. Caroline selected Randolph-Macon in
Lynchburg, Virginia. Since by 1910 it was time for Absalom

to take another furlough, he and Caroline decided that the
whole family would accompany Pearl to the United States by
way of Russia, Poland, Germany, Switzerland, France, and
England.

After leaving the freshman on campus, Caroline and
Absalom and Grace sailed back to China. Pearl felt particularly lonely because her background was so different from that
of her classmates. She was filled with an ancient culture that
did not interest her classmates in the least. During her
sophomore year the Manchu throne was destroyed by young
rebels led by Sun Yat-sen. But again few students or teachers
questioned her. Still she took active part in college life.
After commencement she left with prizes in fiction and poetry.

With a major in psychology, Pearl could not make up
her mind whether to stay in America or return to China, still
in civil turmoil. A letter from Absalom reporting that Caroline was ill with tropical sprue made her decide quickly.
Writing the Presbyterian Board of Missions she asked to be
sent back to China as a teacher. The Board granted her request, and Pearl began teaching in a missionary school for
Chinese boys. At the same time she tenderly nursed Caroline, who became better under a strict dietary regime.
World War I was far away in Europe.

At 25 the still lonely Pearl met John Lossing Buck, a
young American agriculturist working for the Board. Years
later she was to say that she fell in love with a "handsome
face." They really had little in common. She adored books
and was always reading; he did not care for them. When she
announced her plans to marry him, her parents disapproved,
but could not change her mind.

Pearl Sydenstricker married John Lossing Buck in a
simple ceremony in 1917 and went to live in the far north at
Nanhsüchou. For some time she was busy fitting up her
"lovely little Chinese house." From Caroline she had inherited a knack for creating orderly and artistic interiors.
"What a pleasure it was," she later reminisced, "to arrange
the furniture, hang the curtains, paint a few pictures for the
walls, to hang the Chinese scrolls." As a married woman
she was now even freer to walk around town and participate
in the swirling currents of Chinese life. All the same, she
found herself confronted with great personal loneliness. But
these became busy years. She took over a school for young
girls, acted as nurse for an American doctor in town, and

as translator, accompanied John about the countryside on travels which gave her a deep insight into the world of the Chinese peasant.

After three years in Nanhsüchou, John Buck was hired to teach agriculture at the University of Nanking. Pearl was pregnant when they moved. In Nanking on March 21, 1921, she gave birth to a beautiful and apparently normal girl they named Carol. But she did not recover easily from childbirth and made a quiet trip to the United States to enter a hospital, where an operation left her with the bitter knowledge she could never bear another child.

Toward the end of that year her mother died, and Pearl decided to set down the story of vivid Carie, the exile who loved roses, who sang at the piano, who wept at the graves of her dead children, Carie, who was driven by a passion for service although the sign that her sacrifice had been accepted never came. In the telling Pearl did not spare her father, who had not given his wife much help or actual happiness. She wanted to write the biography only so that Carol could read about her grandmother some day. Because she did not want to hurt Absalom's feelings she sealed the manuscript away in a box. It was not to be published for 14 years, five years after he died. She ended The Exile with a rousing tribute:

> I do not think one of us would have called her a
> saintly woman. She was far too practical, far too
> vivid and passionate, too full of humor and change
> and temper for that. She was the most human per-
> son we have ever known, the most complex in her
> swift compassion, in her gusts of merriment and
> in her utter impatiences; she was best friend and
> companion to us.

Pearl Buck, the young mother, was also a busy teacher of English and American literature at the University of Nanking. Artfully she encouraged her husband meanwhile to become an authority on Chinese farming. The first step was to get him to write a textbook based on information his students brought in from the countryside. Actually she wrote most of the book. She had plans as well for her father, who was now at odds with the missionary movement because he had tried to establish a native church led by Chinese preachers. Through her influence he was given a professorship at the seminary in Nanking and came to live with the Bucks. These were the

years when Sun Yat-sen accepted support from Russia's Communist rulers and Chiang Kai-shek began climbing toward
military power.

After Pearl Buck finished her mother's biography she
kept on writing. Three essays with Chinese themes were
published in American magazines. Carol was now four years
old, but something clearly was wrong. She did not speak,
she could not understand, and she was often nervous and
cranky. The Bucks decided to go to the United States for
medical help and enroll at the same time at Cornell University for graduate work. John would continue his agricultural
studies, and Pearl would work for a master's degree in the
English novel and essay. On shipboard she began writing her
first story, "A Chinese Woman Speaks." Its young heroine,
Kwei-lan, is torn between old customs and the modern challenges her doctor husband wants her to accept.

At the Mayo Clinic in Rochester, Minnesota, a German
doctor told Pearl that Carol would never be normal. "It was
as if my very flesh were torn," she said later. The little
girl would grow physically, but her mind would remain that
of a four-year-old. She was suffering from phenylketonuria,
the metabolic inability to assimilate proteins. Today doctors
who detect the disease in time can prevent mental retardation,
but in 1925 they were powerless to do anything. Even with
this appalling news and even though the doctor cautioned
against letting the child consume her, Pearl Buck was not
ready to put Carol into a home for retarded children. That
year in Ithaca she was without servants and had to do her
housework for the first time. To ease their heartbreak over
Carol, the Bucks adopted a three-month-old girl named Janice.
On the way back to China, Pearl Buck began to write "West
Wind" as a companion piece to her Kwei-lan story and continued working in her attic room in Nanking.

The Bucks came home to a difficult period. In 1927
the revolutionary armies of the Kuomintang and the Communists were advancing on the city. When the soldiers marched
in, they killed white people and plundered their houses. At-
tempting to flee, the Bucks were rescued by Mrs. Lu, a poor
woman whose baby Pearl Buck once had saved. Mrs. Lu hid
them in her dark little mud hut. Later the refugees were
discovered and taken to the university to join other white refugees. All were sent to Shanghai on board an American destroyer.

Unhappy there, the Bucks went to Japan and lived for a time in the mountains outside Nagasaki. By winter they could return to China, for the Nationalist Party, led by Chiang Kai-shek, had gained the upper hand and was turning on the Communists. When the Bucks arrived back in Nanking, they found their house looted. The novel Pearl had written had disappeared, but her students had saved the manuscript she had written about her mother. Then in 1929 as she was settling into a more serene existence, Pearl Buck reluctantly decided to bring Carol to America and enroll her in a special school.

While staying with friends in Buffalo, she received word that "A Chinese Woman Speaks" and "West Wind" had been accepted for publication under the title, East Wind, West Wind. The publisher was John Day Co., whose editor, the handsome and winning Richard Walsh, told her that the book was intriguing, but needed some editing. Apart from the manuscript he found its comely author, with her special air of calm and quietness, most fascinating.

Her heart heavy over leaving Carol, Pearl Buck returned to Nanking and within three months wrote The Good Earth. It was to be her most famous book, almost haunting her in after years. It is the story of Wang Lung and his homely, tireless wife O-lan, who deeply love their yellow-brown land. When the drought comes, they wander south to the big city to find work. By chance some gold coins are put into Wang Lung's hands; he becomes richer when O-lan plunders a handful of precious stones. But, as the wealthiest farmer in the district, he feels restless and bored in his new leisure. He takes a concubine, Lotus, from a pleasure house and breaks O-lan's heart. On O-lan's death he loses interest in Lotus, but then falls in love with a little slave-girl, Persimmon, whom his youngest son also desires. As Wang Lung nears death, his two elder sons plan how they will sell his land and divide his profits.

Many readers consider O-lan the strongest character in the book. Her pathetic life sums up the sombre and degrading position of the Chinese woman:

> The woman, when he had gone in the morning, took the bamboo rake and a length of rope and with these she roamed the countryside, reaping here a bit of grass and there a twig or a handful of leaves, returning at noon with enough to cook the dinner....

In the afternoon she took a hoe and a basket and
with these upon her shoulder she went to the main
road leading into the city where mules and donkeys
and horses carried burdens to and fro, and there
she picked the droppings from the animals and carried it home and piled the manure in the dooryard
for fertilizer for the fields.   These things she did
without a word and without being commanded to do
them.   And when the end of the day came she did
not rest herself until the ox had been fed in the
kitchen and until she had dipped water to hold to
its muzzle to let it drink what it would....

The Good Earth, written in a simple, ageless, almost
biblical style, became a tremendous success during the Great
Depression when Americans were seeking roots and certain-
ties.   Sales soared, and eventually Pearl Buck earned a million dollars from it.   The book brought her the Pulitzer Prize
in 1932 and the William Dean Howells Medal from the American Academy of Arts and Sciences in 1935.   It was also made
into a famous Hollywood film.

After The Good Earth, still writing in her attic room
at her Mandarin desk, Pearl Buck finished The Mother, the
story of another Chinese peasant woman, spending her life in
toil and buffeted by tragedy, yet taking hope in the birth of
her grandchild.   But she put away this manuscript for a few
years.   It was finally published in 1934.   Then she became
simultaneously involved in two projects, writing a sequel to
The Good Earth and translating the great classic Chinese
novel of ancient China, Shui Hua Chuan (All Men Are Brothers).

Absalom, toward whom she had become much more
tender in his old age, died in 1931.   Not long afterwards
Pearl began writing his biography, emphasizing his "high, ob-
stinate, angelic tranquility. "   Fighting Angel was published
in 1936 as was The Exile, Carie's story, which had long been
in manuscript.   Later they were brought out together as The
Spirit and the Flesh.

In 1932 Richard Walsh begged Pearl to come to the
United States to receive the recognition due the author of a
best-seller.   John Buck was ready for another furlough and
wanted to use it to complete his Ph. D. degree at Cornell.
Even though she helped him with his studies, especially language, Pearl felt emotionally and intellectually far apart from
her husband.   In New York, Richard Walsh told her, "Here

I am a publisher, and I've fallen in love with my best-selling
author!" Pearl said it was madness and tried to discourage
him.   He too was married, though unhappily.   She also felt a
certain loyalty to her husband of 15 years and resignation to
an unsatisfactory marriage.   Meanwhile she was swept into a
whirl of parties, press conferences, and speaking engagements.

After the furlough year the Bucks returned to China
by way of England and Europe.   On the voyage home from
Italy Pearl Buck was increasingly troubled by the love she
felt for Richard Walsh and decided to tell John about her dilemma.   Although completely amazed, he did agree to a year
of separation, which amounted to a year of freedom for her.
"In six months [Richard] cabled me to meet him in Shanghai
in order to hear 'no' again and this time forever. "

Increasingly restless, she began travels to India, Cambodia and Laos in Indochina, and Siam.   Near Peking she ran
into Richard, who appeared in the midst of a violent dust
storm.   "We parted again eternally. "   Back in Nanking she
felt guilty for having been away so long from Carol, and in
the spring of 1934 she set sail for the United States.   While
the ship was docking at Yokohama, she heard Richard's voice,
"I've turned up again--I shall keep on turning up, you know--
everywhere in the world.   You can't escape me. "   Still she
kept saying "no" every day on shipboard, in Vancouver, and
in New York.   (As Pearl Buck wrote in A Bridge for Passing,
"I am not an easy-to-marry woman, or so I imagine.   I am
divided to the bottom of my being, part of me being woman,
the other part artist and having nothing to do with woman. ")
But, Pearl would comment some years later, "spring in that
magic city was my undoing. "

While arranging to buy an old farmhouse in Bucks
County, Pennsylvania, she finally decided on divorce and re-
marriage.   On the same day, June 11, 1935, she was divorced
in Reno, Nevada, and married Richard Walsh there.   Almost
immediately they began adopting babies, first Robert and Ed-
gar and later John and Jean.   Winters they spent in a ter-
raced New York apartment, summers in Bucks County.   Pearl
Buck wrote of herself as "a mother who laughed too easily"
over naughtiness unless she was angry.   Teachers were unan-
imous in commenting, "Your children are spoiled. "

By this time Pearl Buck, the daughter of Presbyterian
missionaries, felt she had no formal religion.   In the January,
1933 issue of Harper's Magazine she had criticized mission-

aries to China as narrow, uncharitable, unappreciative, ignorant, and insensitive. Rather than being concerned with religious preaching, she wrote, they should be helping with illness
and poverty. The article caused such an uproar that the Presbyterian Mission Board asked her to resign.

Sons and A House Divided, the sequels to The Good
Earth, were published in 1933 and 1935. The trilogy is known
as The House of Earth. In the first sequel Wang Lung's
eldest son leads an indulgent life, and his middle son becomes
an unscrupulous merchant and usurer. The youngest son
evolves into a war lord known as Wang the Tiger, who after
his wife betrays him, tried to mold his son Yuan into a great
warrior. But the boy despises military life and wants to return to his grandfather's old house. A House Divided centers
on Yuan, who quarrels with his father and seeks refuge in
Wang Lung's first earth house. But he does not fit into rural
life and leaves for Shanghai to live with wealthy relatives.
Experiencing the vivid contrast between rich and poor, he
joins a revolutionary band and is captured. His relatives obtain his release and send him to America to study for a doctorate. On his return he is appalled by the conditions he finds,
but accepts his people as they are. These two sequels never
matched The Good Earth in popularity. Many critics found
the simple, almost biblical style ill suited to the stories, especially to the American chapters of A House Divided.

Reviewers complained that Pearl Buck's next book,
This Proud Heart, was full of clichés. The subject matter,
however, seemed compelling--the conflict between Susan Gay-
lord's role as a wife, mother, and homemaker, and her
striving for self-fulfillment as a sculptress.

That same year, 1938, came the Nobel Prize. The
criticism heaped on Pearl Buck's selection wounded her deeply.
When she attended a writers' association dinner as an honored
guest, she spoke very humbly about herself. Sinclair Lewis,
who had won a Nobel Prize in 1930 amid almost as much
furor, scolded her. "You must not minimize yourself," he
said. "Never minimize your profession. A novelist has a
noble function." After that, she never again apologized for
her work. More confident, she left for Stockholm, accompanied by Richard and his daughter Betty. Although they stopped in England and Denmark, she refused to visit Hitler's
Germany.

In Stockholm she was lionized by the press, which

seized on her name, calling her "La Perla." This was the
only time, she remarked, she ever liked it. Newspapers
ran stories and pictures of this handsome, stately woman,
describing her brilliant blue eyes, strong nose, and delicate
cream complexion. Several columns praised her talents--
playing the piano (especially Beethoven sonatas and Chopin),
sculpting, painting, and arranging flowers. Many mentioned
her ready wit.

She would always look back on the Stockholm trip as
the most brilliant occurrence of her life. She sat on the platform with Enrico Fermi, who received the Nobel Prize in
Physics. Her diploma was hand illuminated with beautiful
Chinese figures. And Betty danced with the Crown Prince.
At the same time the experience put into focus the difficulty
of sharing her total life with Richard: "I saw quite clearly
that it doesn't matter how much a woman loves a man and
responds to and respects him, and no matter how indispensable he is, there are parts of life that cannot be shared."

In Stockholm Pearl Buck accepted her Prize with these
words: "I can only hope that the many books which I have
yet to write will be in some measure a worthier acknowledg-
ment than I can make tonight. And, indeed, I can accept only
in the same spirit in which I think this gift was originally
given--that it is a prize not so much for what has been done,
as for the future. Whatever I write for the future must, I
think, be always benefited and strengthened when I remember
this day."

From now on she became exceedingly prolific, not
always with the happiest results. For the next 34 years, in
an easy prose style, she turned out almost seventy books and
scores of newspaper and magazine articles, lectures, and
pamphlets. During wartime she was even writing radio plays.
It seemed time to Americanize her style and content, but
critics compared everything she wrote to The Good Earth.
So between 1945 and 1953 she tried to outwit them by using
the pseudonym John Sedges for five novels, of which The
Townsman, a historical tale set in Kansas, was best received.
Always she stressed the innate goodness of man. But she rejected the modern techniques of stream-of-consciousness invention, symbolism, and deep psychological probing. Many
of her books took up the theme of the strong woman who accepts responsibility for others and must therefore give up her
own desires and independence. Pavilion of Women, written
in 1946, carried this theme over into a renewed Chinese setting.

During World War II, Pearl Buck wrote <u>Dragon Seed</u>
and <u>The Promise,</u> both dramatizing the fighting in China,
Japan, and Burma. In both she predicted that peacetime
would see the white powers losing their dominion over the
colored peoples. In <u>Command the Morning</u> she deplored the
dropping of the atomic bomb by a white nation against a yellow one. When first settling in the United States, she had
been aghast to discover racial prejudice, and through the
years she kept on saying much about the plight of American
blacks. Racial equality and freedom became favorite themes.
Like Wendell Willkie, Pearl Buck dreamed of one world.

Critics charged her with being a propagandist for humanitarian reforms and with writing too much. After 1945
they began to ignore her. But Pearl Buck remained loyal
to her sympathies.

In the early years of the war, trying to explain Asia
to Americans and America, she took over the direction of
<u>Asia Magazine</u> and founded the East and West Association.
Because of her own retarded daughter she was especially
interested in handicapped children. Courageously, in 1950,
she wrote about Carol in <u>The Child Who Never Grew</u>, a small
book intended to give hope to perplexed and despairing parents
of mentally retarded children. And because of her own adopted
family, which had grown to nine, she became deeply concerned
with orphans. With the help of neighbors like Oscar Hammer-
stein, she formed an adoptive agency called Welcome House
to find adoptive homes for children of mixed parentage. The
problem of biracial children was even greater in Asia than in
the United States. Thousands of American servicemen had
left behind countless fatherless children, who were objects
of scorn in their communities. To the Pearl S. Buck Foundation she signed away the considerable fortune she had acquired
through savings, royalties, and real estate. The earnings of
her new books and articles she earmarked for the foundation.
Nor in her love for children did she forget to write for them,
charming books like <u>The Water Buffalo</u>, <u>The Dragon Fish</u>, and
<u>The Big Wave</u>.

In 1953, during a vacation trip, Richard Walsh suffered
the first of several strokes. "The man I knew so well, "
Pearl said, "the wise companion, became someone else, a
trusting child, a gentle, helpless infant, whom no one could
help loving. " He died in 1960 while she was in Japan helping
with the filming on location of <u>The Big Wave</u>. The grief-
stricken widow suddenly thought of her "scholarly parents,

those two who from my earliest years taught me by their example to find release and courage and strength in the use of
the mind. " And she determined, "I carried within my skull
my own implement.   I need not, I must not retreat or pause
or cease to grow because I walk my way alone. " Such thoughts
she put into A Bridge for Passing.   She is filled with memories of her second marriage as she crosses the "bridge from
sorrow to eternity. "

After Richard's death Pearl renewed her friendship
with W. Ernest Hocking, the retired chairman of the Harvard
philosophy department.   Amazingly vigorous at 88, he was
remarkably in tune with her thinking. During his last years
she gave him much affection and companionship, refusing, however, to marry him.   During this period she was living in
Danby, Vermont, a little town she helped revitalize.

Here in Danby on March 6, 1973, after a year of illness, including surgery, she died. Once in speaking of her
friend Eleanor Roosevelt, Pearl Buck defined a sophisticated
person as one who has experienced everything, known everything, and reduced everything to its essence. "Sophistication, "
she said, almost as if speaking of herself, "is the final simplicity. "

Poems at Floodtide

GABRIELA MISTRAL

Gabriela Mistral's poetry has passion as its great
central theme, a passion closely related to tragedy. Four
suicides shattered her life. Little wonder that this Chilean
poet, who came to Stockholm in 1945, looked sad-eyed and
mysterious.

She was the only one of the Nobel lady laureates to
be known by her pen name. For some years she used her
pseudonym interchangeably with her given name. But eventually it passed wholly over to her private life so that after
she became famous she was called simply Gabriela. It was
a name she had chosen from the archangel Gabriel. The
Mistral came from the hot, strong desert wind of Provence.
"I wanted a pseudonym that would evoke the force of nature
that I like the most," she said. Some of her biographers
claim she was honoring two poets she deeply admired, Ga-
briele d'Annunzio and Frédéric Mistral. Usually she signed
her names together as though they were one word.

Gabriela Mistral was 56 when she made the long journey from Petropolis, Brazil, to Stockholm. The ceremony
that December 10 was particularly festive, for this was the
first Nobel presentation after World War II. Indeed, the
Literature Prize had been suspended from 1940 through 1943.
The Prize for 1944 had been awarded to the Danish writer,
Johannes V. Jensen, but he had been unable to leave Nazi-
occupied Denmark. Therefore in 1945 the craggy-faced Jut-
lander sat beside the Chilean poet, who looked majestic and
half Indian in her black velvet gown. A tall, handsome,
dark-complexioned woman with short iron-gray hair, she cap-
tivated the onlookers with her charming smile that belied her
tragic eyes. The city so took her to its heart that newspapers
hailed her as "the lioness of social Stockholm."

Until the poet Hjalmar Gullberg translated her poems

Gabriela Mistral

into Swedish, Gabriela Mistral had been practically unknown in Scandinavia. By 1945 the Swedish Academy knew her poetry well and seemed particularly eager to recognize Spanish-speaking America with a tribute to its leading poet. Gabriela Mistral's citation read, "for her lyric poetry which, inspired by powerful emotions, has made her name a symbol of the idealistic aspirations of the entire Latin American world."

Twenty-six years later Chile would boast of giving Latin America its second winner of the Nobel Prize in Literature. The Whitmanesque Pablo Neruda, honored in 1971, was Gabriela's longtime friend in spite of their great political differences. Indeed, in her last years her fear of the Communism he championed amounted almost to an obsession. Yet she came to his defense several times. Neruda, too, was loyal. Had he not written her, "I shall always revere your life and your poetry"?

Dr. Gullberg made Gabriela's Nobel Prize presentation, hailing her "remarkable pilgrimage from the chair of a schoolmistress to the throne of poetry." Or, as he put it in another way, "the little provincial schoolteacher, the young colleague of Selma Lagerlöf of Mårbacka," had become "the spiritual queen of Latin America." To the "compatriots of Selma Lagerlöf" Gabriela made a gracious acceptance speech, calling herself the daughter of Chilean democracy. "The daughter of a new people, I salute the spiritual pioneers of Sweden.... At this moment, by an undeserved stroke of fortune, I am the direct voice of the poets of my race and the indirect voice for the noble Spanish and Portuguese tongues. Both rejoice to have been invited to this festival of Nordic life with its tradition of centuries of folklore and poetry."

Gabriela Mistral's story, Dr. Gullberg noted, was so well known in South America that, passed on from country to country, it had almost become a legend. It began in northern Chile, in Vicuña, a high Andean village in the grape-growing Valley of Elqui. Here she was born April 7, 1889, and baptized Lucila Godoy y Alcayaga the same day. Her father, Jeronimo Godoy Villanueva, of Indian and possibly Jewish heritage, was an elementary school teacher in the village of La Unión, a pallador or minstrel, who composed verses for festivals, and a vagabond to boot. He had married a beautiful widow of Basque descent, Petronila Alcayaga de Molina, who had a 15-year-old daughter, Emelina. In 1892 Jeronimo abandoned his family, never to return. He left his young daughter with his poetic talent and a great deal of his roaming spirit, for the mature Gabriela was to wander endlessly. Her American friend, the writer Waldo Frank, once described Leon Hidalgo's reaction to her--"a great dark woman wandering through Europe and always bearing Chile, a mysterious treasure, in her hand; reading poems in which a fire of her Andes seems to overwhelm the flowers of her valleys."

Emelina, already a schoolteacher, took a job that year of Jeronimo's leaving. Her mother and sister joined her in Monte Grande, and Lucila became her pupil. In her bright percale apron Lucila was a dreamy, quiet, timid child. She

> talked with the wind,
> and the mountain and fields of cane
> under moons of madness

and

> received a kingdom of her own.

Once in Vicuña she was helping a blind teacher by distributing class materials. Taking advantage of Lucila's absentmindedness, the students stole from her. When the teacher heard of the theft, she accused Lucila and expelled her from school. "Thief! thief!" As the little girl walked away in shame, her classmates jeered and threw stones at her.

When she was 12, her family moved to La Serena, close to her paternal grandmother, Isabel de Villanueva, who was very religious. Here Lucila first saw the ocean. And very clearly she saw her future. Like her father and Emelina, Lucila wanted to be a teacher. For her the profession was always a glorified mission, a way of lifting up the poor and unfortunate. A few years later she became a Socialist, showing her colors in poems and articles for local newspapers. Because of Lucila's radical ideas, however, her application for admission to the normal school in La Serena was turned down.

In 1907, working as an assistant in a school at La Cantera, she met Romelio Ureta, a young railroad employee. They became engaged. But because of frequent and bitter disputes they broke off. Two years later Ureta sent a bullet through his head. Although a postcard from Lucila was found in his pocket, personal honor dictated his suicide. The story went that he acted in despair over not being able to replace a sum of money he had embezzled for a friend. Nonetheless, Lucila felt devastated by his death and began writing with fierce intensity those poems which would appear in Desolación many years later.

The next year, in spite of the tragedy, friends encouraged Lucila, then teaching at Barrancas, to take an examination at a Santiago normal school. It tested her on her knowledge and skill rather than on formal studies. She passed it very successfully and began moving rapidly through the school system.

She was known as a progressive teacher, giving her pupils much freedom to discover themselves. After teaching hygiene at the public school in Traiguén for two months she went to Antofogasta as head inspector and teacher of history, geography, and Spanish. Here she became friends with Pedro Aguirre Cerda, later to be president of Chile. About this time somebody described her as "a young lady of noble bearing who has beautiful green eyes with a limpid gaze, and princesslike hands."

Four months after World War I had broken out, the 25-year-old Lucila competed in the poetic Floral Games, a national contest sponsored by a writers' society in Santiago, and won a laurel wreath and a gold crown for her three Sonetos de la Muerte (Sonnets of the Dead), dedicated to Romelio Ureta. The shy schoolteacher watched unnoticed from a balcony. She had not signed them with her own name because she was afraid that her impassioned and sensuous outcries might jeopardize her position. She had signed them with the name of Gabriela Mistral.

> From that cold ledge where they have laid you by,
> I shall take down and lay you in the ground,
> Where humble and alone myself shall lie,
> Where we shall share dream-pillowings profound.
>
> Beside you stretching I shall show you all
> A mother's yearning for her child asleep.
> So earth shall cradle your pale body's pall
> And sweetness smother half the sobs you weep.

In that single line, "A mother's yearning for her child asleep," Gabriela translated her frustrated love into a longing for motherhood, a theme that would dominate her poetry.

Not long after, she fell in love with a young poet from
Santiago. Mystery cloaks the relationship, even his name.
On Gabriela's side the feeling was intense, but the poet soon
broke her heart by marrying a young heiress. The grief-
stricken teacher asked for a transfer to Punte Arenas (Magall-
anas) in the desolate southern region of Chile, and here from
1918 until 1920 she poured out her heart in poems of intense
lyric emotion, expressing the jealousy, humiliation, and frustration of her loss.

In due time Gabriela was appointed principal of a liceo
for girls in Temuco, in the heart of the rain-drenched Indian
country, where the young Neftali Reyes, who was to take the
pen name of Pablo Neruda, first saw her. At 16 he was
president of the Temuco Literary Club, and Gabriela was
voted an honorary member. She opened the school library
to the shy boy, and he often sat waiting in her office to be
able to talk to her.

About his youth Pablo Neruda later wrote:

> During those years a tall woman, unbecomingly
> dressed, arrived.... The story goes that the ladies
> of the community suggested that she wear a hat--
> everyone wore one then--and she answered smiling:

> 'What for? It would be ridiculous. Like putting a
> hat on the Andes Mountains. '

> That was Gabriela Mistral. I used to watch her
> walking along the streets of my town in flat heeled
> shoes and great, long garments and I was afraid
> of her. But when, overcoming my shyness, I was
> taken to see her, I found her attractive and in her
> well toasted face, where Indian blood predominated,
> as in a beautiful Araucanian vessel, her very white
> teeth shone in a wide, generous smile that bright-
> ened the whole room.

By 1921 the restless young teacher transferred to Santiago as principal of a public high school. She lived on the
outskirts of the city, practiced yoga, studied theosophy, and
received a constant stream of visitors. To those who came
to see her, however, there seemed to be two Gabrielas, the
lonely majestic one who wore a tragic mask and the playful,
happy one who could be capricious at times. That year Dr.
Federico de Onís, a professor at Columbia University in New

York, and a group of his students, all Spanish teachers, were astonished to learn that her poetry had never been collected in book form. Quickly they resolved to publish it.

Gabriela had not been long at her Santiago post when a measure, prohibiting the appointment of teachers without university degrees, became law, and she resigned. Fortunately, just at this time, José Vasconcelos, the Mexican minister of education, invited her to collaborate on a plan of educational reform, including the organization of libraries. Gabriela accepted the offer and came to Mexico, staying much longer than intended, interesting herself in Indian history, and exploring every corner of the country. Here in Mexico she regained her religious faith. Much later she was to write, "I am a Christian, a total democrat. I believe that Christianity in its profoundest sense can save the peoples of the world." In Mexico she also met Palma Guillén, who was to become her lifelong friend.

While Gabriela was in Mexico, the Hispanic Institute under Dr. de Onís's direction collected and published her poems under the title, Desolación. It came from one of the poems which describes a desolate landscape of mist, wind, and fog, which was also a projection of her own anguished mind. "May God forgive me this bitter book," wrote Gabriela, "and may those who find life sweet forgive me too." Desolación contained the Sonetos de la Muerte and her equally famous "El Ruego" (Prayer):

> I tell You he was good, and I say
> his heart like a flower in his breast did sing,
> gentle of nature, frank as the light of day,
> bursting with miracles, as is the Spring.
>
> Unworthy of my pleas is he, You strongly say,
> since no sign of prayer crossed his fevered face,
> and one day, with no nod from You, he went away,
> shattering his temples like a fragile vase.

Her feelings again burst forth in "La Espera Inútil" (The Useless Wait).

> I forgot that your light foot
> had turned to ash,
> and as in happy times
> I set out to meet you on the path.

I crossed valley, plain, and river,
and the singing made me sad.
The evening spilled out its vessel
of light--and you did not come!

If Ureta was the inspiration for those two poems, the
mysterious poet who had jilted her stood behind poems like
"Notturno" (Nocturne):

And now I loosen my martyred sandal
And my locks, for I am longing to sleep
And lost in the night, I lift my voice
In the cry I have learned from Thee:
Our Father who art in heaven,
Why hast thou forsaken me!"

Desolación also contained poems to mothers and children,
religious poems, and a few prose pieces.

A new book, Ternura (Tenderness), dedicated to her
half-sister Emelina, appeared in 1924. It was full of beautiful lullabies that Gabriela called "colloquies the mother has
with her child and with the Earth Spirit around her, visible
by day and audible by night." One of them begins,

Little fleece of my flesh
that I wove in my womb.
little shivering fleece,
sleep close to me!

Dancing their rondas, children throughout Latin America
began to sing Gabriela's lyrics:

The crimson rose
plucked yesterday,
the fire and cinnamon
of the carnation,

the bread I baked
with anise seeds and honey,
and the goldfish
flaming in its bowl.

Her Mexican project a success, Gabriela decided to
go to Spain by way of the United States to personally thank
Dr. de Onís and to deliver a speech to the Pan-American
Union. Following her tour of Spain she visited Switzerland

and Italy and then made a triumphant return to South America.
In Chile she was granted a pension for her work as a teacher.

But she could not settle down. In 1926 she came to
Paris as the Chilean delegate to the League of Nations Committee for Intellectual Cooperation, taking charge of the section on Hispanic-American literature and choosing works of
Latin-American authors to be published in a European series.
Among them she picked some poems by the 22-year-old Pablo
Neruda, then Chilean consul in Saigon, whom she called "our
best young poet. " Already he had published one of his best-
known books, <u>Crepusculario</u> (Twilight Book). In the same
tradition of government recognition of artists, which was to
honor Gabriela, Neruda was appointed Chilean consul in various countries and eventually ambassador to France. Gabriela's
work for the League also brought her into contact with Marie
Curie.

Gabriela did not like living in large cities and by early
1927 had settled into a small house in Fontainebleau. One day
she received a Chilean visitor, who needed help for his small
son. Looking at his papers and reading the name Godoy, she
was astonished to learn that she had a half-brother. Like their
father Jeronimo, he too was a vagabond. His wife was unable
to care for their little Juan Miguel. So quickly and lovingly
Gabriela offered to take her newly discovered nephew into her
home. The four-year-old was nicknamed Yin-Yin. Often he
went with Gabriela on her travels.

In 1929 Petronila died in La Serena at the age of 84.
Gabriela had never been able to persuade her to leave.
Twenty-five years later in one of the poems of <u>Lagar</u> Gabri-
ela evoked her mother's presence:

> My mother was very tiny
> like mint or herbs
> she hardly cast a shadow
> upon things, hardly,
> and the earth loved her,
> because of her being so light
> and because she smiled at it
> when happy and when sad.

The restless feet moved on. But wherever Gabriela went, her
heart reached out to the poor and oppressed, and her door was
always open. In 1930 she was teaching Hispanic-American
literature at Barnard College. Afterwards she spent four months

on the Vassar campus, a summer of lecturing at Middlebury
College, and a term at the University of Puerto Rico. Hearing
that Neruda was in financial trouble, she wrote a letter to
Chilean authorities urging a new consular post for him.

Gabriela was a passionate reader, feeling at home in
the bookshops of Europe and the Americas. Now critics were
recognizing her literary inspirations--Rabindranath Tagore,
the Nicaraguan poet Rubén Darío, the Mexican poet Amado
Nervo, the Bible, and Oriental literature--and seeing her poems
for what they were, pure lyric outbursts, without thematic development or climactic progressions. Gabriela herself once
remarked that she wrote her poems "at floodtide." And still,
paradoxically, she changed and corrected endlessly and waited
long intervals between publishing.

Along with her poems she wrote excellent prose pieces
on sociological and cultural subjects for the best-known Latin-
American journals and newspapers. One of her articles in
1931 declared: "We of North and South America have accepted
with our heritage of geographical unity a certain common destiny which should find a threefold fulfillment in our continent in
an adequate standard of living, perfect democracy, and ample
liberty." Twelve years later in another article she found
race prejudice, "that great paganistic and collective evil,"
and egocentric cultural attitudes to be primary isolating factors leading to disunity. "I write as a prophet when I say
that the century of the common man will be built in the Americas only on common ground in education, regardless of race,
creed, or language."

By 1932 it was time for Gabriela to begin her own consular duties, first in Naples as honorary consul. But Mussolini disapproved of her anti-fascist articles, and she left for
France and Spain and finally Puerto Rico to give more lectures.
Then in 1934 she went as honorary consul to Madrid. Within a
short time she settled in Lisbon as Consul Vitalico, second
class, with the right to choose where she wanted to live. This
honor came after Miguel de Unamuno, Romain Rolland, and
Maurice Maeterlinck asked the president of Chile to offer Gabriela a paid consulate to assure her economic security. But,
ever restless, she could not stay long in Portugal. She had to
move about in Europe and South America, where sometimes
she lectured.

Fourteen years after Ternura there came a new collection of her poetry. Tala (Felling) was dedicated to the Basque,

Catalan, and Castilian child refugees from the Spanish civil
war. She gave the proceeds to a camp for such children at
Pedralbes, in Spain, and angered General Francisco Franco's
followers. Tala continues her old themes and especially
evokes the garden of her childhood in the Elqui valley. Francis of Assisi was her favorite saint, and several poems are
filled with rural speech and a Franciscan love of simple things
like bread and wine and salt and water. But the pathos of
Desolación has been replaced by an air of universal calm.
Often she links the theme of childhood to that of maternity.
Certain stanzas, reflecting her journeys, go beyond her
Chilean memories:

> Like the maguey, like the yucca,
> the Peruvian jug,
> the calabash of Uruapan,
> the century old quena,
> I give myself to you, I yield,
> I open up, I bathe in you!

Just as Tala was published, she returned to Chile after
13 years, her visit an even greater triumph than in 1925.
Schools and libraries had been named after her, and "Gabriela"
seemed to be on everybody's lips. When asked, "Whom do
you want to see?" she simply replied, "I want to talk to the
schoolteachers."

Her next consular assignment, to Nice, came in December, 1938. But with World War II threatening, she asked
for a transfer to Brazil, first to Niteroi and then to Petropolis. In this delightful mountain city she was a neighbor and
close friend of the Austrian writer Stefan Zweig and his young
wife, Lotte. In spite of the terrible war it seemed a time of
happiness for her. Juan Miguel, whom she called "the pine
of Aleppo," showed a talent for writing. But Gabriela loved
plants so much that she hoped he would become an agriculturist.
From her Brazilian home she was also reaching out through
letters to friends like Waldo Frank and Charles and Anne
Lindbergh.

Then tragedy struck again, three times in little more
than a year. One February afternoon in 1942 the Zweigs,
acting in despair over the war and the fate of their fellow
Jews, took massive doses of veronal. Gabriela was shaken
to her depths. Then 18 months later, on August 13, 1943,
her nephew, 18-year-old Juan Miguel, swallowed arsenic.
No one knew why although some of Gabriela's friends guessed

that he had been oversensitive, both to the Zweigs' suicide and
to the taunts of xenophobic schoolmates, who looked down on
his foreign education.   Gabriela lingered one terrible night
by his bedside.   His death broke both her health and her spirit.

When the news came in November, 1945, that she had
won the Nobel Prize, she knelt before her crucifix.   Later
she remarked, "Perhaps it was because I was the candidate
of the women and children. "

Although in ill health, she braced herself to sail to
Stockholm.   On her arrival she endeared herself to the Swedes,
and they won her heart.   The Swedish social democracy, she
exulted, was a century ahead of everything else.

At the ceremony in the Concert Hall, Dr. Gullberg
declared, "In rendering homage to the rich Latin-American
literature, we address ourselves today quite especially to
its queen, the poet of Desolación, who has become the great
singer of sorrow and of motherhood. "   Truly the onlookers
thought she looked like a queen when she received the Prize
from the aged King Gustav.   The only unpleasantness came
when Neruda's wife complained she could not understand why
the Nobel Prize had not been given to a Communist.   By now
Neruda had become a full-fledged member of the party.   In
spite of Gabriela's socialistic sympathies she could not accept Communism and passionately denounced it.

After the Nobel award, Gabriela filled a consular post
in Los Angeles, choosing to live, however, in Santa Barbara.
Subsequently, from a consular post in Italy she would write
her friends there, "Everything I have is a house in California
with two or three thousand books and a one hundred year old
husky tree.   Please look after my good old tree. "

Before long she was very ill with diabetes and harden-
ing of the arteries and accepted the Mexican government's
offer of a house and land in Vera Cruz.   Then in 1951, the
year she won the Chilean National Prize for Literature,
Gabriela resumed her consular duties in Italy and chose to
live in Rapallo, later moving to Naples.   Soon came a short
term as Chilean delegate to the United Nations Commission
on the Status of Women and as a member of its Committee
for Women's Rights.   During her last years she worked as
an advisor to UNESCO, but turned down the directorship of
the South American branch of UNICEF, for which she made
the first worldwide "Appeal for Children. "

Finally ill health forced her into retirement in a house
at Roslyn Harbor, New York, on Long Island, where she lived
with her friend, Doris Dana, who became her trusted translator.   Nonetheless she was able to return to Chile in the fall
of 1954 for yet one more triumphal passage from Valparaiso
to Santiago.   Among her honors was a doctorate from the University of Chile.   At the presidential palace 200,000 Chileans
waited to hear her speak.   Another day in the National Stadium
thousands of children sang her lyrics.   The month after her
return to New York she accepted another honorary degree
from Columbia University.   In all, Gabriela amassed several
such honors.

Lagar (Wine Press), her last book, was published that
year, the record of her personal suffering after the triple
suicides.   "Una Palabra" (One Word) deals with Yin-Yin's
death:

Never again to remember the word between my lips,
that word of iodine and alum stone,
or ever again, that one night,
the ambush in a foreign land,
the lightning bolt at the door,
and my flesh abroad with no soul.

Gabriela Mistral died of cancer of the pancreas on
January 10, 1957, in Hampstead General Hospital, on Long
Island.   In Chile, President Ibáñez ordered three days of
national mourning.   After funeral services in St. Patrick's
Cathedral in New York City, her body, clad in the black
velvet gown she had worn to the Nobel ceremony, was brought
to Santiago.   Three years later her remains were taken to a
mausoleum at Monte Grande.   The vault carried a monolithic
stone inscribed with one of Gabriela's famous axioms, "What
the soul is to the body is what the artist does for his people."

The day following her death Pablo Neruda wrote, "The
heart of Chile mourns.... The wind, the ocean, the trees,
all singing things in our land will sing when they receive her
forever, the only chorus worthy of Gabriela Mistral."

Long ago, in Desolación, Gabriela had herself cried
out, "When I am in heaven may God give me angel wings to
soothe the hurt in my heart; spread instead across the sky
the hair of the children I loved, and let the hair sweep forever in the wind across my face."

Flight and Metamorphosis

NELLY SACHS

A tiny, wispy old woman rose at the Nobel banquet
table the evening of December 10, 1966. "To me a fairy
tale seems to have become reality," Nelly Sachs cried out.
This frail poet with the friendly yet sensitive face moved all
hearts as she paid tribute to the first woman to win the
Literature Prize: "In the summer of 1939 a German girl
friend of mine went to Sweden to visit Selma Lagerlöf, to
ask her to secure a sanctuary for my mother and myself in
that country. Since my youth I had been so fortunate as to
exchange letters with Selma Lagerlöf, and it is out of her
work that my love for her country grew. The painter-prince
Eugen and the novelist helped to save me. In the spring of
1940, after torturous months, we arrived in Stockholm. The
occupation of Denmark and Norway had already taken place.
The great novelist was no more. We breathed the air of
freedom without knowing the language or any person."

Nelly Sachs's diploma commended her for "outstanding
lyrical and dramatic writing which interprets Israel's destiny
with touching strength." She was awarded the Nobel Prize
on her seventy-fifth birthday although she was too modest to
say so. Rather she commented, "Today ... I think of what
my father used to say on every tenth of December, back in
my home town, Berlin. 'Now they celebrate the Nobel ceremony in Stockholm.' "

Gracefully she ended her short speech by quoting one
of her best-known poems, "In der Flucht" (Fleeing);

In der Flucht/ welch grosser Empfang/ unterwegs ...

> Fleeing,
> what a great reception
> on the way--
>
> Wrapped
> in the wind's shawl

Nelly Sachs

feet in the prayer of sand
which can never say amen
compelled
from fin to wing
and further--

This sick butterfly
will soon learn again of the sea--
This stone
with the fly's inscription
gave itself into my hand--

I hold instead of a homeland
The metamorphoses of the world--

It was a happy choice, for the elliptical, metaphorical language summed up so many of her symbols--inscription, flight,
fish, butterfly, and stones.

So far, Nelly Sachs has been the only lady laureate
in Literature to share her Prize. Sitting with her onstage
was 78-year-old Shmuel Yosef Agnon, regarded as the fore-
most writer in modern Hebrew literature. Anders Österling,
member of the Swedish Academy, explained why these representatives of "Israel's message to our time" had been chosen:
"The purpose of combining these two Prize winners is to do
justice to the individual achievement of each, and the sharing
of the Prize has its special justification: to honour two
writers who, although they write in different languages, are
united in a spiritual kinship and complement each other in
a superb effort to present the cultural heritage of the Jewish
people through the written word. Their common source of
inspiration has been for both of them a vital power."

After dwelling on Agnon's unique qualities as a writer,
Österling turned to Miss Sachs: "With moving intensity of
feeling she has given voice to the worldwide tragedy of the
Jewish people, which she has expressed in lyrical laments of
painful beauty and in dramatic legends. Her symbolic language boldly combines an inspired modern idiom with echoes
of ancient Biblical poetry. Identifying herself totally with the
faith and ritual mysticism of her people, Miss Sachs has
created a world of imagery which does not shun the terrible
truth of the extermination camps and the corpse factories,
but which at the same time rises above all hatred of the per-
secutors, merely revealing a genuine sorrow at man's de-
basement."

To all of this Nelly Sachs had her own succinct comment: "Agnon represents the state of Israel; I represent the tragedy of the Jewish people." She was unique in another manner. At the age of 50 she entered an intensely creative period that was to last more than 20 years. At 55 she published her first book of poetry.

When she contributed an autobiographical note for the Nobel records, she wrote in pithy style: "Leonie Nelly Sachs, born in Berlin on December 10, 1891. As refugee arrived in Sweden with my mother on May 16, 1940. Since then living in Stockholm and active as writer and translator." This passion for privacy was lifelong. Often she turned down the idea of giving material for a biography, insisting that her poetry was all that people needed to know. Her closest friends maintained the same tight security about her. Critics could ask questions about her work but not her life.

Her father, William Sachs, a prominent manufacturer and gifted inventor, and her mother, Margareta, born Karger, were cultured and religiously liberal German Jews. Some years her husband's junior, Margareta was only 20 when their daughter was born. Their beautiful home lay in the fashionable Tiergarten section of Berlin. There, near the turn of the century, their only child played with a pet doe and goat in the secluded garden. It was a quiet, protected, and genteel life. Nelly's greatest pleasure was to dance when her father played his favorite Romantic composers on his grand piano. Whirling about the elegant living room, the fragile little girl dreamed of becoming a famous dancer. Some 50 years later she would glorify the "Tänzerin":

> Dancer
> like a bride
> you conceive
> from blind space
> the sprouting longing
> of distant days of creation--

When Nelly was only nine, her parents took her out of the Dorotheen Schule and hired private tutors for her. The reason was her poor health. When she grew stronger, she entered the Aubert Schule and stayed five years.

On her fifteenth birthday in 1906, she received a copy of Gösta Berlings Saga. It so enraptured her that she began corresponding with Selma Lagerlöf. This friendship was to

change her life most decisively 34 years later.   She had already begun writing Legenden und Erzählungen (Legends and
Stories), a collection of tales mostly set in the Middle Ages.
But it was not published until 1921.   Meanwhile the Sachs
family life was so sheltered that only once--at school--did
Nelly Sachs feel the hurt of being scorned as a Jew.   Apart
from dancing for her father, she had a new absorption, a
marionette theater for which she made up little plays.

When she was 17 and suffering from shyness, she went
with her parents to a German spa.   Here she fell passionately
in love with a man, who has never been publicly identified.
The whole affair and setting remain a mystery.   All that is
known is that Nelly Sachs never forgot him.   No other man
ever entered her life romantically.   Years later he died in
a concentration camp, and she hailed him as "der toten
Bräutigam" (the dead bridegroom) in one short poem and
evoked his memory in other poignant verses:

> If I only knew
> On what your last look rested.
> Was it a stone that had drunk
> So many last looks that they fell
> Blindly upon its blindness?

The delicate young Nelly Sachs wrote a different kind
of poetry.   She was never touched by the expressionistic
poets of the early twentieth century.   She found her inspiration in neo-Romantic verse, especially that of the melancholy
and nature-loving Novalis.   None of Nelly's early poetry was
particularly distinctive.   When it was published in Vossisschen
Zeitung in 1923, it predictably caused no stir.   Over the next
few years a few of her poems came out in Jewish publications.
And the Berlin Marionette Theater presented one of her plays.

After William Sachs's death in 1930, his widow and
daughter led an even more secluded life.   Outside their walls
Adolf Hitler, a hater of Jews, rose to power.   Quickly he de-
creed laws to exclude the Jews from German citizenship and
to deprive them of property rights and legal protection.   After
Operation Crystal Night broke in all its ferocity, he began a
systematic campaign of extermination.   Suddenly Nelly and
her mother were living in daily fear of arrest and deportation.
Desperately they watched their panic-stricken friends and
relatives disappear into concentration camps.

As their world began to disintegrate, Nelly mulled

over her books. Martin Buber became one of her favorite
philosophers. She had already formed a taste for Jewish
and Christian mystics, especially Jacob Böhme, the German
cobbler of Görlitz. She had scrutinized the prophets and
psalmists of the Old Testament. She had pored over the
books of the medieval Kabbala and the writings of the Hasi-
dim, which emphasized love and joy in religion. The Kabbala looked for hidden symbolic meaning in every word and
letter of the Hebrew Bible. It was an example not lost on
Nelly Sachs.

By 1939 it seemed almost certain that mother and
daughter would be sent to a forced labor camp. One of
Nelly's young friends, Gudrun Harlan, went to Sweden to
visit the aged Selma Lagerlöf and Prince Eugen and ask for
their help in getting a visa. Soon that help came.

The first plan called for the Sachs women to go by
train to Stockholm. But, showing unexpected heart, a Gestapo official warned them they might be detained at the border. "You must fly," he said. So on May 16, 1940, Margareta and Nelly Sachs arrived at the airport outside Stockholm. Hitler's armies were overrunning Europe, but the
Sachses' torturous months were over. Although Sigrid Undset was fleeing to the Swedish capital at the same time, the
two refugees never met. The Sachses first stopped at a camp
in the suburbs, where the tiny Nelly fitted perfectly into a
child's bed. They had dreamed of going to the United States,
but did not have enough money.

Mother and daughter settled down in Stockholm in a
one-room apartment in the bustling section known as Söder.
Frau Sachs's health was already failing, and as in Berlin
they associated with only a small circle. Nelly remained
painfully shy. Quickly she began teaching herself Swedish.
Later she was able to earn a modest income as a German
translator of many Swedish lyric poets such as Erik Linde-
gren, Johannes Eifelt, Karl Vennberg, and Gunnar Ekelöf,
regarded as Sweden's greatest contemporary poet.

In Stockholm she started writing poetry again. Lyrics
seemed to come to her spontaneously, "like taking a breath,"
she said. So it was that when she was past 50 Nelly Sachs's
poetic career began in earnest. Adolf Hitler had supplied the
final shove. In her lonely exile she had ample time to reflect
on the atrocities against her fellow Jews. The Nazis were
to kill six million of them. From Buchenwald, Dachau,

Auschwitz a torrent of awful pictures came rushing in. "Writing was my mute outcry," Nelly observed later. "I only wrote
because I had to free myself." She also wondered why she
had miraculously been chosen for survival. Was she to be
the representative witness of her people's sufferings? She
decided she had a mission.

During her first years in Sweden she often sat writing
in the dark so as not to disturb her mother. Eli: Ein Mysterienspiel vom Leiden Israels (Eli: A Mystery Play of the
Sufferings of Israel), she said, "was the outcome of a terrible
experience of the Hitler time at the height of its smoke and
flame and was written down in a few nights after my flight to
Sweden." In her own summary Michael, a young shoemaker
(a figure in Hasidic mysticism), "feels, darkly, the inner
call to seek the murderer of the child, Eli, the child who
raised to heaven the shepherd's pipe ... as his parents were
being taken away to their death." In his quiet way Michael
"sees in the shadow thrown by a light on Eli's death shirt
the face of the murderer." The soldier, when the shoemaker
finally meets him face to face, "crumbles to dust before the
divine light shining from Michael's countenance." The time
Nelly Sachs called "after martyrdom." The story, however,
was right out of World War II.

Already she sounds the notes of her most famous poetry. The Voice from the Chimney speaks these words:

We stones were the last things to touch Israel's
        sorrow.
Jeremiah's body in smoke,
Job's body in smoke,
the Lamentations in smoke,
whimpering of little children in smoke,
mothers' cradle songs in smoke,
Israel's way of freedom in smoke--

After being published in a limited edition, Eli was
broadcast on two West German stations, performed on stage
a few years later, and made into an opera by the Swedish
composer, Moses Pergament. It was always designed, Nelly
Sachs said, "to raise the unutterable to a transcendental
level." Eventually it appeared with Abraham im Salz (Abraham in Salt), Nachtwache (Night Watch), other short plays
and "szenischen Dichtunge" (dramatic poems) in Zeichen im
Sand (Signs in the Sand).

During 1944 and 1945 Nelly Sachs worked on a volume
of poetry, <u>Dein Leib in Rauch durch die Luft</u> (Your Body in
Smoke through the Air), which was published in 1947 with a
new title of <u>In den Wohnungen des Todes</u> (In the Habitations
of Death). Its first poem, "O die Schornsteine" (O the Chimneys), piercingly echoes the Eli words:

> O the chimneys
> On the ingeniously devised habitations of death
> When Israel's body drifted as smoke
> Through the air--
> Was welcomed by a star, a chimney sweep,
> A star that turned black
> Or was it a ray of sun?
>
> O the chimneys!
> Freedomway for Jeremiah and Job's dust--
> Who devised you and laid stone upon stone
> The road for refugees of smoke?
>
> O the habitations of death,
> Invitingly appointed
> For the host who used to be a guest--
> O you fingers
> Laying the threshold
> Like a knife between life and death--
>
> O you chimneys,
> O you fingers
> And Israel's body as smoke through the air!

"O die Schornsteine" became one of Nelly Sachs's most famous
poems, but at first it attracted little attention. The book
showed a new untraditional style for her, unrhymed, irregular,
rich in abstract metaphors and symbols which, one reviewer
said, "may carry seven shades of meaning." It was a tragic
lamentation in psalm-like rhythms. Dust, ashes, smoke--
the terrible crematory ovens of the concentration camps in
Germany and Poland. She inscribed <u>In den Wohnungen des
Todes</u> "to my dead brothers and sisters." Smoke becomes
dust, and dust becomes the sand of the burning Sinai desert:

> But who emptied your shoes of sand
> When you had to get up to die?
> The sand which Israel gathered,
> Its nomad sand?

Sometimes the dusk becomes the sand in the hourglass:

> Build, when the hourglass trickles,
> But do not weep away the minutes
> Together with the dusk
> That obscures the light.

She inscribed her second volume of poems Sternverdunkelung (Eclipse of the Stars) "in memory of my father."
Here Nelly Sachs, who had once said:

> Time roars with our longing for home
> like a seashell

can also write:

> But we have found a friend
> In exile; the evening sun.
> Blessed by its suffering light
> we are bidden to come to it with our sorrow
> which walks beside us:
> A psalm of night.

Although she finds it necessary to ask the terrible question,

> Why the black answer of hate
> to your existence, Israel?

she believes that the Jewish people will survive.

The dust also becomes the dust on the butterfly's
wings in "Schmetterling," one of her most quintessential
poems:

> What lovely aftermath
> is painted in your dust,
> You were led through the flaming
> core of earth
> through its stony shell,
> webs of farewell in the transient measure.

> Butterfly
> blessed night of all beings!
> The weights of life and death
> sink down with your wings
> on the rose
> which withers with the light ripening homewards.

What lovely aftermath
is painted in your dust.
What royal sign
in the secret of the air.

Long an invalid, Margareta Sachs died in 1950. Nelly
now faced the world alone, but kept on writing. After Und
Niemand weiss weiter (translated as And No One Knows How
to Go On) appeared in 1957, followed by Flucht und Verwandlung (Flight and Metamorphosis) two years later, her reputation began to grow markedly. Now she was no longer obsessed with the hideous details of the Jewish torture. She
looked for more universal understanding. She saw the Jewish
suffering as a chapter in a long history of martyrdom, which
in itself is a kind of catharsis, leading toward reconciliation
with God. It is little wonder that Stephen Spender once epit-
omized her poems as "catastrophe and redemption."

Some critics have pointed out that Nelly Sachs actually
wrote a single book. Beda Alleman showed that the idea of
"the book" has a religious origin, stemming from the Kabbala,
especially from The Sohar, a commentary on the Pentateuch.
In one poem from Und Niemand weiss weiter she specifically
mentions "the scribe of The Sohar":

> opening the words' mesh of veins
> instilling blood from stars
> which circled, invisible, and ignited
> only by yearning.

In another poem from the same book she questions:

> Who knows where the stars stand
> in the creator's order of glory
> and where peace begins
> and if in the tragedy of earth
> the torn bloody gill of the fish
> is intended
> to supplement with its ruby red
> the constellation of Torment,
> to write the first letter
> of the wordless language--

With each new volume Nelly Sachs spoke more and
more of reconciliation. And she yearned for her homeland.
Twenty years after her flight to Sweden she realized her
dream. In 1960, the 68-year-old exile stood in Dortmund

to receive the Annette von Droste-Hilshoff Prize for Poetry.
Her reception was rapturous.   When she turned 70, the city
established an annual Nelly Sachs Award for Literature and
gave her a lifetime pension.   That year critics hailed <u>Fahrt</u>
<u>ins Staublose</u> (Journey into a Dustless Realm), a comprehen-
sive collection of her poems.   Earlier she had used the same
title for a slender collection.   One of the poems spoke of

> Craters and parched seas
> drenched with tears
> journeying through starry stations
> on their way to a dustless realm.

Still highly productive at 71, Nelly Sachs brought out
the first of her four-part series, <u>Glühende Rätsel</u> (Glowing
Enigmas).   The fourth part she finished in 1966.   Some critics
consider it one of her most important poem sequences.

> In the bewitched wood
> with the peeled-off bark of existence
> where footprints bleed
> glowing enigmas gaze at each other
> intercept messages
> from grave vaults--

Many of these poems are concerned with pain--

> The beds are being made for pain
> The linen is pain's close friend

and with illness and death.   They reflect Nelly Sachs's own
stay in the hospital for a nervous breakdown that struck in
the midst of her German triumphs.   The chain of flowing
enigmas, inscribed in drifting metaphors of dust and sand,
raises to a cosmic plane the fate of the Jews slaughtered in
the concentration camps.

The year before Nelly Sachs went to the Nobel ceremony she was awarded one of West Germany's top honors, the
Peace Prize of the West German Booksellers' Association.
On that occasion President Heinrich Lübke called her poems
"works of forgiveness, of deliverance, of peace." A Hamburg
newspaper noted, "To the millions of nameless and voiceless
who are generally recalled only in the form of merciless,
six-digit figures, Nelly Sachs has given mouth and voice."

Twenty-six years after she had arrived in Sweden as

a frightened exile, Nelly Sachs became a Nobel laureate.
She heard Ingvar Andersson, a member of the Swedish Academy, say: "Your lyrical and dramatic writing now belongs
to the great laments of literature.   But the feeling of mourning which inspires you is free from hate and lends sublimity
to the suffering man.   We honor you today as the bearer of
a message of solace to all who despair of the fate of man. "

Nelly Sachs lived for three and a half years after the
Nobel ceremony.   She was not lonely any more.   She had
numerous influential Swedish friends, and she exchanged letters with literary persons throughout the world.   Above all
she delighted in greeting the younger German writers who
filed through her apartment.

Agnon, her co-laureate, died February 17, 1970, and
almost three months later on May 12, she herself was dead
in Stockholm.   Only four days later Nelly Sachs, "glowing
enigma, " could have celebrated the thirtieth anniversary of
the flight that led to her poetic metamorphosis.

The Science Prizes

Pale Glimmer of Radium
MARIE CURIE

On December 11, 1903, Marie Curie wrote to her brother, Joseph Skłodowski, about the honor that had just come to her and her husband Pierre. "We have been given half of the Nobel Prize. I do not know exactly what that represents; I believe it is about sixty thousand francs." She called it a huge sum, adding, "I don't know when we shall get the money, perhaps only when we go to Stockholm."

Soon the Curies would renounce all "material profit" from their discovery of radium. But that December Marie was deeply concerned about Pierre. In the Nobel Prize money she saw a chance to get him out of the School of Physics and Chemistry, where he was clearly unhappy, and to give him better medical treatment.

Poor health was the main reason they did not go to Stockholm to share the Nobel Prize in Physics with Henri Becquerel. Marie had been ill during the summer, and Pierre suffered acute pains, which his doctor called rheumatism. Neither welcomed the long railroad journey in wintry weather. "Forty-eight hours without stopping," wrote Marie, "and more if one stops along the way." It did not seem to matter very much to her that she was the first woman to win a Nobel Prize.

The Curies finally went to Stockholm in 1905 so that Pierre could give their Nobel lecture. Six years later Marie won the Nobel Prize in Chemistry and took her sister Bronya and her own daughter Irène with her. For that 1911 ceremony the frail, almost ethereal widow with the sad ash-gray eyes and the wavy ash-blonde hair wore a simple dress without jewels.

In 1903 one of the co-laureates was Svante Arrhenius, the Swedish chemist, whose theory of electrolytic dissociation

177

Marie Skłodowska Curie

or ionization in the conductivity of aluminum was important
to the Curies' achievement.   The diploma they received in
absentia read, "In recognition of the extraordinary services
they have rendered by their joint work on the radiation phenomena discovered by Professor Henri Becquerel. "   Marie
Curie's diploma in 1911 was given "in recognition of the services to the advancement of chemistry by the discovery of
the elements radium and polonium, by the ionization of radium, and the study of the nature and the compounds of this
remarkable element. "

     She was only 36 when she won her first Nobel Prize.
She had earned her first degree at the Sorbonne only nine
years earlier, for she had not begun her university studies
at the usual time.   Only because of her family's devotion
had she been able to begin at all.

Marya Skłodowska was born into a remarkably close-knit and intellectual family on November 7, 1867, in Warsaw. She was the last child in the circle of three other girls and one boy.   Since all the children had nicknames, Marya became Manya or sometimes Manyusya.   When she was a year old, her father, Władisław Skłodowski, became under-inspector at the high school where he taught physics.   Manya's mother, Bronisława Bojuska, was the principal at a girls' school. But when she showed signs of tuberculosis after her last pregnancy, she had to give up her work.   At home, staying rather remote from her children, she sat and made shoes. Manya could never remember being kissed by her mother.

The curly-haired little girl was healthy and bright, with a prodigious memory.   Although she was two years younger than her classmates, she quickly became the star pupil in Mlle. Sikorska's school.   And in her father's workroom she stood entranced by the instruments, tubes, scales, mineral specimens, even an electroscope.   But in the classroom an onerous shadow threatened.   The bulk of Poland was under Russian dominion.   Inspectors regularly visited the schools to check that no Polish was taught, and Manya learned to mock and hate them.   Harassed by his Russian superiors, Professor Skłodowski was demoted and lost part of his salary so that the family had to move to poorer lodgings.

Unfortunately he also invested his life savings of 30,000 rubles in his brother-in-law's steam mill, which went bankrupt.   He was soon reduced to taking in boarders, whom he instructed.   Thus it was possible for the ailing Mme. Skłodowska to stay for a year in Nice on the French Riviera.   But there was no cure, and a tragic period began. In 1873 Zosia (Sophie), the eldest daughter, died of typhus caught from one of the boarders.   Two years later Mme. Skłodowska was gone.

Manya's world was shaken but she kept on being an achiever.   Like her beloved sister Bronya (Bronisława) and her brother Jozio (Joseph), she won a gold medal at the Gymnasium, or secondary school.   Yet there was no hope for any girl to enter the University of Warsaw.   And so after graduation Manya was sent to stay for a year with country relatives with whom she had spent many delightful childhood holidays.   One of her persistent memories would be of a "kulig"--an all-night sleigh ride, carnival and fancy dress ball, where she went disguised as a peasant Cracow girl. Then she and her beautiful sister Hela (Helena) were invited

by one of their mother's former pupils to spend two months
at her country estate. Again there were jolly times, and one
night at a ball Manya danced so much she wore out her fine
new shoes. As Eve Curie says in her splendid biography,
Madame Curie:

> Many years later my mother sometimes evoked
> those happy days for me. I looked at her tired
> face, worn out by nearly half a century of care
> and immense toil. And I thanked the destiny
> which, before it dictated this woman's austere and
> inexorable summons, had allowed her to follow by
> sleigh after the wildest kuligs, and to use up her
> shoes of russet leather in one night of dancing.

All too soon Manya had to return to her father's Warsaw apartment. More than ever she became attached to this
kind, erudite man, who gathered his children around the tea
table in the evening, translating English, French, and German
books with remarkable ease. Since the university remained
closed to her, Manya decided to give private lessons. At the
same time she joined a "floating university," begun by sympathetic teachers, who privately instructed young students.
Inspired by Auguste Comte and Herbert Spencer, she and
Bronya were now calling themselves "positivists" and following underground political movements and discussing reform.
For a while she read aloud to the women in a dressmaking
shop and collected a little Polish library for them.

But she and Bronya really longed to go to Paris to
study science and medicine. Manya broached the following
plan. She would work as a governess to help pay for Bronya's
studies. When Bronya was well on her way, she would help
Manya, who dreamed of attending a university in a free country. The deal was struck. Bronya left for Paris, and 18-
year-old Manya went to work as a governess. She hated her
first job in Warsaw.

Then she took one with a family on a distant country
estate in Szczuki. Soon Mlle. Manya and Bronka, her eldest
pupil, became close friends and cooperated in teaching the
illiterate village children. She also found time for her own
studies of physics and mathematics. "I ... teach myself a
little or a lot, working alone," she wrote a friend.

When Bronka's handsome brother Casimir came home
on vacation, he and the pretty young governess fell in love.

But his parents were aghast when he told them he wanted to
marry the girl. Casimir did not oppose them, and left. In
spite of her humiliation Manya stayed on for three more years
because she desperately needed money for Bronya.

Finally she returned to Warsaw and took a job with a
rich industrialist's family. Belong long Bronya wrote that
it was time for her to come to Paris. Their father had accepted a rather demeaning but better-paying position so that
he could help more with his daughters' education. Bronya,
now a consultant in gynecology, had married a young Polish
doctor, Casimir Dłuski. The couple invited Manya to stay
with them while she studied at the Sorbonne.

But Manya did not leave right away. She was intrigued
by the "Museum of Industry and Agriculture" that one of her
cousins was running as a front for scientific and nationalistic
ventures under the very nose of the Russian authorities. The
test tubes and electrometers and various pieces of equipment
Joseph Boguski kept there riveted her attention. One more
reason she hesitated was that she had not yet put Casimir
out of her mind. She met him again at Zakopane in the Car-
pathian mountains, but again he could not make up his mind,
and Marie gave him up for good.

In November, 1891, the 24-year-old Manya enrolled
at the Faculty of Science at the Sorbonne, writing her name
in the French style as Marie Skłodowska. Living with the
Dłuskis was pleasant, but she had too little chance to concen-
trate. After the first year the shy young student moved out
on her own into a cold, dark attic room, where she managed
so frugally that one day the Dłuskis found her ill of malnutrition. They took her home with them and fattened her up.
But when Marie went back to her attic, she resumed her
frugal ways and hard study. She had great gaps to fill in
her knowledge of mathematics and physics.

Iron-willed, persistent, obsessed with perfection,
Marie Skłodowska passed first in the master's examination
in physics in 1893 and second in the master's examination
in mathematics in 1894. During those three years she had
also mastered the French language. But she had firmly decided that love and marriage were not for her.

One January evening in 1894 Marie met a brilliant
French scientist in the boarding-house room of a Polish
professor, who happened to be in Paris on his honeymoon.

It was Joseph Kowalski's thought that the bearded visitor from the School of Physics and Chemistry might have a workroom available; for Marie needed a laboratory to carry out a study on the magnetization of steel.

She first saw Pierre Curie "standing in the window recess near a door leading to the balcony." Though he was 35, she thought him very young. "I was struck by the expression of his clear gaze and by the slight appearance of carelessness in his lofty stature." She felt that his "rather slow reflective words, his simplicity, and his smile, at once grave and young," inspired her confidence.

That very evening Marie Skłodowska and Pierre Curie held an interesting scientific dialogue on quartz crystals. She also told him about her ambition to become a teacher in Poland. She felt that Poles had no right to abandon their country when it was struggling against Russian tyranny.

Pierre was already a physicist of note. While working on the physics of crystals, he and his brother Jacques had discovered the phenomena of piezoelectricity, which came to have manifold applications. Together they invented the piezoelectric quartz balance, an apparatus for making precise measurements of small quantities of electricity. In the School of Physics and Chemistry he was developing new equipment that all physics laboratories would eventually use. He was also working on experimental and theoretical problems of crystallography.

Within the next few weeks Pierre and Marie met a few times. Then, strongly attracted by this remarkable and very pretty young woman with her intense gray eyes, he asked to call on her. She too was attracted. The grave, sensitive, and naturally elegant Frenchman was also gentle and kind and as unconcerned with material comforts as Marie. Their courtship was carried out in true scientific style. The suitor's first gift was a copy of his pamphlet, "On Symmetry in Phenomena; Symmetry of an Electric Field and of a Magnetic Field."

After her master's examination in mathematics, Marie announced she was taking a holiday in Warsaw. Before she left, Pierre asked her to marry him. But she refused, convincing herself she could not abandon country or family. Nonetheless she returned to Paris in the autumn, and Pierre kept pressing her. In March, 1895, he defended a brilliant

doctoral thesis, his study of the magnetic properties of substances at various temperatures. The results form the basis
of all modern theories of magnetism.

Finally Marie accepted Pierre's proposal, and on
July 26, 1895, they were married, without a gold ring, in
the city hall of Sceaux, a Parisian suburb. Casimir Dłuski's
mother had offered to buy the wedding dress, and Marie
asked only that it "be practical." Since Pierre was a free-
thinker and Marie had given up her religious faith, there
was no religious ceremony. Afterwards the few guests, who
included Professor Skłodowski and Hela from Warsaw, gathered
in the garden of Pierre's parents. Then the newlyweds took
off on a pair of sturdy bicycles to roam the roads of France.
Pierre was a superb naturalist, who could point out all the
interesting trees and flowers. In the middle of August the
honeymooners joined the Dłuskis, Professor Skłodowski, and
Hela at a farm in Chantilly, where Pierre's parents came
visiting. After Pierre was given the "Polonization" treatment, it was Marie's turn to become "Gallicized."

By October the young couple was settled in a Paris
flat, and Marie had found a place to work in the laboratory
of the School of Physics. In Eve's words, "two hearts beat
together; two bodies were united; and two minds of genius
learned to think together." Twenty-two months later, though
highly pregnant, Marie left with Pierre on another long bi-
cycle trip, which was cut short by Irène's birth September 12,
1897. The baby was delivered by her grandfather, Dr. Eugène Curie; then, sadly, only a few days later, the new
grandmother, Mme. Sophie Claire Curie, died of breast cancer. Even though she was now a mother Marie Curie did
not intend to give up her scientific work. In her free time
she tended Irène; otherwise a nurse took over. Within three
months Marie finished and edited her work on magnetization.

Deciding to go ahead with a doctoral dissertation, she
looked for a suitable subject. She found one in Henri Becquerel's experiments. Shortly after Wilhelm Röntgen's discovery of X rays in 1895, Henri Poincaré put forth a hypothesis that these rays might be emitted by fluorescent bodies
under light. Working with this problem, Becquerel placed
a uranium salt, potassium uranyl sulphate, in the sun till
it showed significant fluorescence and then set it on a photographic plate wrapped in black paper. When developing the
plate sometime later, he found it had been blackened even
though it had not been exposed to light. When he tried to

find out how long the effects of the fluorescent light lasted,
he saw that the plates were blackened even after the fluorescence stopped. Here, unaffected by external conditions, was
a new type of radiation from the heart of a solid material.
Of special importance to the Curies' later research was his
observation that this radiation could discharge an electroscope,
the rate of discharge giving a measure of the radiation's
strength. The nature and origin of radiation, however, remained a fascinating mystery, and Marie decided to investigate
the radiation of uranium.

The only laboratory she could get was a glassed-in
storeroom on the ground floor of the School of Physics. In
summer it was steaming, and in winter the temperature was
often a little above the freezing point. But, grateful for any
place, she quickly set to work, using the new methods of
precise electric measurements that showed Pierre Curie's
trademark. First she had to measure the power of ionization of the uranium rays, that is, their power to make the
air a conductor of electricity and thus discharge an electroscope. Here she could use an ionization chamber, the Curie
electrometer, and Pierre and Jacques Curie's most ingenious
invention, the piezoelectric quartz balance, which supplied
amounts of electricity proportional to the weights suspended
from it.

As the work progressed, Marie Curie found that the
intensity of the radiation was proportional to the amount of
uranium examined and that this radiation was not affected by
lighting or temperature or by the chemical state of combination of the uranium. And so gradually she became convinced
that radiation was an atomic property. To test whether it
occurred elsewhere, she carefully examined every other known
element, both in the pure state and in compounds, and discovered that compounds of thorium also emitted rays like
uranium. Now she began using the term radioactivity for
the power to give off rays.

Next she examined the minerals which contained thorium and uranium--pitchblende, chalcolite, and uraninite--and
put them through an electrometer test. As she measured their
radioactivity, she discovered that it was stronger than what
she would have predicted from the amounts of thorium and
uranium present. After innumerable experiments she could
come to only one stupendous conclusion: an even more powerful radioactive substance existed in these minerals. That
substance, she decided, must be a new element. On April 12,

1898, in a preliminary note to the Academy of Sciences, Marie Skłodowska Curie announced the possible presence in pitch-blende ores of a new, powerfully radioactive element. She was opening the Atomic Age.

At this point Pierre gave up his studies of crystals and began to collaborate with his young wife. From now on they worked as a team. The Curies began prospecting for the new element by examining pitchblende, which in the crude state was more radioactive than the pure uranium oxide extracted from it. They knew that the new element must be present in very minute quantities and calculated that the ore contained the new element to a maximum of 1 per cent. Hundreds of experiments later they found that the element they were seeking was only a millionth part of pitchblende ore. Now they had some help from G. Bémont, the laboratory chief.

First they separated all the elements in pitchblende by chemical analysis, using acids and hydrogen sulfide. Then they rapidly but accurately measured the radioactivity of every separation product. Thus by careful elimination they knew that the radioactivity existed only in certain parts of the ore. When they observed that the radioactivity was concentrated in two different chemical fractions of the pitchblende, one containing bismuth and the other containing barium, they theorized there must be two new elements. In July, 1898, they announced the discovery of one of these elements. It had chemical properties resembling those of bismuth. Ever the ardent patriot, Marie called it polonium after her homeland. At the time she was still trying to be a good housewife and describing in the margins of a cookbook her success with gooseberry jelly.

Only now did the Curies interrupt their research for a holiday in the country with Irène. By fall they were back in their cold damp laboratory in the rue Lhomond. On the day after Christmas they announced the discovery of another "new element to which we propose to give the name of RADIUM."

Although their discovery was widely hailed, there were still some incredulous scientists, who said that radium and polonium existed only in imperceptible traces in the products the couple had prepared. Pierre and Marie therefore decided they must try to obtain pure radium and polonium. Because polonium is far more unstable than radium, they decided to isolate radium first. It was necessary to work with huge quantities of crude ore. Although pitchblende itself was too expensive, they believed that the residue left after the extraction of uranium would contain polonium and radium. But how to obtain this residue? Finally the director of the St. Joachimsthal mines in Bohemia offered to send the Curies a large amount at a reasonable price.

They began their exhausting work in a derelict shed in the School of Physics. To their happy surprise the Austrian government suddenly decided to give them a ton of the residue free if they would pay the transportation costs. This they were more than willing to do. The huge, coarse sacks of residue arrived. And now the backbreaking procedures began, to last almost four years. The Curies filled the shed with jars of precipitates and liquids, which were carried outside and poured into a basin smelter. With smoke-stung eyes Marie stood stirring the boiling material with a rod almost as big as herself. Pierre meanwhile worked in the makeshift laboratory, studying the properties of radium.

Finally the concentrated products were brought back into the shed, and Marie purified them and began the fractional crystallization of radioactive solutions. In the shed it was difficult to protect the equipment from heat, cold, wind, dust, and air. There were times when Pierre urged her to give up what seemed like an insurmountable task, but Marie steadfastly refused. In 1902, 45 months to the day on which she had announced the possible existence of radium, Marie Curie prepared a decigram of the pure element, about enough to fill the tip of a teaspoon. She calculated the atomic weight at 225.

On that never-to-be-forgotten night Pierre and Marie walked into their dark workshop to see the luminous particles in their tiny glass containers. As Eve writes, the "phosphorescent bluish outlines gleamed...." Then "two faces turned toward the pale glimmering, the mysterious sources of radiation, toward radium--their radium." Pierre tenderly touched his wife's hair.

Of this period Marie later wrote, "We had no money, no laboratory, and no help.... And yet it was in this miserable old shed that the best and happiest years of our life were spent, entirely consecrated to work."

Subsequently she isolated a few milligrams of polonium

from several tons of pitchblende. But she could not obtain
it in a pure state. It proved to be a product of radium decay.
She had given such a symbolic name to this unstable element.
She always regretted that it became less important than
radium.

Meanwhile in 1900 the Curies had moved to a house
on the boulevard Kellerman, and here Pierre's father settled
down with them and became Irène's special teacher and friend.
That same year Marie was appointed lecturer in physics at
the Girls' Normal School in Sèvres. In order to teach there
and commute on a slow train she had to steal long hours from
her laboratory work.

Although her life was incredibly busy, she was a loving,
warm, and careful mother. Between 1899 and 1904 the Curies,
sometimes singly, sometimes together, sometimes with their
new assistant, André Debierne, published 36 scientific reports. Debierne had discovered actinium, another radioactive element, in 1899. Moreover, they were constantly communicating with other scientists, who hurried into experiments
on radioactivity. Already in 1903 Ernest Rutherford and
Frederick Soddy put forward their theory that radioactive
elements go through successive changes in which new elements
are formed.

In June, 1903, Marie took her doctoral examination,
delayed by her long research. Her thesis on "Researches on
Radioactive Substances" was undoubtedly the most stunning
dissertation ever submitted to the examiners. In honor of
the occasion she bought herself a new black dress.

The same month Pierre received an invitation to lecture on radium at the Royal Institution in London. He and
a pregnant Marie attended an endless round of banquets and
receptions. In August their second child was born prema-
turely and died. Marie implored Bronya, "Write to me, I
beg of you, if you think I should blame this on general fatigue
--for I must admit that I have not spared my strength. I had
confidence in my organism, and at present I regret this bitterly, as I have paid dear for it. The child--a little girl--
was in good condition and was living. And I had wanted it
so badly!"

At the end of the year Pierre returned to London to
accept the Davy Medal. On the heels of this honor came the
announcement of the Nobel Prize. And the dreams began to

be realized.   With 70,000 francs in the bank, Pierre could
give up his lectures at the School of Physics and see better
doctors.   With the leftover money Marie could make a loan
to the Dłuskis for the sanatorium they had built in Zakopane.
She and Pierre could buy presents for Jacques Curie and
Bronya and Hela and Joseph.

Suddenly there were 25,000 more francs, Marie's
half of the Osiris Prize she shared with Edouard Branley.
Now she helped some Polish friends and secretly paid for a
trip home to France for a teacher she had known in her girl-
hood.   Finally she installed a modern bathroom in the house
and repapered a small room.   But, Eve complains, she did
not even buy a new hat.   "She did not know how to be famous."

Nor did Pierre.   As the therapeutic uses of radium
for curing malignant tumors became known, technicians in
several countries made plans to exploit the new element.
But Marie and Pierre decided "to take no material profit"
from their discovery.   They wanted to offer their research
freely to the world.   To patent their technique, Marie said,
"would be contrary to the scientific spirit."

Even more broadly, their work led scientists to change
their whole idea of matter.   Elements were no longer considered immutable.   Rutherford identified two of the three rays
given off by radium and named them alpha and beta rays.
The third kind was called gamma.   The rays, found to be
exactly the same in all radioactive elements, suggested another theory.   Every atom is made up of the same kinds of
particles, is in fact a little galaxy.   The result was the
planetary atom.

In 1904 Pierre accepted a professorship at the Sorbonne.   For the first time Marie gained official status in
her husband's laboratory by being appointed chief-of-work in
the chair of physics.   On top of their success Marie, pregnant again, felt exhausted and suffered a mild depression.
Most of her worries centered on Pierre and his terrible attacks of pain.   Then after Eve was born in December, 1904,
she regained her spirits.   In June, 1905 she and Pierre went
to Stockholm for the Nobel lecture.   At the podium Pierre
discussed the effects their discovery of radium had in chemistry, geology, meteorology, and biology.   But he also reflected on possible misuse: "We might still consider that in
criminal hands radium might become very dangerous, and

here we must ask ourselves if mankind can benefit by knowing the secrets of nature, if man is mature enough to take advantage of them, or if his knowledge will not be harmful to the world. " Yet he concluded optimistically, "I am among those who think with Nobel that humanity will obtain more good than evil from the new discoveries. " As requested, the Swedes gave the Curies a visit without pomp.

Back in Paris they spent most of their evenings in dressing gowns and slippers, reading scientific journals and making complex calculations. Sometimes they relaxed at the theater or at concerts, and once Loie Fuller, with her lavish costumes and elaborate lighting devices, danced in their house. She introduced them to her friend, Auguste Rodin, whose studio they often visited. But most of their friends were scientists.

Easter, 1906 was a happy holiday in the country. Irène chased butterflies with Eve toddling behind. Pierre whispered to Marie, "Life has been sweet with you. " A few days later, on April 19, on a sullen, rainy afternoon, Pierre was walking rather absentmindedly along the street. A horsedrawn cab struck him down, killing him instantly. When Marie heard the news, Eve Curie says, "she seemed as inanimate and as insensible as a woman of straw. " Her loss was devastating. Once she had exulted, "He was all I could have dreamed at the moment of our union and more. " Eve comments:

> Marie Curie did not change from a happy young wife into an inconsolable widow. The metamorphosis was less simple and more serious. The interior tumult that lacerated Marie, the nameless horror of her wandering ideas, were too virulent to be expressed in complaints or in confidences. From the moment when those three words, 'Pierre is dead, ' reached her consciousness, a cape of solitude and secrecy fell upon her shoulders forever. Marie Curie on that day in April, became not only a widow, but at the same time a pitiful and incurably lonely woman.

Though the widow refused any official ceremony or national pension, she did accept the offer to replace Pierre at the Sorbonne. Thus she became the first woman to be given such a post. In November she took up Pierre's lectures exactly at the point where he had left off--"When one

considers the progress that has been made in physics in the
past ten years. . . . "

     She could not, however, stand the memories of the
house on the boulevard Kellerman and rented a house in
Sceaux, where Pierre was buried. Dr. Curie, now 79,
remained with her and the two girls. If outwardly she played
the icy automaton, privately she wept and despaired. Eve
describes the time the widow showed Bronya a terrible packet,
"a hideous mass of clothing, of linen, of dried mud and blackened blood, " the clothes Pierre had worn when struck down.

          The silent widow took the scissors and began to cut
          up the dark coat. She threw the pieces one by one
          into the fire and watched them shrivel up, smoke,
          be consumed, and disappear. But suddenly she
          stopped, struggling in vain against the tears that
          darkened her tired eyes. In the half-congealed
          folds of the cloth appeared some viscous fragments
          of matter, the last scraps of the brain in which,
          a few weeks before, noble thoughts and the dis-
          coveries of genius had been born.

          Marie contemplated these corrupt remains fixedly;
          she touched them and kissed them desperately until
          Bronya dragged the clothing and the scissors away
          from her and began in her turn to cut and throw the
          pieces of cloth into the fire.

     Along with Dr. Curie, Marie had another ally in Manya
Kamienska, Joseph Skłodowski's sister-in-law, who became
both governess and housekeeper. Unfortunately, she soon returned to Warsaw because of poor health, and less reliable
Polish governesses took her place. Then in February, 1910,
Dr. Curie died, after being bedridden a year. Marie was
now solely responsible for Irène and Eve. Well aware of the
challenge, she wrote down detailed instructions for their study
and leisure hours and filled notebooks with her observations
of their progress.

     She could also cling to her professorship. In 1910
she published Traité de Radioactivité (Treatise on Radioactivity), whose title page carried a photograph of Pierre, the
same picture she had placed in the Oeuvres Complètes de
Pierre Curie (Complete Works), which she collected in 1908.
And she still had her old collaborator, André Debierne. In
1910 they succeeded in isolating pure radium in the metallic

state. Debierne also helped her study the rays emitted by polonium. Later she worked out a method for measuring the emanations from radium. She was likewise busy preparing the first international standard of radium--21.99 milligrams of pure radium chloride, which served as a model for the standards of five continents.

In 1910, just as Pierre had done before her, Marie Curie refused the cross of chevalier in the Legion of Honor. But she did allow her champions to present her for admission to the Academy of Sciences the next year. One of the academicians declared indignantly, "Women cannot be part of the Institute of France," and Marie Curie missed being elected by one vote.

In 1911, however, came the solace of her second Nobel Prize, this time in Chemistry. The Swedish Academy of Sciences wished to recognize her discovery of radium and polonium since only radioactivity was mentioned in the 1903 award. Marie was characteristically modest over her position as the only person in the world to have won two Nobel medals.

In her Nobel lecture she said: "... I wish to recall that the discovery of radium and that of polonium were made by Pierre Curie in common with me. We also owe to Pierre Curie, in the domain of radioactivity, some fundamental studies which he carried out either alone or in common with me or in collaboration with his pupils. The chemical work which had as its aim the isolation of radium in the state of pure salt and its characterization as a new element was carried out especially by me, but is intimately linked with the work in common. I therefore believe I shall interpret exactly the Academy's thought in admitting that the high distinction bestowed upon me is motivated by this work in common, and thus constitutes an homage to the memory of Pierre Curie."

Even before her first Nobel Prize, those envious of Marie Curie's success began a whispering campaign against her. After her return to Paris rumors against "that foreign woman" intensified. Besides, she suffered excruciating pains from a kidney ailment. She had really dragged herself to Stockholm. Following major surgery, she hid in a small house near Paris to recuperate, later taking Irène and Eve to the English coast to spend a summer with a friend.

As a break in the gloom the Sorbonne and the Pasteur

Institute were combining forces to build an institute for her.
In July, 1914, just as World War I was looming, the Institute
of Radium, Pavilion Curie, on avenue Pierre Curie was finished. Marie Curie presided over its laboratory of radioactivity and Professor Claude Regaud, a noted physician, over
its laboratory for biological research and Curietherapy (radiation therapy).

Soon the Germans were advancing on Paris, and Marie
Curie decided she must contribute to the national defense by
supplying radiological stations to follow the troops. First,
however, she had to protect from the enemy the precious
gram of radium in her laboratory. She carried it to the
safety vault of a Bordeaux bank. Then from her laboratory
she began to equip 20 radiological cars nicknamed "Little
Curies," keeping a Renault for her own use. In this car,
with her driver, she now moved about in the war zones, "all
flame," as one of her friends said. If the chauffeur was un-
available, she drove the Renault herself. Besides equipping
the cars, Mme. Curie installed 200 radiological rooms.
Thus there were 200 fixed and mobile posts for examining
over a million wounded men.

She had left the money from her second Nobel Prize
in a Swedish bank. Now she ordered that it be used for war
bonds. She also wanted to send her medals to be melted
down, but a Bank of France official refused them. For most
of the war Irène accompanied her mother on the field trips.
While studying at the Sorbonne, she had been initiated into
radiology.

After the war Marie Curie rented a summer house in
l'Arcouest, a Breton village on the Channel coast. So many
Sorbonne professors vacationed there that it was dubbed "Port
Science." Here she liked to sit in a lighthouse, sail, swim,
work in her garden, and watch her daughters having fun. By
the end of 1920, rejoicing in Poland's liberation, she wrote
her brother Joseph: "So now we, 'born in servitude and
chained since birth,' we have seen that resurrection of our
country which has been our dream.... But can the clouds
of the present situation be compared with the bitterness and
discouragement that would have crushed us if, after the war,
Poland had remained in chains and divided into pieces? Like
you, I have faith in the future."

She had declared, "My most ardent desire is the
creation of an institute of radium in Warsaw," and in 1925

she traveled to her birthplace to lay the cornerstone for
such a building. But first there was a never-to-be-forgotten
visit to the United States. In the spring of 1920 a rich American woman, Mrs. William Brown Meloney, a magazine editor from New York, interviewed Mme. Curie at the Radium
Institute in Paris. When asked what she wanted most, the
great scientist said, "A gram of radium to continue my researches." Mrs. Meloney then decided to ask ten rich women
to contribute ten thousand dollars each to the project. But
when she found only three willing to make this donation, she
began a subscription among all American women, rich and
poor. In less than a year the Marie Curie Radium Fund had
enough money for one gram of radium. The committee members invited Marie Curie to come to the United States to accept it from President Warren G. Harding's hands.

Marie Curie was already troubled by failing eyesight.
But with her daughters she sailed to New York. The country
welcomed her with a great rush of affection. Honorary doctorates, titles, and medals were heaped on her, but she was
so easily fatigued that Eve and Irène often had to act as her
stand-ins. Before going to Washington, D. C., she visited
several campuses and attended a huge gathering of the American Association of University Women in Carnegie Hall. More
exhausting ceremonies followed, but finally she reached the
White House. Actually the President put an imitation of the
radium into her hand. The tubes of real radium, which gave
off dangerous radiation, had been left in the factory. Five
hundred men had worked to provide that gram. Money left
over from the fund supplied Mme. Curie with a life income.

After this she was asked to make trips to many countries on official duties. Irène accompanied her to Brazil,
Eve to Spain. When not traveling, she was still involved in
complicated research. In 1922 she became a member of the
Academy of Medicine and devoted much of her time to the
medical applications of radioactive substances.

She worked on Pierre's biography and about this time
she wrote, "We cannot hope to build a better world without
improving the individual. Toward this end, each of us must
work toward his own highest development, accepting at the
same time his share of responsibility in the general life of
humanity--our particular duty being to help those to whom we
feel we can be most useful."

As the years passed, money was needed to buy radium

for the cancer treatment at the Radium Institute in Warsaw. Once again Marie turned to the United States and Mrs. Meloney, who collected enough money for a second gram of radium. In 1929 Mme. Curie sailed once more for New York to thank America in Poland's name. This time she was the guest of President and Mrs. Hoover at the White House for several days.

In 1926 Irène married Frédéric Joliot, one of the laboratory assistants. Within a year Marie Curie rejoiced over a granddaughter. She was equally proud of a grandson born in 1932. The Joliot-Curies continued to work at the Radium Institute with Marie. Her heart leaped with joy when they discovered artificial radioactivity in 1933. Eve had already made her debut as a concert pianist.

The failing eyesight was finally diagnosed as double cataract. Several operations were necessary, but finally with glasses Marie regained almost normal sight. Eve quotes the source of her courage: "Nor do I know whether, even by writing scientific books, I could live without the laboratory." Back in her laboratory toward the end of her life, she wrote a huge volume called Radioactivité.

People often noticed Marie Curie's radium-pitted hands. The long years of research finally took a more vicious toll. On July 4, 1934, in a sanatorium at Sancellemoz she died of pernicious anemia, caused by radium poisoning. She was buried at Sceaux with her coffin above Pierre's. In spite of the tragedy, it had been one of the world's most magnificent love stories.

Triumph and Rebuff

IRÈNE JOLIOT-CURIE

It was almost a scientific fairy tale. A shy, solemn-faced French girl of 14 sat in the auditorium of Stockholm's Royal Academy of Music on December 10, 1911, to watch her famous mother receive the Nobel Prize in Chemistry. Exactly 24 years later that girl, matured into a shy, solemn-faced matron, stood beside her handsome husband in the Concert Hall to receive the same Prize.

The Chemistry award to Irène and Frédéric Joliot-Curie read, "In recognition of their synthesis of new radio-active elements." At the same ceremony James Chadwick received the Prize in Physics for his discovery of the neu-tron to which the Joliot-Curies had decisively contributed. They were hailed: "The results of your researches are of capital importance for pure science, but in addition, physi-ologists, doctors, and the whole of suffering humanity hope to gain from your discoveries remedies of inestimable value."

But they were a modest pair--Irène, as reserved as Marie Curie, and Frédéric, three years his wife's junior, with a patient, easy manner. At 38 Irène was, like her mother, comparatively young to become a Nobel laureate; Marie had been 36 at the time of her first award.

But early achievement was to be expected in Irène's case. What other girl had such a scientific heritage? She was born in Paris September 12, 1897, just in those stirring days when both of her parents were busy with their brilliant research. That day Marie and Pierre Curie's account book carried what was for them a rather extraordinary expense: "Champagne 3 francs, telegrams, 1 franc, 19." For the most part the baby was turned over to a nurse's care al-though Marie tried to change and feed her morning, noon, and night. Many a day she would fly from the laboratory to the rue Montsouris, where the nurse was trundling the baby

Irène Joliot-Curie

carriage, to make sure Irène was not lost. When Irène was
only a few months old, her mother began her monumental researches into radioactivity. The baby girl, whom Marie
called "my little Queen," took her first steps in the garden
at Sceaux under the watchful eye of her grandfather, the wid-
owered Dr. Eugène Curie. In a school notebook Marie kept
track of the little Queen's weight and appearance of teeth.
She also pictured a singing child, a toddler chasing the cat
"with wild war cries."

At night Irène would not go to sleep without her mother
beside her cot, and if she did not feel her close by would
scream incessantly, "Mé! Mé!" This name eventually became the substitute for Mama. As was to be expected with
such extraordinary parents, Irène was precocious. But she
was not sophisticated. When Pierre Curie returned from
London in 1903 with the heavy gold Davy Medal, engraved
with his and Marie's names, he gave it to his six-year-old
daughter, who looked on it as a "big new penny" to be played
with.

After a sister, Eve Denise, was born in December, 1904,
the jealous little Irène became more possessive than ever.
"Apples! Bananas!" she cried, and her mother made long
journeys across Paris to find the fruit Irène demanded. She
was painfully shy though, and Marie organized many special
parties to draw her out. Still, Irène did have playmates,
especially Jean and Hélène Perrin's children, Alene and Francis, who lived next door, separated from the Curies only by
a railing full of rose vines.

When Pierre Curie was killed in April, 1906, Marie
at first reported that "Pé," as Irène called him, had hurt
himself in the head. The day after the funeral Marie told
Irène everything: "She did not understand, at first, and let
me go away without saying anything," Marie noted in her
diary, "but afterward, it seems, she wept and asked to see
us. She cried a great deal at home, and then she went off
to her little friends to forget. She did not ask for any details and at first was afraid to speak of her father. She made
great worried eyes over the black clothes that were brought
to me.... Now she no longer seems to think of it at all."

That summer Marie rented a house near Sceaux for
her daughters, her father-in-law, and herself. Irène had inherited her mother's love of flowers. Now she could grow
anything she wanted on her square of earth in the large garden.

For her and Eve there were numerous Polish governesses;
the best of the lot, Mlle. Kamienska, fell ill and had to return to Warsaw all too soon.   Fortunately, there was always
that marvelous friend and preceptor, their tall, ungainly old
grandfather.   He taught Irène botany and natural history and
filled her with his radical political beliefs that went back to
the revolution of 1848.   He was, Eve Curie wrote, "the in-
comparable friend ... of that slow, untamed child so profoundly
like the child [Pierre] he had lost." With his "mocking
spirit" he "polarized her intellectual life in a decisive way."
In 1937 Eve could write, "The spiritual equilibrium of the
present Irène Joliot-Curie, her horror of suffering, her im-
placable attachment to the real, her anti-clericalism and
even her political sympathies come to her in the direct line
from her grandfather."

After Dr. Curie's death in 1910, Marie was for the
first time in full charge of her household.   Eve has described
in detail her mother's definite ideas about educating her
daughters.   Each day both girls had to do an hour's work,
physical or intellectual, which Marie tried to assign in the
most attractive manner possible.   Next they exercised in the
open air, especially partial to long walks in all kinds of
weather.   If not walking, the girls were performing on a garden crossbar with cord, trapeze, and flying rings.   Later
they went regularly to a gym to work out and brought home
prizes.   Governesses continued to supervise their lessons.
Proudly Marie noted down Irène's mathematical and Eve's
musical precocities.   They also learned gardening, cooking,
sewing, and modeling with clay.

Most of their holidays they spent in France with their
Aunt Hela and their cousins, since Mé could never be long
away from the laboratory.   They were never baptized, and
Marie gave them no spiritual education.   Deliberately, she
never mentioned their father to them because she found it
too painful to speak his name except to strangers.   The careful program she mapped out, however, never considered social graces and etiquette.   Eve seemed to come by them
naturally, but out in society Irène was panic-stricken.

In 1911, the year Mme. Curie won her second Nobel
Prize, they accompanied her to Poland and stayed with Aunt
Bronya at her sanatorium.   Here the girls learned to ride
horseback and carry rucksacks in the mountains.

In Stockholm young Irène may have been slightly disappointed that the literature laureate, Maurice Maeterlinck, was too ill to appear. Her own poetic nature could respond to The Blue Bird and that "poetic fancy, which reveals sometimes in the guise of a fairy tale, a deep inspiration."

She had now passed beyond governesses. But Marie Curie did not like the cramped, poorly ventilated classrooms she saw and tried to protect her daughters from them. Irène and Eve were to study very little, but very well. For Irène's sake Mme. Curie began a teaching cooperative in which Sorbonne professors allowed their children to enter their laboratories for lessons. Paul Langevin taught mathematics; Jean Perrin chemistry; the Polish-born Mme. Perrin, who was Marie's best friend, showed the children how to sculpt; and Marie Curie, using live experiments, taught the group physics. Among the ten boys and girls Irène soon became a "scientific star." This teaching, says Eve, "gave Irène in default of a complete literary equipment a first-class scientific culture, which she could not have obtained in any lyceum." After two years, however, the parents were overworked, and the collective teaching ended. Irène was then enrolled at the Collège Sévigné, a private school, for two years of study toward the baccalaureat. Eve was to follow her there a few years later.

In the summer of 1913, Irène accompanied Mé and Eve on a walking tour in the Engadine Mountains in a party that included Albert Einstein and his son. Often, remarks drifting out of context from the high level of abstruse conversation between Einstein and Mme. Curie made the girls double up with laughter. Deep down, however, Irène was increasingly serious.

The next summer she and Eve stayed with a governess and cook in a little villa on a Brittany beach, expecting their mother for the month of August. But by August 1 the war was on, mobilization had begun, and the Germans were advancing. The girls had to give up Mé's company to the national war effort. Marie had written, "If [war does break out], I shall stay here and I shall send for you as soon as possible. You and I, Irène, shall try to make ourselves useful." Later she had this thought for her elder daughter, "If you cannot work for France just now, work for its future.... Do your mathematics and physics as well as you can." She also told her, "You must feel responsible for your sister and take care of her if we should be separated for a longer time than I expected."

By fall they were all back in Paris together at an apartment in the quai de Béthune, Eve in school and Irène working for a nurse's diploma at the same time she was beginning her studies at the Sorbonne. Irène had a reputation for punctuality and a perfect record for doing homework neatly and well. Wrote Eve in later years: "This young person, so unsociable, so slow-moving, and hard to approach, lacked the dash of the brilliant pupils. She had something better; knowledge once acquired was fixed firmly in her mind. The examination periods for the bachelor's and master's degrees, which had made even our mother in her time feverish and nervous, were for Irène Curie just like any other day. She went quietly to the Sorbonne, came back certain of being accepted, and then waited without much emotion for the results of which she was always sure in advance. "

By 1915 Marie was off on her radiological duties at the front. Trained to be self-reliant, the "beloved daughters" kept house as best they could and knitted sweaters for the soldiers. During bombardments they stayed in bed instead of going down to the cellar.

Then Irène was trained to operate X ray equipment, became her mother's "manipulator, " and eventually went on some missions of her own to Furnes, Hogstrade, Amiens, and Ypres. The wounded soldiers warmed to her constant good humor and unruffled calm. For a while in 1916 she and Eve, only 11, enlisted in a gang of harvest workers in Brittany, replacing men who had gone into the army. That year also Irène joined her mother in giving instructions in radiology to nurses at the Radium Institute in Paris. Wrote Eve: "An intimate and charming companionship linked Mme. Curie and this young girl. The Polish woman was solitary no longer. She was able to talk of her work or of her personal worries now with a collaborator and friend. "

At the end of the war Irène was 21, sturdy, calm, "marvelously balanced" (according to Eve), and positive that she wanted to be a physicist and study radium. "The fame and the achievement of her parents neither discouraged nor intimidated her..., " Eve said. "Her sincere love of science, her gifts, inspired in her only one ambition: to work forever in that laboratory which she had seen go up. " Because of her competence she was named her mother's preparateur, or assistant.

Irène inherited her father's aptitude for using ingenious

devices and was particularly skillful at operating the Wilson
cloud chamber, which makes the tracks of high-speed atomic
nuclear particles visible by water droplets condensed on the
ions produced along their trails. Through the long working
days she always looked calm.

By now the Curies could take summer holidays together
in Brittany, at l'Arcouest, with its stimulating Sorbonne colony often gathered at Taschen, the thatched cottage presided
over by Charles Seignobos, their energetic septuagenarian
friend. As part of the fun, Irène and Eve helped Mé master
a good crawl stroke in swimming. Eve describes herself
and her sister ready for a sail--"with bronzed arms, in their
cheap little dresses, their hair ornamented by red pinks from
the garden which Charles Seignobos, according to an unalter-
able tradition, had given them. "

In May, 1921, all three Curies boarded the Olympic
for the triumphal tour of the United States. The two girls
spoke pleasantries in English, Polish, and French though
Irène had to fight her shyness. As Mé grew increasingly
exhausted, they became more than her escorts. Sometimes
Irène had to steel herself to double for her mother, donning
a university cap and gown to receive the honorary degrees.
Still, the ever solicitous Mrs. Meloney, who arranged the
trip, saw to it that the girls were offered tennis games,
swimming and boating parties, evenings at the theater, and
one splendid fling at Coney Island. At the White House,
Irène was photographed standing at the left side of President
Harding, who presented her mother with the symbolic gram
of radium. As a grand climax to their tour, Mrs. Meloney
shepherded all three Curies on a tour of the Grand Canyon,
where the two sisters rode Indian ponies and mules to the
bottom of the canyon.

Back in the Paris laboratory, Irène performed several
experiments on radium with Fernand Holweck, chief of staff
of the Radium Institute. Her first paper on physics appeared
in 1921. By this time the Curies were settled in a rather
charmless apartment on the Île St. Louis. Irène had inherited
her mother's indifference to money and clothes and living
quarters and felt perfectly comfortable. It was Eve, always
looking as though she had stepped out of a fashion magazine,
who indulged in rather fruitless bouts of interior decorating.

Meals, Eve remembered, were often reduced to "scientific dialogues between the scientist and her elder daughter. "

Years later Eve marveled, "It used to dismay me to see
Irène Curie get a box of bonbons, put it away in her small
yellow pine cupboard, always in such meticulous order, take
it out once to eat a single bonbon, and finally forget all about
the existence of this treasure, which I should have devoured
in a few hours. I have seen her accumulate| in her savings
bank, franc by franc, sums which seemed enormous to me
but which she never spent--simply because she never wanted
anything." Eve also admired her sister's marvelous emotional
control. "I have never succeeded in making Irène angry, nor
have I ever heard her say anything nasty, and to my knowledge
she has never told a lie in her life."

Irène took her doctorate in 1925 with a thesis on the
alpha rays of polonium, the element her parents had discovered.
Marie celebrated the event with a "laboratory tea, " using
laboratory glasses for tea or champagne and stirring rods
for spoons.

That same year Irène met her future husband. Among
the workers at the Radium Institute was a handsome, slight,
darkhaired young man with a kind and sensitive expression.
In spite of his shyness he was brimming with vitality. Frédéric Joliot, a recent graduate of the School of Physics and
Chemistry, had long idolized Marie and Pierre Curie, had
even pinned up their pictures in his home laboratory. Hired
on Paul Langevin's recommendation, he was regarded as the
most brilliant of Mme. Curie's assistants. Still the young
man had much to learn about radioactivity, and Irène was
willing to help him. Sometimes though she forgot to say "Good
morning," and many in the laboratory considered her a "block
of ice." But beneath the young woman's cool exterior Frédéric discerned "an extraordinarily sensitive and poetic nature."
He also believed she had the "same purity, the same good
sense, and tranquility" as Pierre Curie. She gave him the
impression of being 'the living replica of what her father
had been."

In Fred, as he preferred to be called, Irène found
someone who shared her love of science, sports, and the
arts. Even when working her hardest, she took time to ski,
canoe, swim, and climb mountains, with her camera as an
important part of her equipment. Friends admired her way
of adapting her dresses to the exigencies of a hike. Invariably Irène transformed sleeves and belts into pockets. Fred
too excelled in sports and was besides a skilled pianist and
landscape painter. Both of them hated city life.

The "daughter assistant" and the "engineer assistant" began taking long walks together in the forest of Fontainebleau and after a few months realized that they were in love. They were married October 9, 1926. To perpetuate the name of her famous parents they decided to adopt the combined names of Joliot-Curie. In 1927 their daughter Hélène was born. Marriage, says Eve, made Irène "more human and tractable."

At first the Joliot-Curies lived with Mme. Curie but before long moved to a flat of their own. Still they came to lunch at least four times a week and of course continued to help "La Patronne" in the laboratory. In 1932 Irène succeeded her mother there as Chief of Work.

Like Marie and Pierre before them, Irène and Frédéric became inseparable in research and beginning in 1928 jointly signed their scientific papers. In 1930 Frédéric presented his doctoral thesis on the electrochemical properties of radioactive compounds of polonium.

The new team now showed great interest in the study of nuclei or cores of atoms. During their lifetime an exciting world of atomic physics had opened up. The year that Irène was born J. J. Thomson demonstrated that a current of electricity passing through a gas consists of a stream of lightweight, negatively charged particles, which came to be called electrons.

In 1903, the year that Marie and Pierre won their Nobel Prize, Ernest Rutherford and Frederick Soddy put forward their theory of radioactivity, postulating that radioactive elements undergo a series of successive changes to form other chemically different elements. The intermediate products are mainly characterized by a decrease in their radioactivity. The disintegration, Rutherford noted, was accompanied by the emission of radiation. Testing to see if the radiation would pass through a thin sheet of aluminum, he found that some of it was slightly slowed down by the sheet and some was more penetrating. The less penetrating rays he called alpha rays. Eventually he found them to be helium nuclei. Alpha radiation became a valuable tool for studying the structure of the atom. The more penetrating rays, negatively charged electrons, Rutherford called beta rays. Finally there were gamma rays, akin to very penetrating X rays.

In 1911, the year that Marie Curie won her second Nobel Prize, Rutherford, a prizewinner in 1908, published

a new theory of atomic structure, stating that the mass of
the atom is located in a small central core he named the nucleus. From his experiments he concluded that it is positively charged. Two years later Soddy, who was also re-
warded with a Nobel Prize, developed his theory of isotopic
radioactive elements. Isotopes are varieties of a single element with different atomic weight.

By 1920, when Irène began her research in earnest,
scientists had given the name proton to the hydrogen nucleus,
which had been produced some years earlier when a current
of electricity was passed through a gas in a cathode-ray tube.
In the stream of positively charged particles the one with
the lightest weight was shown to have the same mass as the
hydrogen atom and a charge equal to the negative charge of
the electron. Eventually it was determined that this particle
actually was the nucleus of the hydrogen atom. During the
same period Rutherford and James Chadwick proved that the
nuclei of most light elements could be disrupted by fast alpha
particles and thus eject protons.

The Joliot-Curies were fascinated by Rutherford's
pioneering techniques. Marie Curie had built up an impressive stockpile of intense radiation sources, and her daughter
and son-in-law had the largest polonium supply in the world.
Both were highly skilled in the use of radiation detectors
such as the ionization chamber, and Irène taught Frédéric
how to use the Wilson cloud chamber, which became his
favorite instrument. Eugénie Cotton tells how one day Frédéric was so filled with enthusiasm that he cried out, "Irène,
this is the most beautiful experience in the world!" To this
his wife replied, "I would share your opinion, my dear, if
I had not had the experience of maternity."

Soon a German study intrigued the Joliot-Curies. In
1930, Walther Bothe and Hans Becker showed that beryllium,
when bombarded with alpha particles, gives off a form of
mysterious, penetrating radiation ten times stronger than
that from any other light element. The Joliot-Curies repeated this experiment and proved that the radiation could
eject protons from an absorption screen of paraffin placed
between the beryllium and the ionization chamber. They also
saw that the radiation produced proton tracks in the cloud
chamber containing hydrogen. Curiously, the tracks started
at various places inside the chamber. But it was Chadwick
who showed that this radiation included electrically neutral
particles of about the same mass as the protons. He called

them neutrons. (Rutherford had predicted their existence
years before, and the Joliot-Curies had just missed discovering them.) A quarter of a century later, when speaking of
Irène's contributions to science, Chadwick referred to this
"very strange effect, " which provided the clue for his discovery.

The Joliot-Curies also just missed discovering the
positron, found by Carl Anderson the same year, 1932, in
which Chadwick discovered the neutron.   The positron is an
electric subatomic particle which has the same mass as an
electron, but has a positive rather than a negative charge.
Carl Anderson, too, became a Nobel laureate.   In their white
smocks husband and wife kept on making important studies of
how protons materialize and how positrons are annihilated
when they encounter electrons.   In the midst of all the exciting experiments, Irène announced that a new baby was coming.
Pierre Joliot-Curie was born in that remarkable scientific
year of 1932.

Continuing to work with alpha particles, the Joliot-
Curies conducted still more famous experiments in 1933.
They bombarded aluminum with alpha particles, emitted from
polonium.   Then, using a sensitive Geiger counter, they recorded that their alpha particles striking aluminum atoms
were producing positrons, which lasted for one billionth of
a second.   But after they had sealed up their polonium
source, the Geiger counter kept clicking, indicating that positrons were still being emitted.   Quietly Frédéric said to his
wife, "I wonder if we have not created artificial radioactivity. "

They had in fact created a new radioactive substance.
By chemical analysis they proved it was phosphorus 30. A
stable aluminum atom has 13 protons, 14 neutrons, and an
atomic weight of 27.   In the Joliot-Curie experiment it "swallowed" an alpha particle, which consists of two protons and
two neutrons.   The too-heavy intermediate nucleus threw off
a neutron.   The new substance had 15 protons and 15 neutrons with a mass of 30.   What the young couple had made
was a phosphorus lighter than common phosphorus, which
has an atomic weight of 31.   Even as they were making their
chemical tests, the new isotope was decaying.   Phosphorus
30 has a half-life of only two and a half minutes; the final
product was silicon.

In the same way the Joliot-Curies obtained radio-
nitrogen from the alpha bombardment of boron and radio-

silicon and radio-aluminum from two isotopes of the metal
magnesium. On January 15, 1934, they announced their discoveries to the Academy of Sciences. Marie Curie's tired
face lit up with intense joy when she saw the first artificial
radioactive elements.

Since then more than a thousand radioactive isotopes
have been prepared, at least one and sometimes as many as
12 for each element. They have become medically important
as tracers and are widely used in radiotherapy. In certain
cases they are more effective than the natural radium preparations. Also in industry they have often proved more useful
than the materials which are naturally radioactive. Even
more, the Joliot-Curie discovery opened a new avenue of research, inspiring Enrico Fermi to perform experiments that
finally led to the controlled release of nuclear energy.

That year of great triumph was also one of sorrow.
On July 4, Marie Curie died in a sanatorium, with Irène
and Eve beside her. She had felt certain that Irène and
Frédéric would go to Stockholm.

The very next year they received a telegram, beginning, "I have the honor to inform you...." Strictly speaking,
they were physicists, but the Nobel Committee decided that
their achievement was of enormous importance to chemistry.
At the ceremony Irène followed her mother's example of
wearing a simple black gown without any jewels. Eve often
complained. "All my efforts to get her to take care of her
fine hair and to make up her face, with its firm and beautiful features, like a primitive portrait, have been in vain."
The names of her parents cropped up several times in the
presentation speech, and she heard herself and Fred praised
for "worthily" maintaining these brilliant traditions.

Two days later the Joliot-Curies gave their joint lecture, Irène on "Artificial Production of Radioactive Elements"
and Frédéric on "Chemical Evidence of the Transmutation of
Elements." Irène began by noting her parents' awards. Then
remembering that her father had not always been given his
due, she said firmly that the experiments had been carried
out by Monsieur Joliot and herself, working together. The
way in which they had divided up their Nobel lecture, she
explained, was simply for convenience.

Just as Pierre Curie had warned in 1905 that radioactivity "in criminal hands" lays a heavy burden on mankind,

so Frédéric in 1935 insisted that the use of radioactivity must
be a "matter of conscience. " He and Irène were committed
to the idea of using scientific discoveries in the cause of
peace.   More than coincidentally, the Greek goddess of peace
was named Irene.

The Joliot-Curies used part of the prize money to
build a home on the edge of the Parc de Sceaux. Fred hung
his father's hunting horns and fishing trophies in the large
drawing room.   Friends would long remember relaxed Sunday
afternoons at Sceaux as perfectly delightful--lively conversation, card games, tennis, walks in the neighborhood.   Fred
liked to sit at the piano and play Mozart and Beethoven.   Often he improvised.   Sometimes for Irène he would put a
Gustav Mahler record on the gramophone.

For vacations they went to l'Arcouest to live the simple life of their Breton fishermen friends, to whom Fred even
introduced the music of Bach.   Eugénie Cotton recounts how
with a smile Irène remarked, "Other men carry a picture of
their wives in their wallets.   But what does Fred carry?
Not a picture of Irène.   He carries a picture of the big pike
whose catch so enraptured him. "   The Joliot-Curies also acquired a chalet in the mountains near Courcheval and went
there during winter vacations.

Irène gave much time to the children's upbringing.
She and Fred had high hopes for them.   When Hélène was
only four, her proud father showed Albert Einstein some
"proton tracks" the tiny girl had scribbled on a piece of
paper.   Einstein smiled and said, "If you don't watch out,
she will become a theoretical physicist. "   About that time
Hélène, a vivid little figure in red, was meeting her doting
grandmother, Mme. Curie, for a short playtime--with sand
pies--every afternoon in the Luxembourg Gardens.

Hélène did in fact become a physicist like her brother,
who proudly bore his grandfather's name.   Irène sweetly reported, "My mother and my husband held discussions with
such eagerness and answered each other with such rapidity
that I could not get in a word and was obliged to insist on a
chance to speak when I wanted to express an opinion.   Now
it is frequently the same thing when my husband and my son
talk together. "   Two great French scientific families were
united in 1950 when Hélène married Michael Langevin, Paul
Langevin's grandson.

After the Nobel Prize the honors poured in. Irène
and Frédéric became members of several academies and
scientific societies. Individually they were given honorary
doctorates at several universities. Both were named officers
of the Legion of Honor. But fame did not change Irène. According to Eve, "she would not do anything that bored her
such as seeing importunate people, taking interest in clothing,
or showing interest in public receptions. "

Poetry relaxed her. One friend remarked, "Poetry
was the common denominator for the three of us, Irène, Fred,
and myself. " She knew French, English, and German poetry
well. In quiet even tones she liked to quote Kipling's "If":

If you can trust yourself when all men doubt you,
But make allowance for their doubting too;
If you can wait and not be tired by waiting....

As a poet of British imperialism, Kipling did not impress
her. She saw him, however, as a poet of great variety, who
admired peasants, workers, sailors, engineers, explorers,
and artists, contributors to the progress of humanity.

Irène took a keen interest in women's social and intellectual advancement. Like her mother she was convinced
that they did not have the place in society they deserved. "I
think that the decision to give women the right and eligibility
to vote is a means of justice that has been too long postponed, "
she wrote. In 1936 she gladly joined Leon Blum's Popular
Front government as undersecretary of state for scientific research and helped lay the foundations for the National Center
for Scientific Research. Helping to shatter a precedent, two
other women became undersecretaries in the Blum cabinet.

Politics now became more important. The impassive
scientist found herself excited by social questions. Irène
had been influenced by her Grandfather Curie's radical politics and anti-clericalism, and Fred by his liberal-minded
mother. In 1936 the couple firmly supported the republicans
in the Spanish civil war. And in 1937 they joined the Socialist party. That year Frédéric was made a professor at
the Collège de France and Irène a professor at the Faculty
of Science, where she had lectured since 1932. In his new
laboratory of nuclear chemistry, Frédéric, his head full of
idealistic thoughts, built the first cyclotron in Western Europe.

Already Irène's health was showing signs of radiation

exposure. Nonetheless, the brilliant experiments continued.
In 1938 she and Pavlo Savic bombarded uranium with slow
neutrons. Analyzing the products, they reported one similar
to lanthanum. This led Otto Hahn and Fritz Strassman to
their idea of nuclear fission.

As early as January, 1939, Frédéric was demonstrat-
ing fission by physical means. He proved that many neutrons
are produced by fission, that such reactions can be developed
in explosive chains, and that nuclear reactions can be controlled to release great quantities of energy. But that same
year, fearful of Adolf Hitler's power and the misuse of the
chain reaction, the Joliot-Curies suddenly stopped publishing
papers. That fall, after World War II had broken out, they
recorded the principle of nuclear reactors and deposited the
paper in a sealed envelope at the Academy of Sciences. It
remained secret until 1949.

Now staunchly they turned to fight for France. Frédéric became an artillery captain and was ordered to coordinate
the work of various research laboratories. Almost immediately he sent a representative to Norway to buy that country's stock of heavy water, the world's largest, to be used in
atomic research. Shortly before the Nazis rolled into Paris,
the Collège de France received the heavy water on loan.
After sending it to England in the care of two assistants, he
lied to Gestapo agents to get them off the track. He was just
as successful in a grueling 12-hour session with the Gestapo
when he dissuaded the Germans from seizing France's only
cyclotron and its valuable store of radium.

In 1940 the Joliot-Curies denounced the imprisonment
of their longtime friend, Paul Langevin. In 1942, in reaction
to the Nazis' execution of P. Solomon, a brilliant young theoretical physicist, who was Langevin's son-in-law, Frédéric
Joliot-Curie joined the Communist party. "I was impressed,"
he said, "by the generosity, courage, and hope for the future
that these people in my country had. They seemed willing to
do the most to give France social reform."

Meanwhile, as a leader of the National Front, centered
at the university, he stood in the forefront of the resistance
movement. Pretending to be still busy with theoretical in-
vestigations of the atom, he was actually directing the manu-
facture of explosives and radio equipment for the maquis, or
resistance fighters. Often on his laboratory benches he himself made incendiary bombs. For a time he hid the staff

members of a clandestine newspaper in his laboratory. Through this dangerous period Irène supported and comforted him.   But when the Nazis became more suspicious, Frédéric urged her to take Hélène and Pierre to Switzerland while he lived on in Paris using the name of Jean-Pierre Gaumont.

Only two days after the city's liberation, Frédéric Joliot-Curie was appointed director of the National Center for Scientific Research.   Quickly he was promoted to Commander of the Legion of Honor, awarded the Croix de Guerre, and elected to the Academy of Sciences.   But Irène would appear two times before the Academy, all in vain, to affirm the "right of women" to become members.

In 1946 General Charles de Gaulle named Frédéric Joliot-Curie as French High Commissioner on Atomic Energy and appointed Irène a commissioner.   In this role she turned her administrative abilities to acquiring raw materials and detector installations.   Frédéric summed up the couple's philosophy: "French science does not want to have anything to do with atomic research other than for peace.   All our efforts are being utilized in the development of this tremendous energy for the advancement of humanity."   Speaking of her mother, Irène said that like Pierre Curie she believed that science should resolve human problems in the sense of making happier lives possible.   "Its use for destruction seemed to her a desecration.   In her eyes any political consideration would not have been an excuse to use the atomic bomb."

In that same year of 1946 Irène was appointed director of the Radium Institute.   She was now 49 years old and in failing health.   But nothing could keep her away from duties or work.   Her 10- to 12-hour days in the laboratory resulted in many new papers on radioactivity.   James Chadwick has given this picture of her: "Her parents were both persons of strong and independent mind, and Mme. Joliot-Curie inherited much of their character as well as their scientific genius.   She knew her mind and spoke it, sometimes perhaps with devastating frankness, but her remarks were informed with such regard for scientific truth and with such conspicuous sincerity that they commanded the greatest respect in all circumstances.   In all her work, whether in the laboratory, in discussion, or in committee, she set herself the highest standards and she was most conscientious in the fulfillment of any duties she undertook."   In any argument, in fact, Irène would not make the slightest concession.   Fred, on the other hand, put opponents in a state of mind in which they were ready to accept his arguments.

In 1949 Irène proudly watched Frédéric direct the construction of France's first atomic pile. But now their political sympathies were beginning to be suspect. During the cold war, in 1950, Frédéric was removed from his post on the Atomic Energy Commission. Irène served her full term of five years, but was not included in the reorganization in 1951. The painful disgrace coincided with increasingly severe health problems for them both.

From now on the Joliot-Curies devoted themselves and all their scientific works to the cause of peace. Time and time again Irène denounced scientific secrecy and appealed for the free circulation of scientific ideas and discoveries. She was a member of the World Peace Council, which Frédéric later served as president. Idealistically, they made several trips to the Soviet Union. And the hostility mounted. In 1949, on a visit to the United States, Irène was detained for a day or so on Ellis Island, then released without explanation. In 1954 she found her application for membership in the American Chemical Society rejected because of her politics.

In the 1950s Irène had to undergo several operations, and her health deteriorated rapidly. Still she was willing to play tennis with her son. And in 1955 she drew up a plan for the new nuclear physics laboratories at Orsay, south of Paris, where scientists could work with large particle accelerators in much more spacious quarters.

Finally she was unable to go on her customary long walks all over Paris, and a friend drove her about in a car. Smilingly she said, "I think I am becoming lazy." But she knew she was becoming progressively enfeebled.

Early in 1956 she was sent to the mountains, but showed no improvement. "Breathing, eating, all the most elementary functions, are becoming painful," she told a friend. She had wasted away from too much radiation. A victim of leukemia, she died on March 17 at the Curie Hospital. In a letter to Queen Elizabeth of Belgium, Frédéric wrote, "Marie Curie, helped by Irène, had energetically undertaken the task of organizing X-ray examinations of the wounded at the front in order to facilitate the location of projectiles embedded in their bodies. It was doubtless when

Irène was engaged in examinations of this kind, notably on the Belgian front near Ypres, that she received the massive doses of X-rays which were to cause the terrible ravages to which she succumbed. "

So unpopular in a political sense were the Joliot-Curies that Irène, the second-most famous woman scientist in France, was little mourned. The French cabinet, however, finally decided to give her a state funeral.

That same year Frédéric became a member of the Central Committee of the French Communist party. While keeping his own chair at the Collège de France, he accepted Irène's vacant chair at the Sorbonne. Also in her memory he finished planning the Orsay laboratories. But his own days were numbered. In July, 1958, he presided at the beginning of the International Congress of Nuclear Physics, making his final plea to use atomic energy for peaceful ends. One month later, also a victim of leukemia, he was dead, like Irène, generally unmourned. Science and politics had exacted a heavy toll.

Cycle of Courage
GERTY CORI

Nobody in the Koncerthus in Stockholm knew that the vivacious, radiant woman, who accepted a Nobel Prize on December 10, 1947, was suffering from an incurable disease. Nobody, that is, except her husband, who shared the award with her. Shortly before they came to Sweden, Gerty Cori learned she had myelosclerosis, a bone-marrow disease. As she carried off the Nobel ceremonies, so Gerty Cori continued to work in the laboratory for ten more years with courage, grace, and what her friends called almost superhuman willpower.

The Cori name is forever linked to a physiological cycle that helps explain the body's metabolism of sugar. As her illness became known, her associates thought her name should also be tied to a cycle of courage. She did many brave things in her life, but enduring her illness was the bravest.

Dr. Gerty and Dr. Carl Cori shared their award in Medicine or Physiology with Dr. Bernardo Houssay of Argentina, whose research at one point dovetailed with their own. The Coris, who flew to Stockholm from St. Louis were honored "for their discovery of the course of the catalytic conversion of glycogen." Coming from Buenos Airea, Houssay received his half of the Prize "for the discovery of the importance of the anterior pituitary hormone for the metabolism of sugar."

Professor H. Theorell, head of the Biochemical Nobel Department of the Caroline Institute, explained that the work of these prizewinners lay within the same centrally important sphere, the metabolism of sugar in the body. They had, he said, "elucidated the enzymatic reaction between glucose and glycogen and ... shown that these reactions are caused by physiological factors." Faulty sugar metabolism often leads

213

Gerty Theresa Cori

to diabetes.   Theorell pointed out that it had been possible
to keep the disease in check by insulin since its discovery
by Banting and Macleod.   Then he commented, "It would be
a grave mistake, however, to believe that this brilliant discovery unravelled the immense complex of problems concerning sugar metabolism.   Certainly it is long known that insulin decreases the blood sugar level, but until recently the
mechanism of this effect was veiled in mystery. "

The Coris threw a clear light on previously obscure
points in the knowledge of sugar metabolism, which supplies
energy for life activities.   Gerty and Carl Cori shared the
Nobel lecture they gave the next day on "Polysaccharide
Phosphorylase, " Carl giving the first and third parts and
Gerty the second.   Only Carl spoke at the Nobel banquet:
"To have thus been singled out among so many worthy scientists must evoke a feeling of humility and at the same time
renew the determination to go on with the work. " He looked
at Gerty and said, "That the award should have included my
wife as well has been a source of deep satisfaction to me.
Our collaboration began thirty years ago when we were still
medical students at the University of Prague and has continued
ever since.   Our efforts have been largely complementary,
and one without the other would not have gone as far as in
combination. "

The year was 1914 when Gerty Theresa Radnitz and
Carl Cori met during the first semester in the anatomy class
of the medical school at Prague's famous old Carl Ferdinand
University.   The tall, shy, handsome Carl, fair-haired and
blue-eyed, had grown up in Trieste, where his father, a zoolo-
gist, was head of the Marine Biological Station.   But he had
returned to his birthplace, Prague, to enter medical school.
He had spent many a summer in the Tyrol with his maternal
grandfather, Ferdinand Lippich, a professor of theoretical
physics at the university.

The pretty, vivacious, brown-eyed Gerty with a mass
of reddish-brown hair and a tall, slender figure was just 18,
a few months older than Carl.   She was also a native of
Prague, that city of colorful towers, an architectural show-
piece of ten centuries still under the control of the Hapsburg
emperor.   The two soon found out they had even more in common than Austrian blood and a passionate absorption in science.
Both loved sports, such as mountain climbing in the Austrian
Alps, swimming, skating, and tennis.   But it was hardly the
time for such pleasures.   World War I had just broken out.

Carl quickly learned the background of this brilliant
and energetic girl. Rather coincidentally, in light of the
Coris' famous research years later, her father was the manager of several sugar refineries. Gerty was born August 15,
1896, the eldest of three daughters of Otto Radnitz and his
wife Martha, born Neustadt. The family was moderately
wealthy, and Gerty, Lotte, and Hilda grew up in a comfortable Prague apartment and had private teachers. From these
childhood years they were especially fond of remembering a
vacation on the Belgian coast. But nothing could really equal
Prague, that "city of a thousand faces, " with its streets filled
with history--medieval lanes, Renaissance churches, rococo
and baroque palaces, all set among hilltops and gardens along
the Vltava river.

At ten Gerty was considered quite an independent child.
It was time for her to enter a lyceum for girls, which gave
very small place to science and mathematics, but laid great
stress on the development of cultural and social graces. Then
at 16, because of her special interest in chemistry, she decided to study medicine even though she was quite unprepared.
But her Uncle Robert, professor of pediatrics at Carl Ferdinand University, encouraged her. To be admitted to medical
school Gerty needed a great deal more academic work--eight
years of Latin and five more of mathematics, physics, and
chemistry. On top of that, medical school would last six
years. But she could not be held back, for she was as
courageous and ambitious as she was pretty and charming.

That summer, vacationing in the Tyrol, she met a
teacher from the Tetschen Realgymnasium who helped her
work off three years of Latin in just three months. Gerty
took just one year to master the courses she needed to pass
the examinations for medical school, "the hardest examinations I was ever called upon to take, " she said later. Just
after her eighteenth birthday, while the Prague newspapers
were carrying banks of headlines about invasions and battles,
Gerty was enrolled as a student at Carl Ferdinand University.
She was now part of a proud and longstanding heritage, for
it had been founded in 1348. There were two branches,
Czech and German, and Gerty chose the German branch.

After their meeting in the classroom it did not take
long for Gerty Radnitz and Carl Cori to fall in love. But
both were determined to get their medical degrees before
they married. In the laboratory they collaborated on an im-
munological study and made what Gerty called a "modest

contribution to the knowledge of the complement of human blood. " Their paper was published in a scientific journal.

As the war intensified, Carl entered the Austrian Army as a lieutenant in the Sanitary Corps and served on the Italian Front, where he did bacteriological and chemical work in a hospital for infectious diseases. About the same time Gerty became an assistant in the medical school, taking case histories, giving physical examinations, and doing some routine laboratory work.

Carl finally returned to Prague to resume his studies, and in 1920 he and Gerty received their medical degrees. That summer, on August 5, they were married. Free of school at last, they could indulge in the sports they loved. Both were still intrigued by mountain climbing, and the intrepid Gerty, blessed with great endurance and skill, climbed many glaciers.

After a war so devastatingly lost, the new nation of Czechoslovakia greatly needed medical doctors. The two young Coris, however, were much more interested in doing biochemical laboratory research. Carl Cori quickly found a job at the University of Vienna working half time at the Pharmacological Laboratory and half time in the Internal Medicine department. His bride joined the staff of the Carolinen Children's Hospital, also in Vienna. Here she did chemical work and research and published several papers on her studies of the thyroid and the spleen.

The next year Carl was appointed an assistant in pharmacology at the University of Graz. But a shattered postwar Austria was really not a very promising place for research. The war and its aftermath had left what Carl called "indelible impressions. " Suddenly a job offer came from the United States and promptly he accepted it. He felt a "strong urge" to do scientific work in an environment "free of strife. " As Dr. Helen Porter would say, Gerty too "had experienced at first hand the conflicts and the sorrows and suffering of mankind at war, and it became her determination to make in some field a contribution to their alleviation. "

Carl had to leave by himself because Gerty had not been hired. He began as a biochemist with the New York State Institute for the Study of Malignant Diseases, located in Buffalo. Soon, however, the good news arrived that he had found an opening for Gerty as assistant pathologist in

the same place. Young Dr. Gerty sailed for New York, came
to Buffalo, where she passed the necessary civil service examinations, and received her appointment. In 1925 she was
named assistant biochemist. Five years later Carl added to
his duties by accepting the post of assistant professor of physiology at the University of Buffalo. The young emigrants
never regretted their move. Years afterwards Gerty Cori
was to comment, "The high state of development of biochemical methods in the United States came as a revelation. The
Institute offered good equipment and complete freedom in the
choice of problems. "

And so the Coris donned their white lab coats together,
ready to begin their remarkable joint research. The first
of a series of important papers appeared by 1923. Their
early work in Buffalo centered on the metabolism of tumors,
but soon they became interested in normal carbohydrate metabolism. What chemical processes, they asked, are involved
when the body burns sugars to sustain life? Banting and Macleod's discovery of insulin, made about the time the Coris
settled in Buffalo, now suggested further research, for this
hormone was an exciting tool.

In their laboratory the Coris worked with white rats
which were all fed a known quantity of sugar. Some were
also given insulin. To determine how much of the sugar had
been oxidized they put the rats into respiratory chambers
and later analyzed the bodies for carbohydrates. Their findings indicated that half of the absorbed sugar was converted
to glycogen and stored in the liver and muscle, that some of
the sugar was transformed to fat and stored in this form, and
that the rest was burned, leaving water and carbon dioxide.
The Coris concluded that insulin decreases the amount of
sugar stored as glycogen in the liver and increases the amount
oxidized in muscle, most useful information for doctors treat-
ing diabetics. Epinephrine was another hormone the Coris
studied.

The French physiologist Claude Bernard discovered
glycogen (animal starch) in 1857. About 70 years later the
Coris picked up the threads of his discovery, along with more
recent facts established by a Kiel professor, Otto Meyerhof,
a Nobel prizewinner in 1922. Meyerhof studied the chemical
changes involved in the contractions and relaxations of mus-
cles. Eventually, the Coris showed that glycogen in the mus-
cles is metabolized to lactic acid, which is carried by the
blood stream to the liver, where it becomes liver glycogen.

This in turn is released from the liver into the blood as glucose, which becomes the original muscle glycogen. Such a continuous process came to be known as the Cori cycle. In their subsequent research the Coris provided more detailed, even step-by-step explanations of the chemical processes involved in the transformations.

They became naturalized in 1928. Three years later new job offers came to the new Americans from Washington University Medical School in St. Louis, where Carl accepted the position of professor of pharmacology and biochemistry. Gerty became a research assistant in pharmacology, allowed to work in the laboratory as an equal with her husband. A New York Post article once reported, "... it is hard to tell where the work of the one leaves off and that of the other begins. They talk over their problems together, decide what is to be done, and then parcel the tasks out between them, checking and correlating with each other all the way."

The chemical changes that glycogen undergoes during the cycle that the Coris had begun to formulate in Buffalo are due to certain proteins called enzymes. Like the hormones, insulin and epinephrine, they are manufactured in normal bodies. To understand the transformation of glycogen, the Coris now tried to isolate the enzymes, which are extremely complex in their chemical structure. Meyerhof's experiments gave them some leads. They minced muscle taken from frogs' legs and extracted the tissue with distilled water three times, each time pouring off the water. Thus the phosphorylated (bound to phosphorus) glucose was removed, leaving the muscle glycogen behind.

In a series of complicated chemical steps they next removed from this extract a glucose phosphate that was slightly different from the activated glucose that releases its energy in normal muscle tissue. The Coris named this compound glucose-1-phosphate, later to be called the Cori-ester. It was the first step in the conversion of glycogen into glucose, and--because the process is reversible--sometimes the last step in the conversion of blood glucose to glycogen. Later they identified two new enzymes, polysaccharide phosphorylase and phosphoglucomutase, which catalyze the glycogen-Cori ester-reaction. Finally, using a third enzyme, hexokinase, discovered by Meyerhof in 1927, the Coris could give a more complete picture of the Cori cycle.

The discovery of phosphorylase was the basis for the

220 The Lady Laureates

Coris' Nobel award and caused Dr. Arthur Compton, Nobel
laureate in physics and chancellor of Washington University,
to say: "The fame of Carl and Gerty Cori is based upon the
reliability of their careful measurements. Thus, when earlier
investigators had demonstrated within experimental error that
sugar in the liver is released to the blood by the action of
the enzyme diastase the Coris found that this was indeed an
experimental error, that the true catalyst was instead a substance which they named phosphorylase." Later they crystallized and studied other enzymes present in muscle tissue. In
1943, using rabbit muscle phosphorylase, they achieved the
testtube synthesis of glycogen.

The same year the Coris moved to St. Louis, Bernardo Houssay explained from his laboratory in Buenos Aires
that a certain substance in the anterior pituitary lobe inter-
feres with the proper utilization of sugar. He continued with
years of brilliant experimental work on the pituitary gland.
In 1945, the Coris and three co-workers announced that hormones intervene in the hexokinase reaction, which is part of
the glucose-glycogen cycle. This reaction, they discovered,
is promoted by insulin but checked by another hormone in
extracts from the anterior lobe of the pituitary gland.

The triumphant year of 1936 in which the Coris isolated the Cori-ester was climaxed in July by the birth of
their only child, a son named Thomas. Gerty was now 40,
and this first birth took a certain courage. Although she remained a dedicated scientist, she was so superbly organized
she could be a splendid wife and mother at the same time.
In Houssay's phrase the three roles were the "triple crown
that adorned her life." He also praised her for a personality
that combined "an astonishing drive to act with unusual gen-
tleness, kindness, and charm."

Gerty was an accomplished hostess in a beautiful home
filled with flowers, art, books, and music. Even more, she
filled it with wit. Gardening was a special hobby for both
Coris, and again it was team work, Gerty taking over the
flowers and Carl the vegetables. Her sister Lotte was a successful painter in Venice, and Gerty herself loved the paint-
ings of Dürer, Rembrandt, and the Impressionists. She read
widely, biography, history, and modern novels. With her
Prague and Vienna backgrounds she delighted in the music of
Mozart and Beethoven. Bach was another favorite. Above
all, she loved Beethoven's opera Fidelio with its moving outcry, "Es gibt eine Gerrechtigkeit" (There is a justice), which

summed up her own passionate beliefs about justice in every
form.   "I believe that in art and science are the glories of
the human mind, " she once wrote.   For all her busy schedule
Gerty Cori somehow always took time to be a warm friend to
many and to carry on a large correspondence.

As the Cori research team continued to work, the
laboratory became an outstanding center of metabolism research.   "The physiology of today is the medicine of tomorrow, " as Ernest Starling said.   Severo Ochoa, Arthur Korn-
berg, Earl Sutherland, Jr. , and Christian DeDuve, all to become Nobel winners in Physiology or Medicine and Luis Le-
loir, a future Nobel laureate in Chemistry, worked enthusiastically in the St. Louis laboratory.

Edward Doisy, still another Nobel laureate, once told
some fellow scientists: "Genius the Coris have, there is no
question about it.   But their capacity for hard work has aided
that genius to blossom and to benefit mankind.   They are
good Americans, excellent companions, the kind that fishermen like to take to the woods with them.   They are swimmers
as well and all-around outdoor people. "   Having climbed the
Austrian Alps, the Coris were in no sense intimidated by the
American Rockies, which they climbed in summer vacations
over a period of 16 years.

In 1946 Carl received the Lasker Award and a gold
statuette of the Winged Victory of Samothrace to symbolize
victory over disease and death.   The next year was a banner
one, too.   Carl was named professor of biochemistry and
head of the department, and Gerty was appointed a full professor.   Then in November came the news that they were to
share the Nobel award with Houssay.   At the Nobel Banquet
in the Golden Hall, Arne Tiselius, vice-president of the
Nobel Foundation, called the awards "an expression of the
gratitude of mankind. "   And he gave a special accolade: "The
intricate pattern of chemical reactions in the living cells,
where everything appears to depend on everything else, re-
quires for its study an unusual intuition and a technical skill
of which the Coris are masters. "

In his little speech Carl Cori did not forget his and
Gerty's adopted country.   "While still very young we had the
good fortune to go to the United States.   Our adopted country
has treated us with the utmost generosity and has been of
great importance for our scientific development and our outlook on life.   It is our belief that art and science can best

grow and develop in a society which cherishes freedom and which shows respect for the needs, the happiness, and the dignity of human beings. " On another occasion Gerty remarked, "I believe that the benefits of two civilizations, followed by the freedom and opportunities of this country, have been essential to whatever contributions I have been able to make to science. "

At the time his parents went to Stockholm, young Tommy was only 11 and more interested in baseball than in science. But his father was not discouraged, remembering that he himself had not turned to science until he was 12. Eventually Tommy gained a Ph. D. degree and became a research chemist.

In 1947 the vigorous Gerty Cori was ailing. The doctors found she had myelosclerosis, which causes a type of anemia, requiring frequent blood transfusions. Ironically, she who had done so much for medical science was suffering from an illness for which there was no cure. Through her last ten years she had to slow down her activities, put away her tennis racket and ice skates and climbing equipment. But the more she weakened the more courage she showed. She must have often looked at the Winged Victory statuette Carl had received. To the very last she continued working in her laboratory, showing extra kindness to foreign students who felt lonely. "Honesty, which stands for intellectual integrity, courage, and kindness are still the virtues I admire though with advancing years the emphasis has been slightly shifted, and kindness has seemed more important to me than in my youth, " she wrote.

The Coris did not always work as a team. Each did important individual research. In 1954, almost 100 years after Claude Bernard's discovery of glycogen, Gerty Cori used the enzymes involved in the biological cleavage of glycogen as tools to chemically define the molecular structure. The next year she did important research in glycogen storage diseases in children, a hereditary disorder caused by the absence of certain enzymes. In her last years, too, honors and degrees streamed in on Gerty and Carl Cori singly and jointly. A very special event occurred in 1947, when she was one of 12 women honored at Hobart and William Smith College in Geneva, New York, during ceremonies marking the centennial of the first medical degree conferred on a woman. Included in the honors for Gerty were elections to the National Academy of Sciences and the American Philo-

sophical Society.   In 1952 President Harry Truman named
her to the science board of the National Science Foundation
and, despite her deteriorating condition, she made many
trips to Washington, D. C.

Gerty Cori died on October 27, 1957, of complications
of the myelosclerosis she had suffered so long.   Twenty-one
year-old Tom came home from his studies at the University
of Wisconsin, and fellow scientists arrived from afar for the
memorial service.   Houssay described her life as "a noble
example of dedication to an ideal--to the advancement of
science for the benefit of humanity. " She was cremated, and
her ashes rest in St. Louis.

Fittingly, at the service a Beethoven string quartet
was played.   Just before the music began her voice was heard
in a "This I Believe" recording she had once made: "For a
research worker the unforgotten moments of his life are those
rare ones, which come after years of plodding work, when
the veil over nature's secret seems suddenly to lift and when
what was dark and chaotic appears in a clear and beautiful
light and pattern. "   Gerty Cori had known several such moments.

Madonna of the Onion
MARIA GOEPPERT-MAYER

The prettiest girl in Göttingen in the 1920s happened also to be the brainiest, and eventually Maria Goeppert-Mayer became the first woman to win a Nobel Prize in theoretical physics. One half of the 1963 award went to Eugene Wigner for contributing to the theory of the atomic nucleus and the elementary particles and the other half to Maria and J. Hans D. Jensen "for their discoveries concerning nuclear shell structure." Wigner, once sceptical of the Mayer-Jensen theory, eventually had come around to recognizing its logic. As for Maria Mayer and Hans Jensen, they had arrived at their conclusions independently, but had later joined forces to write a book.

Maria's achievement was remarkable because she had done her work when she was well into her forties. Most theoretical physicists get their flashes of genius before their fourth decade. Wolfgang Pauli had affectionately dubbed her "Madonna of the Onion." For in utterly feminine words she once described the inner workings of the atomic nucleus: "Built up like an onion in layers, with the protons and neutrons revolving around each other and spinning in orbit, like couples in a waltz around a ballroom."

At 57 "the Madonna" was short and plump and still pretty, but suffering from the effects of a stroke three years earlier. It had left her with a slightly blurred speech, a slowed-down walk, and some paralysis. When she walked toward King Gustav VI, an aide followed her to hold the half-pound gold medal and heavily bound diploma. Although Maria Mayer could offer the king her right hand, which still had a little strength and feeling, her left hand and arm were almost completely paralyzed. At the banquet in the Town Hall she sat beside the king and worried that he might find her stupid because she was deaf in one ear. Of course, he did not. By turning her head, one of the most brilliant women scientists in the world was quite able to keep up a conversation.

224

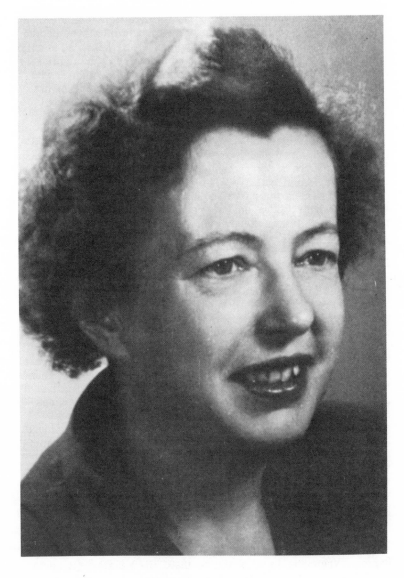

Maria Goeppert-Mayer

Staying close to her through all the festivities was her husband.
Dr. Joseph Mayer, an internationally famous chemist, had
tears in his eyes when he saw Maria sitting onstage with the
other laureates.

At the moment she stood in the spotlight she felt overcome by her customary shyness. "I thought of all the people
who stood there before me, the names I had heard as a child
and those who were my teachers and friends." And then she
thought of her father, "a great gentle bear of a man," who
had wanted her to make something of her life. Still, in his
most ambitious dreams he had never envisioned the Nobel
Prize for his daughter.

Maria was an only child, born June 28, 1906, in Kattowitz (now Katowice), Upper Silesia (then Germany), to Dr.
Friedrich Göppert, * a professor of medicine, and his wife,
the former Maria Wolff. When she was four years old she
came with her parents to live in the charming medieval university town of Göttingen, where her father became a professor of pediatrics. (In her autobiographical note in Les
Prix Nobel Maria Mayer proudly states, "On my father's
side I am the seventh straight generation of university professors.")

Maria grew up in an old-fashioned house, which the
musical Frau Göppert--"delightful woman and wonderful hostess"--liked to fill with guests and flowers. As the director
of the children's hospital and the founder of a free baby
clinic, her father had some rather unusual theories on child
rearing. Dr. Göppert believed that mothers should not limit
their children's freedom and encouraged his blonde and round-
faced little Maria to be adventurous. But she was really not
a good guinea pig. The pale little girl, suffering a succes-
sion of children's ailments and frequent headaches, had to
spend a lot of time indoors. Still with her father she enjoyed
a special relationship, for he encouraged her scientific curiosity and took her on "enchanting" long science walks. He
was the one who admonished her, "Never be a woman," meaning that she should not drown herself in domesticity. Meanwhile Maria went to private and public schools and "had the
great fortune to have very good teachers."

---

*After her marriage Maria Mayer retained her proud family
name. When she immigrated to the United States, it became
Goeppert.

On her eighth birthday, Archduke Franz Ferdinand and his wife were assassinated in Sarajevo. Within a couple of months Germany was on war footing, with consequent deprivations for Göttingen's citizens. Like them, Maria had to eat a lot of watery turnip soup, sometimes flavored with a pig's ear.

At the Hohere Tochterschule, Maria showed special promise in mathematics and languages, particularly French, which her mother had once taught. Then in 1921 she entered the Frauenstudium, a small private school run by feminine suffragists to prepare girls for the university. Two years later, in the midst of the wild postwar inflation, the women lost all their money and had to close their school. During this period, which was even worse than the war for many German cities, a reporter from the New York Times wrote a story about Dr. Göppert's clinic and commented that the good professor was suffering from malnutrition like all his young patients. As a result, food packages began arriving from the United States, a loving gesture Maria never forgot.

The teachers at the Frauenstudium suggested that Maria attend the preparatory school for boys, which that year was opened to girls. Instead she decided to take the abitur or university entrance examination at once, although she had only two years of preparation instead of three. She pulled the necessary strings, and at Hannover in 1924 went through the grueling work of written examinations and the one day of oral testing.

That spring a slim and graceful Maria entered the famous university, where she was immediately singled out for her beauty. The Göpperts' house lay just above that of the famous mathematician David Hilbert, and the family was socially allied to many of the noted mathematicians and physicists at the university, especially to Max Born and James Franck. Quantum mechanics was exciting the scientific world. Until 1920, Göttingen had been considered the mathematical center of the world. Now it was in the forefront of the new physics. One day in 1927, Born invited Maria to attend one of his seminars. Though a mathematics student, she found physics so exciting she switched her field. That year her father died, and to honor his memory she felt she must take her doctorate, which she wanted to do under Born. At the beginning of her studies in physics she spent a term at Girton College, Cambridge, and met Ernest and Mary Rutherford. Her greatest profit there, she said, was to learn English.

After Dr. Göppert's death his widow, in good Göttingen tradition, began to take in boarders. But Maria, who had the reputation of being cool and reserved, remained rather aloof from them. One day when her mother was ill, she opened the door to a lanky, tanned Californian named Joseph Edward Mayer, who was looking for a room. When recovered, Frau Göppert gave him one. Joe Mayer had come to Germany that extremely cold winter of 1928-29 to study with Franck on a Rockefeller grant. The friendly, witty, opinionated young American dearly loved to argue and to tease. Other students envied him because of his generous bankroll and new car.

Maria did not give the new boarder much attention till one day she saw him swimming in splendid style at the municipal pool. Joe, she learned, had been captain of his swim team at the California Institute of Technology in Pasadena. Soon he found that she returned his interest, and he wooed her with rounds of dancing and strenuous athletics--swimming, hiking, skiing, and playing tennis. Teasingly, Joe was to say long afterwards that in spite of her reputation for aloofness she had been a "terrible flirt." More seriously he was to add that she was "lovelier and brighter" than any girl he had ever met.

In mid-January, 1930, Maria and Joe were married at the city hall and feted at a party in the Göppert home. They honeymooned in Berlin, where Maria looked up a childhood nurse. Shortly after her marriage she finished her doctoral dissertation, "Über Elementarakte mit zwei Quantensprüngen" (On Elemental Processes with Two Quantum Jumps). On her committee were Franck and Adolf Windaus, already Nobel laureates in Physics and Chemistry, and Born, who was to become another laureate in Physics.

Only a month later the young couple was sailing from Cherbourg across the Atlantic. Joe had an appointment as assistant professor of chemistry at Johns Hopkins University in Baltimore, succeeding Dr. Harold Urey, who was going to Columbia. Whatever her expectations, Maria now ran up against a wall of nepotism laws. Although she had come from the birthplace of quantum mechanics, she was offered no post at the university. Maria Mayer was what Joan Dash calls the "fringe benefit" wife, "the academic wife, whose husband has a fairly secure position, so that the university considers her a captive, who can be hired with no guarantees for as little as possible, and dropped whenever it becomes expedient."

Her only assignment, with a minimum salary and an attic
office, was to help a member of the physics department with
his German correspondence. Actually, in her nine years at
Hopkins the uncomplaining Maria never had any other rank
than that of volunteer associate. "I would have fought if I
had had to," she said later, "but I only wanted to learn, to
teach, to work."

But, as Joe Mayer would remember, "everybody in
the physics department was helpful, especially Karl Herzfeld,
Gerhard Dieke, and the famous R. W. Wood." Immediately
Maria began to work with Herzfeld. Between him and Joe
she learned a lot of physical chemistry, collaborating with
both of them on several papers. With Herzfeld she worked
on energy transfer on solid surfaces and on the behavior of
hydrogen dissolved in palladium. After Herzfeld left Hopkins
she and one of his former students worked on the quantum
mechanical electronic levels of benzene and later of some
dyes. Meanwhile Maria taught Joe all the quantum mechanics
she knew, the Born-Heisenberg system of particle mechanics.

Soon after the Mayers came to Baltimore, Frau Göppert paid them a long visit. But the young wife was still so
homesick she returned to Germany in the summer of 1931,
accepting an appointment from Born. Maria had always wanted
children, and despite her longing for Göttingen wanted them to
be born to American citizens. "I think Hitler was the main
reason," Joe Mayer would comment later. "Also, having
lost German citizenship by marrying an American, Maria had
no passport, a situation which caused many difficulties in
1931 on our trips in Europe outside Germany."

So, shortly before Marianne was born in the spring
of 1933, Maria Mayer became naturalized. For a year the
new mother, who called having a child "a tremendous experience," spent most of her time with her baby. But then, because she had excellent help in the house and a husband who
encouraged her at every turn, she decided to go back to work.
In their leisure time she and Joe canoed and sailed on Chesa-
peake Bay.

Although Maria was not at all interested in politics,
she grieved over what Hitler was doing to the Jews, especially to academic Jews like Born, who had to leave Göttingen.
So the Mayers began opening their home to streams of German
exiles.

When Maria became pregnant again, she hoped for a boy. To give her something to do, she and Joe began collaborating on what they thought would be a short-term project, a book on statistical mechanics. Actually, it took them four years to finish. Meanwhile in 1938 Maria did give birth to a boy, who was named Peter.

When the manuscript was ready for publication, however, the title page brought its problems. Joe, of course, had a title after his name, associate professor of chemistry at Columbia. During Maria's second pregnancy he had been let go at Johns Hopkins after a change of administration and had gone to New York. But Maria had nothing to put after her name. The sympathetic Urey assigned her to lecture to chemistry students so that the title "lecturer in chemistry" could be used. The book, Statistical Mechanics, became a classic text, but in spite of his protestations Joe Mayer got more credit for it.

One day after the attack on Pearl Harbor, Sarah Lawrence College in New York offered Maria Mayer her first paid teaching job, a half-time position. There, on her own initiative, she organized a unified science course that brought together astronomy, chemistry, and physics. Soon Joe was away much of the time at the Aberdeen Proving Grounds in Maryland, working on "classified" weapons systems.

That spring of 1942 Urey invited Maria to join the secret research group at Columbia. It was involved in separating the fissionable isotope uranium-235 from the more abundant uranium-238. Part of the widespread secret bomb research, the project was called SAM. When asked what SAM meant, Urey and others gave "Substitute Alloy Materials" as a cover. At SAM, because the government did not discriminate against women, Maria at last felt like an equal among equals. Soon she had 20 persons working under her. Still, she remembered, "Urey assigned me not to the main line of research in the laboratory, but to side issues, for instance, to the investigation of the possibility of separating isotopes by photochemical reactions. That was nice, clean physics although it did not help in the separation of isotopes." During those busy and successful years Maria had to take time off, however, for thyroid and gall bladder operations.

At the beginning of 1945, as part of his work at the Aberdeen Proving Grounds, Joe Mayer was sent to the Western Pacific. Meanwhile Edward Teller wanted Maria in Los

Alamos, but she went only after VE Day in May.   Joe moved about so rapidly that her mail addressed to his Army PO number never got to him, and for a while he was uncertain whether she was at home or in New Mexico.

The bomb work was going on at Columbia, Oak Ridge, the University of Chicago, on the Columbia River in Washington, and in Los Alamos.   "It was impossible to hide the existence of these as big secret war work," Joe Mayer would say later, "but every effort was made to hide that each was a part of the same big project."

In Los Alamos, where the bombs were assembled, the secrecy was so intense that the only address was a Santa Fe post office box.   Later the Mayers would laughingly recall that "at least one grand piano (Teller's) was delivered to that P. O. box and babies were born in it!"   The more famous nuclear physicists, whose presence would have indicated the nature of the research, were given false names.   So Maria found herself working with Farmer (Fermi), Wagner (Wigner), and Baker (Niels Bohr).   It had been a hard time for her, keeping the painful secret of the atomic bomb, which, except for VE Day, might well have been used on her homeland. Some of the other German scientists in exile had mixed feelings about their country, but Maria continued to love Germany and the Germans and insisted that Hitler was "an aberration."

As the summer wore on, Joe still had not heard from her.   Long afterwards the Mayers would chuckle over their attempt to catch up with each other.   As Joe would tell it, "Toward the end I wrote her to send mail to general delivery, Honolulu.   When I arrived after a 36 hour flight from New Caledonia, I first went to the post office.   The clerk looked at my crumpled uniform, duffle bag, unshaven and atabrine-yellow face and said, 'Jesus Christ, I'm sorry.   I just bundled a big package of your mail and stamped it undeliverable.'"

He finally managed to get through to Maria by telephone.   On arrival in San Francisco he booked a commercial flight via Albuquerque to Washington and New York.   Maria boarded his plane in Albuquerque, and their reunion was joyful.   Only after Hiroshima did she say to Joe that--by only two days--she had missed watching "Trinity," the world's first atomic explosion.

After the war Maria returned to her half-time position at Sarah Lawrence.   During the war years she had been

nagged by the feeling that she should have been home more.
Peter and Marianne were tended by a bossy English nanny,
and now their mother tried to spend more time with them.
But even during her busiest days she had tried to parcel her
time so that she could read aloud to them at night. Peter
seemed to need help with his homework. But from the circle
of his parents' brilliant friends what an educational experience he and Marianne had already had--learning Italian history from Laura and Enrico Fermi, their neighbors in Leonia,
New Jersey; hearing the story of the dinosaurs from Urey,
another neighbor; and, academics aside, playing Ping-Pong
with Edward Teller.

In 1946 the Mayers left for the University of Chicago,
where Joe was offered a full professorship in chemistry and
Maria, to her surprise and delight, an associate professorship in physics. Later she became a full professor. On
the Chicago campus Fermi's new Institute of Nuclear Studies
was attracting many of the famous scientists who had worked
on the bomb project. Joe and Maria joined Fermi, Urey,
Franck, and Willard Libby there. Said Maria, "This was
the first place where I was not considered a nuisance but
greeted with open arms by the administration." Robert
Hutchins was the chancellor. And yet there was no salary
because of the university rule that both husband and wife,
even in different departments, could not be hired by the university. Not until 1959, when the Mayers were being wooed
by the University of California at San Diego, did the University of Chicago pay Maria Mayer a full professor's salary.

The Mayers found a handsome old three-story brick
mansion on Chicago's South Side, and here Maria could grow
the orchids she loved in a greenhouse Joe fitted up for her
on the third floor. Summers she became an excellent outdoor
gardener. It was a splendid house for entertaining, and the
Mayers gave many parties. One friend described Maria of
the bright, blue eyes as "a woman who makes people happy
in her home." Into their social life the Mayers also fitted
many rounds of bridge and charades with their scientific
friends. Camping was a summer recreation.

Soon Maria had another job, with half-time salary, at
the Argonne National Laboratory, which was building a nuclear
reactor. Much of her learning in nuclear theory came from
the Argonne. Puffing her endless cigarettes, she attended
weekly sessions there. Admittedly, Maria almost always enjoyed the company of men more than that of women, both
professionally and socially.

She was fortunate in having easy access to Fermi and Teller. In about a year Teller asked her to work with him, doing the involved mathematics, on a paper discussing the origin of the elements. Teller had a theory, later discarded, that they had been formed when the universe was very young. Afterwards he came to accept the hypothesis that they are the result of continuing supernova explosions. While working on the paper, he and Maria were struck by the fact that certain isotopes such as those of the elements tin and lead were more abundant than allowed by any smooth curve of abundance against atomic number or weight. Besides being abundant, they were remarkably stable, indicating that abundance was related to stability, which would not be unexpected.

At a time when Teller was out of town, Maria decided to inspect all the information they had about these abundant isotopes and their nuclei. Then she discovered something remarkable. All the abundant isotopes had either 82 or 50 neutrons, the nuclear particles that have weight but no charge, or 82 or 50 protons, the positively charged particles that determine the identity of the elements. Soon she was using the term "magic numbers" to describe the mystery. Hans Bethe told her to look up a paper written by a German professor from Göttingen named Elsasser. He too had tried to find some meaning in this regular occurrence of numbers, and she felt encouraged.

When Teller returned, he got busy with nuclear weapons and lost interest in the project. Maria began taking her questions to Fermi. She studied the data on the nucleus under bombardment and continued collecting and studying data from cyclotrons and nuclear reactors. Now she had more numbers, 2, 8, 20, 28 and 126, making seven "magic numbers" in all. Joe urged her to publish, and after she had carefully collected all the available data, "On Closed Shells in Nuclei, I and II," appeared in Physical Review in 1948-49.

"Theoretical physicists hate numerology," Joe Mayer would later comment. "There are more crackpots seeing magic in accidental numerical relations than almost any other kind." At home he pushed Maria to solve the mystery. More and more she began thinking of a shell model of the nucleus something like the model of the planetary atom. According to this model, just as planets orbit the sun, so the electrons, each carrying a negative electrical charge, orbit the nucleus, which carries positive electrical charges. In certain elements, notably the five "noble" gases of the periodic table,

helium, neon, argon, krypton, and xenon, the concentric
shells are very stable, and the electrons do not easily go
into higher energy states. Hence these elements normally
do not enter into combination with other elements. The
heavier the atom the greater the number of completed or
closed shells. The noble gases have definite numbers in the
table of elements, indicating the number of protons contained
in the nucleus, the same as the number of electrons in the
planetary system. Thus they can be said to have "magic
numbers" of electrons.

The question Maria Mayer asked herself was this:
"Does the repeated occurrence of stable numbers of particular nuclear particles mean the same?" Shell models for the
nucleus had already been worked on by a number of physicists, including Eugene Wigner, but seemed contradictory to
Niels Bohr's drop model. The Bohr model, which likens the
nucleus to a drop of liquid held together by surface tension,
with protons and neutrons moving about in haphazard fashion,
had successfully explained other phenomena. Maria Mayer
began to wonder if the protons and neutrons orbited within
the nucleus in certain shells, held in place by the average
nuclear force field millions of times greater than that bind-
ing electrons to the nucleus.

Wigner and another physicist named David Inglis had
given some thought to spin-orbit coupling with the nucleus,
suggested by the fact that the nucleon (proton or neutron)
spins on its axis while it orbits. But they assumed the splitting to be very small.

One day the revelation came. Maria and Fermi were
talking in her office when he was called to the phone. As
he was heading out the door he asked her, "Is there any in-
dication of spin-orbit coupling?"

Her thinking crystallized at that moment, Maria answered at once, "Yes, of course, that will explain everything." While Fermi was at his phone call, she took up her
pencil and started thinking. She worked the rest of the day
and that evening was able to tell Joe that she could explain
the magic numbers. Soon Fermi taught her "onion theory"
to his nuclear physics class.

Maria's flash of genius was her concept that a measured spin of a nuclear particle will correspond to one of two
different orbits. According to the article she wrote later in

Scientific American, "... the spins and nuclear magnetic moments lead to a description of the nucleus in terms of orbits
of single particles. One can then picture the building of the
structure of the nucleus as the gradual filling up of single
particle orbits by neutrons and protons in the same way as
electrons built the atom. " The point was that single particle
orbits without strong spin-orbit coupling gave magic numbers
at the wrong places.

In the scheme Maria Mayer worked out, the magic
numbers correspond to closed shells, indicating the boundaries where the level is filled and the next level is appre-
ciably higher. The larger magic numbers occur at the places
where the spin-orbit coupling has its greatest effect. In that
same article Maria likened the electronic structure of an atom
to that of an apartment house. At the end she pointed out
that the shell model would explain the phenomenon of isomer-
ism, "the existence of long-lived excited states in nuclei. "
But she thought the most important application would be in
the study of beta-decay, emission by a nucleus. "The lifetime of a nucleus that is capable of emitting an electron depends on the change of spin it must undergo to release the
electron. Present theories of beta-decay are not in a very
satisfactory state, and it is not easy to check on these theories
because only in a few cases are the states of radioactive nuclei known. The shell model can help in this situation, for
it is capable of predicting spins in cases in which they have
not been measured. "

In April, 1950, Physical Review published Maria's
"Nuclear Configurations in the Spin-Orbit Coupling Model.
I. Empirical Evidence and II. Theoretical Considerations. "
Generously she had wanted to include Fermi's name. But
he too was generous. "No. Because ... I am a famous
man. If I put my name on it, it will always be attributed
to me--it is really not my work. It is yours. "

Then Maria had an experience similar to that of Charles Darwin, who a little less than a century before had found
out that quite independently Alfred Wallace had formulated a
theory of natural selection and duplicated his own long years
of effort. Only two days after Maria's papers arrived at the
Physical Review office, there came a paper from Hans Jensen,
a well-known Heidelberg physicist, also setting forth a shell
model based on spin-orbit coupling. Jensen's co-authors
were his colleagues, Haxel and Suess. As Joe Mayer gave
the background some years later, "Suess was interested in

the abundance of elements and isotopes and recognized the
anomalies at 50 and 82 (maybe also at 126 neutrons). He
went to the experimental nuclear physicist Haxel, who recognized the agreement in nuclear measurements. Then together
they went to Jensen, their favorite theoretician, who was impressed by the facts but could think of no explanation. Only
later he recognized that large spin-orbit coupling would do it. "

But, unlike Darwin, Maria had invested only one year
in her work. Actually, Darwin and Wallace, both of magnani-
mous spirit, presented papers on their theory jointly at a
meeting of a British scientific group shortly before The Origin of Species was published. So too Maria Mayer was gentle, not bitter, and prepared to work with Hans Jensen.

In the summer of 1950, sponsored by the State Department, which was sending scientists to German universities,
the Mayers returned to Germany. Maria met Jensen and
found him a "dear, gentle man. " The next year, having been
selected a member of the Heidelberg Academy of Sciences,
she returned. Next Niels Bohr invited Maria and Jensen to
his Institute in Copenhagen. By then Maria and Jensen were
such good friends she could quip, "We look at things in the
same way; even our eyeglass prescriptions are identical. "

With his mind set on the Nobel Prize, Jensen now
suggested to Maria that they write a book on the shell model.
She agreed, and when he arrived in the United States, they
began their collaboration. It would take them four years,
however, to complete Elementary Theory of Nuclear Shell
Structure because their habits were so different. Maria was
conscientious, methodical, and orderly in the best German
academic tradition. Jensen was a procrastinator. But they
did agree that the dedication should read, 'to our most patient and most constructive critic, Joseph E. Mayer. "

While Maria was writing her part of the book, the
Mayers were invited to Japan by the Japanese Physical Society for a meeting of the International Union of Pure and
Applied Physics. At Hiroshima she could have been haunted
by her involvement in the bomb project. But, long used to
controlling her emotions, Maria kept her feelings back. Still
Fermi's death from cancer in 1954 saddened her tremendously.
Then suddenly on her fiftieth birthday she lost most of the
hearing in her left ear.

In 1959 the new San Diego campus of the University

of California offered the Mayers two full professorships--Joe
in chemistry and Maria in physics. Before they left she
planned a beautiful wedding for Marianne, who married Donat
Wentzel, an astrophysicist. Marianne herself did research
in astronomy.

Shortly after the Mayers had settled into their beautiful home in La Jolla, Maria had a stroke, seemingly the result of a virus complication. Two months later she was out
of the hospital in time for Christmas, a holiday she always
made particularly festive. Despite her paralysis and other
impairments she swallowed both fear and unhappiness and
kept on living.

Three years later, one November morning in 1963,
the telephone rang at the Mayer home at four o'clock in the
morning. The call came from a Swedish newsman, who said
that Maria and Hans Jensen had been jointly awarded half the
Nobel Prize in Physics. In Joe Mayer's words, the Prize
was given "for the explanation based on the single assumption
that spin-orbit coupling (which had been assumed to be very
small) was prodigious, especially in the heavy elements. "

At first Maria was incredulous. "Is it really true?
I still can't believe it's true. Oh, how wonderful!" After
Joe ran for a bottle of champagne, she said, "Good! I've
always wanted to meet a king. " Soon she received the formal announcement in a telegram.

Maria and Joe flew to Scandinavia alone. Peter, who
was studying economics, could not leave his classes, and
Marianne had her own home duties. First, though, to conserve Maria's strength, Joe suggested a vacation in Denmark.
In Stockholm, at the Grand Hotel, Maria found flowers from
her old teacher, Max Born. For the ceremony she wore a
green brocade gown, and for the king's banquet she changed
into a long red chiffon gown.

Later she was to say, "To my surprise winning the
Prize wasn't half as exciting as doing the work itself. That
was the fun--seeing it work out. " Jensen would comment,
"By the time the Prize came, it really didn't matter much.
The big moment for me had come years before when I learned
that Fermi had put my name in nomination. I didn't get it
that year, but I really didn't care. It was Fermi's regard
that was the ultimate honor for me, not the medal. "

On December 12 Maria gave her Nobel lecture on
"The Shell Model. " She ended with the observation, "The
shell model has initiated a large field of research. It has
served as the starting point for more refined calculations.
There are enough nuclei to investigate so that the shell mod-
elists will not soon be unemployed. "

Some friends wondered if Joe Mayer ever regretted
that he had purposely kept himself from collaborating with
his wife. They just might have formed an exciting research
team like Marie and Pierre Curie, Irène and Frédéric Joliot-
Curie, and Gerty and Carl Cori. But Joe was not sorry.
He had his own triumphs, and he wanted Maria to make it
on her own. As for Maria, she saw their marriage as an
exciting partnership, one of the chief spurs to her success.
Joe, she said, "always understood. "

She finished out her life in La Jolla, teaching, doing
research, gardening, growing orchids, reading poetry, giving
parties. Among the faculty wives the soft-voiced Maria had
the reputation of being the most elegant hostess. "Elegant"
was, in fact, her favorite adjective. In these years the Went-
zels presented the Mayers with a granddaughter, and Peter
became an assistant professor of economics, causing Maria
to say proudly that he represented the eighth generation of
university professors in her family. Academic honors came
to both Mayers. Maria was a member of the National Academy of Sciences and had honorary doctorates from several
colleges.

In the mid 1960s, doctors found that Maria had some
heart irregularity and in 1968 inserted a pacer. In December, 1971, she suffered sudden heart failure and lay in a
partial coma until her death February 21, 1972. Recalling
the "Madonna of the Onion, " her friends and admirers could
bring to mind several adjectives such as gentle, thoughtful,
complex, intriguing. But all could agree on one word--
modest. As Chancellor Herbert York of the University of
California, San Diego, once said, "She just doesn't wear fame
lightly; she is unaware of it. "

Wizard with Crystals

DOROTHY CROWFOOT HODGKIN

Dorothy Crowfoot Hodgkin was in Ghana on October 29,
1964, when she learned that she had won the Nobel Prize in
Chemistry. Her husband Thomas had been director of the
Institute of African Studies at the University of Ghana since
1962, and she was paying one of her annual visits that usually lasted two or three months. Leaving their bungalow on
the university site at Legon, a green and pleasant district
near Accra, the Hodgkins flew from an equatorial climate to
a chilly England before going off to a much colder Sweden.

On their last night in London they were entertained at
an Arabian party, to which Dorothy Hodgkin gracefully alluded
in her acceptance speech at the Nobel banquet: "My hosts
advised me, then, telling me how one should reply in Arabic
to congratulations that one receives, congratulations on some
very happy event: the birth of a son, perhaps, or the marriage of a daughter. And one should reply: 'May this happen also to you.' And now even my imagination will hardly
stretch so far that I can say this to everyone in this great
hall. But at least, I think, I might say to the members of
the Swedish Academy of Science: 'In so far as this has not
happened to you already, may this happen also to you.'"

When the Hodgkins landed at the Stockholm airport,
they rushed into the arms of their daughter Elizabeth, a history teacher at a girls' school in Zambia. Liz had flown
and hitchhiked to get there. The next day the Hodgkins'
younger son, Tobias, spending a preuniversity year in India,
flew in from New Delhi "after various difficulties." Toby
was followed by Dorothy's sister Elizabeth with her 16-year-
old son John, as well as by two nieces, Susanna and Victoria,
and another nephew, Sebastian, all teenagers, who with their
mother Joan shared the Hodgkins' old Victorian house in Oxford.

For the Nobel ceremony the light-haired Dorothy

Dorothy Crowfoot Hodgkin

Hodgkin with her beautiful English complexion and bright smile
was an elegant figure in a gown of pale gold Chinese silk.
The material had been "bought from an Indian shop in Accra
and made up ... by a Ghanaian girl named Charity Hesse."
While admiring the lady laureate, the Swedes also warmed
to her genial, pipe-smoking husband Thomas, who had a
"Beatles" haircut. Swedish newspapers commented that if
there had been a Nobel Prize in African Studies, he would
have won one.

Dorothy Hodgkin was given the Nobel Prize for "her
determination of the structure of biochemically important substances by X-ray methods" and the following accolade: "You
have solved a large number of structural problems, the majority of great importance in biochemistry and medicine, but
there are two landmarks which stand out. The first is the
determination of the structure of penicillin, which has been
described as a magnificent start to a new era of crystallography. The second, the determination of the structure of
vitamin B_{12}, has been considered the crowning triumph of
X-ray crystallographic analysis, both in respect of the chemical and biological importance of the results and the vast com-
plexity of the structure." Only the year before Thomas's
cousin, Alan L. Hodgkin, had shared the Nobel Prize for
Physiology or Medicine.

Missing from the Nobel ceremony in 1964 was the
Hodgkins' older son, Luke, already the father of three, who
could not leave his job as a mathematics teacher at the University of Algiers. Luke in Algeria, Liz in Zambia, Toby
in India, Thomas in Ghana--no wonder a relative could say,
"They are the most peripatetic family I've known of. Nobody
ever knows where they'll be next." Dorothy herself called
the Hodgkins "widely dispersed."

A spread-out family was a pattern long familiar to
her. She spent her own childhood in Egypt and England, and
her parents traveled ceaselessly between Africa and England.
Egypt had been under British suzerainty since 1882; in 1889
Britain and Egypt established a condominium or jointly
administered protectorate over the Sudan. In these two countries, Egypt and the Anglo-Egyptian Sudan, Dorothy's father,
John Winter Crowfoot, carved out a distinguished colonial
career.

A classical scholar and archaeologist, he was an inspector in the Ministry of Education in Cairo when Dorothy

Mary, the eldest of four daughters, was born there May 12,
1910. His wife, Grace Mary, born Hood (and called Molly
in the family), was deeply involved in his career. But in
her own right she later became an internationally known authority on the weaving of Coptic textiles. She was also an
excellent botanist. In her early married life she wandered
with her husband across the Sudan and drew flowers for that
country's official Flora.

In 1914 John Crowfoot became director of education
and antiquities and principal of Gordon College in Khartoum.
But the First World War caused an uprooting of the Crowfoot
family. Dorothy and her two younger sisters, Joan and Elizabeth, sailed away on a boat heading for England. Eventually
they came to Worthing, a Sussex seaport, close to the South
Downs. Here they lived under a nanny's care and not far
from their Grandmother Crowfoot's watchful eye. They did
not see their parents again until the end of 1918 when Molly
Crowfoot brought a new baby, Diana, from the Sudan to England. Feeling it necessary to reacquaint herself with her
other daughters after three years' separation, she spent the
next year with them in her old home, Nettleham Hall, in Lincoln. She became their teacher as well. Molly Crowfoot's
chief interests were history and natural history. So, as
Dorothy Hodgkin later explained, she had her daughters write
out their "own history books under her guidance, the different
reigns of the kings of England, and what people wore and
what homes they lived in and the poetry they wrote." The
girls also prepared books about flowers and birds for themselves. In addition, their mother asked them to memorize
long poems like "The Revenge" and "The Forsaken Merman"
--"the sort of things," a mature Dorothy would comment,
"which one says to oneself and remembers ever afterwards."

After the war Molly Crowfoot and her husband followed
a pattern of going to England every summer, she staying on
for six months and he for three. John Crowfoot became a
Commander of the British Empire in 1919. After 1921 the
family home was in Geldeston in Suffolk. The Crowfoot family had been established in that East Anglian shire for several
centuries. Dorothy attended a variety of small schools.
Then at 11 she was enrolled at the Sir John Leman School
in Beccles and lived with friends in town during the winter
months. She remained a pupil there until 1928. For almost
200 years several Crowfoots had practiced medicine in Beccles.
All had antiquarian and literary interests. One Doctor Crowfoot was celebrated for early experiments in artificial respira-
tion.

Already at the age of ten a poised and self-reliant child with remarkable large blue eyes, Dorothy felt a curious excitement about crystals and chemistry. Just before she entered the Leman school, she went to a small private class in Beccles with a governess trained in Parents National Educational Union methods. Here she did some elementary chemistry and first grew crystals, the "flowers of the mineral kingdom," as Abbé Haüy, the "father of crystallography," called them. To be sure, scores of nonmineral substances also form crystals. These "flowers" are solids with tidy geometric shapes, with plane faces meeting at characteristic angles, and with characteristic symmetry. The visible regularity results from an orderly array of molecules and atoms making up their structure. The elegance and beauty and mystery of crystals intrigued Dorothy from the start. She was very glad when she and another girl at school were allowed to join the boys doing chemistry.

Now she began learning something about the history of crystallography. In the late eighteenth century Abbé Haüy theorized that crystals are made of small solid blocks, an idea that foreshadowed the concept of unit cells made up of molecules. A later crystallographer named Bravais decided that the interior of crystals could best be described by putting dots at the corners of hypothetical unit cells and drawing lines between the dots. Such an imaginary three-dimensional arrangement, which is regularly repeated, is called a space lattice or crystal lattice. Little did Dorothy dream that in her life work she was to discover the complex lattice structures of penicillin, vitamin B_{12}, and insulin.

Her appetite for chemistry was whetted still more in 1923 when she and her sister Joan went out "to see Father" in Khartoum for six months. He was by now a member of the Governor General's Council. The girls learned some mathematics from a family friend and went on all kinds of visits. Dorothy was especially interested in the Wellcome Laboratory, where she met her father's good friend, Dr. A. F. Joseph, the soil chemist.

To entertain the young guests from England the laboratory geologists threw a few grains of gold into a pile of sand and showed them how to pan away the sand. Promptly Dorothy and Joan wanted to try the same experiment on the sand at the bottom of a little channel running through their garden. There they found a black shiny substance. At school in England Dorothy had already begun qualitative analysis.

Suspecting that the substance might be manganese dioxide, she went back to the laboratory and asked to test it. She needed help, which she got from Dr. Joseph. In the end the substance turned out to be ilmenite, containing titanium, not one of the elements she had learned to test for up to that point. The little experiment led Dr. Joseph to give the eager young Dorothy a "beautiful box used by surveyors for doing chemical experiments." It became the foundation of the laboratory she set up for herself in the attic as soon as she was back home in England.

In 1925 she first met up with X-ray crystallography, the intricate science that was to dominate her life. Molly Crowfoot gave her young daughter a children's book by W. H. Bragg called Concerning the Nature of Things. One statement in particular caught her fancy: "Broadly speaking, the discovery of X-rays has increased the keenness of our vision over ten thousand times and we can now 'see' the individual atoms and molecules."

X-ray crystallography was still in its formative period. It had evolved only because scientists began speculating as to whether X rays were tiny particles or lightlike waves. Some thought that if X rays could be diffracted (forced to change direction) by a diffraction grating (a series of fine parallel scratches on a polished surface), they could be considered waves. But as it turned out, no man-made diffraction grating could bend the powerfully penetrating X rays since the distance between adjacent fine scratches could never be small enough, that is, equal to the size of "waves" in the radiation.

Then in 1912 a young physicist in Munich, Max von Laue, got the idea that the invisible particles of a crystal might be a natural and far finer three-dimensional diffraction grating. Calculations had showed that the distance between a crystal's adjacent atomic layers is very much smaller than the wavelength of visible light. Von Laue reasoned that if X rays have wavelengths comparable to the interatomic distances within a crystal, they could be diffracted. Acting on his suggestion, two colleagues found, indeed, that a pencil of X rays passing through a crystal of copper sulfate formed a pattern of small spots on a photographic plate. With some further calculations von Laue conclusively proved that these spots were due to diffraction of the wave-like X rays. The experiment was a double breakthrough, for it also proved that the remarkable order of crystal shapes arises from the harmonious arrangement of the basic units.

That same year in Cambridge, young Lawrence Bragg, working with his father, W. H. Bragg, noted the geometrical shapes of the Munich photographs and theorized that this kind of diffraction could be regarded as cooperative reflections of the internal planes of the crystal. This led to his famous mathematical formula, known as Bragg's law. The Braggs were true pioneers in the field. The senior Bragg designed a spectrometer which made possible the direct comparison of the intensities of diffracted rays. Lawrence Bragg, studying sodium chloride, showed the first structural determination by X ray and quickly moved to other structures. Von Laue received a Nobel Prize in 1914. The next year the Braggs, father and son, were honored, and at 24, Lawrence became the youngest Nobel laureate in history.

In 1927 John and Molly Crowfoot left for Palestine, where he served as director of the British School of Archaeology in Jerusalem and excavated Byzantine churches at Bosra, Samaria, and Jerash, the Roman "city of a thousand columns" on the desert's edge. After finishing the Leman School, Dorothy, at 18, came out to Palestine on what she considered one of the most marvelous journeys of her life. She helped her parents in the exciting dig and showed great skill in drawing the mosaic pavements of the ancient churches. She enjoyed the experience so much that she seriously considered giving up chemistry for archaeology.

John Crowfoot had been to Oxford, and within the family it was somehow understood that Dorothy should go there too. But her preparation at a small country school was far from complete. Before coming to Transjordan, she hastily learned some Latin and botany for the Oxford Entrance. While in Jerash she received a letter from her worried tutor in Oxford, saying that she should be studying some physics if she really were intending to read chemistry. Dorothy wrote back, "I'm sorry, but I'm here." The tutor did send out a physics textbook, which Dorothy studied evenings, helped by an architect friend.

Most of her first year at Oxford she spent doing more physics and thinking how lucky she was "to know very little more than Faraday." Thus she could really find the answers for herself over again. At Somerville College she became devoted to its principal, Margery Fry. This younger sister of Roger Fry, the famous art critic, was a noted penal reformer and campaigner against the death penalty. That first year at Oxford, Dorothy spent most of her afternoons finishing

the drawings she had begun in Transjordan.   Sundays she went
on archaeological expeditions.   Gradually she became more
and more involved in chemistry although Somerville was not
used to having many science students around.   During vacations, since her parents were away, she stayed on at the university to work in the laboratories with the various demon-
strators.   The well-known E. G. J. Hartley encouraged her
to make a series of chemical analyses of the colored glass
tesserae from Jerash and lent her his platinum crucible and
a key to the laboratory.

       Then after she had attended a special course in crys-
tallography, her tutor encouraged her to do her research in
X-ray crystallography.   After paying a short visit to Professor Victor Goldschmidt's laboratory in Heidelberg, she returned to Oxford and became H. M. Powell's first research
student.

       This science was a strict discipline, demanding the
utmost patience.   A flow sheet for a structure determination
would show as many as 30 separate steps, many of them
mathematical.   Crystallographers often had to take hundreds
of pictures of a single crystal, rotating it in sequence.   From
the position and intensity of the spots on the photographic film
it was possible through a complicated mathematical procedure
to calculate the positions of all the atoms and molecules in
the one-unit cell.   Crystallographers had to analyze the patterns in a technique similar, somebody has said, to determining the shape of a jungle gym from studying the shadows
of its bars.   Measurements had to be made of unit cell dimensions, the density of the crystal, and indices and intensities
of all observable reflections.   Then a trial structure had to
be determined--a lengthy and complex process--and later refined.

       One day in 1932 a "chance meeting" steered Dorothy
toward Cambridge.   Dr. Joseph, who had helped her with
chemistry in the Sudan, happened to be visiting at Oxford.
On a local train he met T. S. Lowry, professor of physical
chemistry at Cambridge, who had just appointed John D.
Bernal to a lectureship.   With Dorothy Crowfoot's future
clearly in mind, Dr. Joseph suggested to Lowry that arrange-
ments be made for her to study with Bernal.   She had listened
to Bernal lecture on metals at Oxford, and when she heard
that he was working with sterols, her course was settled.
For she had become fascinated by such complicated molecules
as sterols and strychnine.   Those sterols which especially

interested her were solid cyclic alcohols found in plant and
animal tissues.

Later when the physicist Peter Debye passed through
Cambridge, he teased Dorothy that she had acquired a European reputation by tidying Bernal's microscope desk. "There
was 'gold' all over it, " she remembered later, "very interesting crystals sent to Bernal from many different places,
after his initial success with the sterols. He was very widely
exploratory in those days; together we took X-ray photographs
of early preparations of vitamin B_1, vitamin D, several of
the sex hormones, and pepsin crystals. There is a sense in
which all my subsequent work started from looking at crystals with Bernal. "

Dorothy's generous aunt, Dorothy Hood, was paying
most of her college bills. There was also a small scholarship from Somerville. Then in 1933 Somerville gave her a
research fellowship to be divided between Cambridge and
Oxford. So she was able to spend two happy years at Cambridge. She returned to Oxford in 1934 as Official Fellow
and tutor in natural science at Somerville and soon was teaching chemistry at the women's colleges at the university.

Assigned to the Department of Minerology and Crystallography, she decided she wanted new apparatus. With
the help of Sir Robert Robinson, professor of organic chemistry and a future Nobel laureate, she obtained a grant, which
bought two X-ray tubes, a Weissenberg camera, and two os-
cillation cameras. But a limited budget allowed her only one
or two research students and no real laboratory. The little
team was housed in scattered rooms in the university museum,
even in the basement. Often pretty young Miss Crowfoot had
to climb a precariously placed ladder while carrying her delicate crystals to the gallery.

Here she continued the researches on sterols she had
begun with Bernal and then began looking into insulin. But
reluctantly she postponed the study until the experimental
methods were more fully developed. Meanwhile she was
showing that she fully possessed the unusual combination of
qualities crystallography demands--precision, ease in mathematical analysis, and a very special kind of imagination.

In 1935, deciding that the results of crystal structure
must be made readily available to organic chemists, she
wrote for the Annual Reports of the Progress of Chemistry

of the Chemical Society of London the first separate section
on organic molecular crystals. It set a standard for concise
and accurate reporting.

The year of 1937 was a banner one. She got her doctorate and married within the twelvemonth. Her thesis was
on the chemistry and crystallography of the sterols. That
spring she went to London to photograph insulin at the Royal
Institution. While staying with Margery Fry, who had retired
from Somerville, she met Margery's charming cousin,
Thomas L. Hodgkin, the son of Robert H. Hodgkin, historian
and provost of Queen's College, Oxford, and the grandson of
two other historians.

Indeed, Thomas came from a most remarkable family
network that sprouted, someone has said, "with solid Victorian
qualities of social responsibility and intellectual seriousness
and independence. " His great-great-grandfather was Luke
Howard, the father of meteorology. His grandfather's uncle,
Dr. Thomas Hodgkin, first described the malignant disease
of lymph tissue that bears his name. One of his father's
cousins married Robert Bridges, the poet laureate. On the
other side, Thomas Hodgkin's maternal grandfather was a
master of Balliol who had seven daughters, each of whom
married a man of distinction.

Thomas, always considered a "terrific talker, " had
been educated at Winchester and Oxford. At the time he
met Dorothy he had just left government service in Palestine
and was trying to become a schoolteacher. They were married December 16, 1937, in Geldeston and had a large party
afterwards in the Village Hall. For two months they honeymooned in the south of France and then had to spend alternate
weekends visiting each other, for Thomas was teaching at
Whitehaven, and Dorothy remained at Oxford. He moved on
to a Workers' Education job in North Staffordshire, but the
two-home arrangement had to continue until 1945, when Thomas became director of Extramural Studies at Oxford.

The Hodgkins' first son, Luke, was born in 1938, followed by a daughter, Elizabeth, in 1941, and a second son,
Tobias, in 1946. Fortunately for Dorothy Hodgkin's remarkable dual career of science and domesticity there was always
household help. First there were "nice girls staying with
us. " Then "sometime in the war Edith and Alice came, elderly refugees from the blitz, and stayed helping us the rest
of their working lives. " And Thomas's mother whisked the

children off to Queen's College one day every week. "During
the war," Dorothy would later comment, "the children were
very young, but I had no sense of guilt in continuing with
scientific work--it seemed the natural thing to do at that
period."

World War II created an enormous demand for penicillin, the antibiotic discovered by Alexander Fleming, Ernst
Chain, and Howard Florey, all future Nobel laureates. As
a prime research goal chemists and crystallographers in
England and the United States were put to work to see if penicillin could be produced by chemical synthesis. Dorothy
Hodgkin started directing her research team as soon as
crystalline specimens of salts and degradation products were
available.

The penicillin molecule contains one sulphur atom.
After many experiments the Oxford crystallographers determined the position of the sulphur atoms in the crystal lattice.
Halfway through the war they began doing their calculations
for electron density maps on punched-card machines.

For this complex project Dorothy Hodgkin used all her
imagination and insight, which her colleagues said amounted
to genius. She impressed everybody in the laboratory by arriving at a correct initial interpretation, tenaciously sticking
to it, and ending up with a detailed, accurate, and thoroughly
convincing picture. As an associate remarked, she thought
about the complex molecule "in mental stereo."

Although she had fully established the chemical constitution of penicillin, large-scale production by chemical
synthesis proved too difficult because the substance is very
sensitive to acid solutions. But Dorothy Hodgkin's research
had laid a firm foundation for future development. Meanwhile penicillin derivatives and allied compounds with greater
stability in acids were synthesized. Some were produced on
an industrial scale.

While she was in the midst of her studies of penicillin,
none other than W. H. Bragg singled out the work on choles-
teryl iodide she had finished at the beginning of the war. He
said it had passed the "sound barrier," meaning that by a
physical method she had surpassed the boundaries of the organic chemist's knowledge about the arrangement of atoms in
the molecule. In 1946 she became a university lecturer and
demonstrator. Ten years later she was to be appointed university reader in X-ray crystallography.

Fresh from her triumph with penicillin Dorothy Hodgkin found a new and very exciting research project in 1948. That year, at the very same time, medical research laboratories in the United States and England were growing crystals from the factor in the liver material that protects against pernicious anemia. This substance is named vitamin B_{12}. Although produced by microorganisms and molds in the alimentary canals of certain animals, particularly the ruminants, it is produced only in insignificant quantities in humans.

The B_{12} molecule proved to be a very complex structure with a cobalt heart. By introducing various heavy atoms into the crystals and by using an experimental method recently developed by J. H. Bijvoet, the Dutch crystallographer, Dorothy Hodgkin and her colleagues finally clarified the molecular structure of vitamin B_{12}. They had to amass and process a vast amount of experimental treatments, varied according to circumstances. Fortunately they had the help of three of the first electronic computers, one of which was in Los Angeles. The final paper was dated 1957. Bernal called the structure determination "the greatest triumph of crystallographic technique that has yet occurred." He went on to say that the achievement was a remarkable instance of the way research can be pushed forward when led by a worker of genius, helped by keen young collaborators.

After the war Thomas Hodgkin's career developed in new directions. Indeed, the 1950s began the travel years. In 1957 Thomas was a visiting lecturer at Northwestern University in Illinois; in 1958 he was at the University of Ghana, and that same year took up a post as research associate at the Institute of Islamic Studies at McGill University in Montreal. By this time he had become an expert in African and Arabian history and politics. In that same decade Dorothy Hodgkin made her first trips to China and the Soviet Union and her second visit to the United States, where she had first come in 1947 on a Rockefeller Fellowship to see various laboratories. She had been named a fellow of the Royal Society that same year. In 1956 she was to become a Royal Medalist. Through the 1950s and 1960s she accepted memberships in many learned societies, including the American Academy of Arts and Sciences in 1958. There were many honorary degrees.

In 1958 she moved from the Ruskin Natural History Museum, a building described as "bizarre" both inside and outside, to a modern wing of the chemistry building at Oxford.

Visiting scientists commented both on the informality of the
laboratory, where everybody was on a first-name basis with
her, and on the rather large number of "charming young ladies
intent on becoming distinguished crystallographers." Dorothy
Hodgkin always had a quiet way of speaking and sometimes
so absorbed a manner that a relative could say she had "an
almost dreamy appearance." Also in 1958 came an especially
moving ceremony. Her 85-year-old father, John Winter
Crowfoot, was granted an honorary doctorate by Oxford.

Thomas Hodgkin had gone to Ghana several times to
lecture and had served on a commission charting the future
of the new university. In 1962 he was appointed the first
director of African studies at the University of Ghana in
Legon, some 3300 miles south of Oxford. He was by now
a distinguished Africanist and the author of pioneer books on
Africa's past and present. Legon is one of the most beautiful campuses in Africa, its rambling white stucco buildings
with red clay tile roofs spread out in lawns and gardens.
There Thomas had a front-row seat to study the rise of African nationalism, for in 1957 Ghana became the first former
colonial nation in black Africa to gain independence. He also
had a splendid chance to follow the rise to power of the charis-
matic Kwame Nkrumah, prime minister and then president,
who tried to develop his own brand of African socialism.
Shortly after Thomas left Ghana, the Osagyefo or "redeemer"
was overthrown in a military coup.

For three years Dorothy flew out to Ghana for two or
three months each year. She spent much time in the chemistry library and did some crystallography in the laboratory,
helping one of the research students. But she also took time
to enjoy this vital, happy country with its "plumpy," handsome, and immaculate people. She was intrigued by the geometric designs of kente and adinkra cloths, made in Ashanti-
land.

When the Hodgkins came to Stockholm in 1964, the
Swedish press was delighted to have such a large family en-
tourage to photograph. In her acceptance speech Dorothy
Hodgkin said, "My breath is quite taken away by the succes-
sion of impressions, this beautiful city and this beautiful
golden Byzantine hall, the meeting with very many old friends,
and the making of very many new ones, the coming of my
children by adventurous journeys from different parts of the
world." Her use of "Byzantine" to describe the Golden Hall
with its symbolic mosaics was quite appropriate because the

study of Byzantine churches had been her special hobby since 1928.

Later that evening, speaking on behalf of the 1964 laureates to a large group of Swedish students she said: "I was chosen to reply to you this evening as the one woman of our group, a position, which I hope very much will not be so very uncommon in the future that it will call for any comment or distinctions of this kind, as more and more women carry out research in the same way as men." She went on, "But I might have been chosen for you for other reasons to reply to your speech, as a countrywoman of Tom Paine, who wrote an early book on the rights of man, from whom the declaration of human rights which you mentioned today derives."

After commenting on the Ghanaian commitment to work for peace and progress, she told of the enormous party that was given in her husband's Institute of African Studies to celebrate her award. There were court dances, hunter dances, and "quite modern dances symbolizing work and happiness." Then "under the stars in Africa" Dorothy Crowfoot Hodgkin made a speech, saying that never before had a Nobel Prize been celebrated in just such a way. By contrast, her sister, Diana Rowley, the wife of a Canadian geographer, was at the North Pole when she heard about her sister's honor.

The day after the gala ceremonies Dorothy Hodgkin delivered her Nobel lecture on "The X-Ray Analysis of Complicated Matter." At its end she remarked that her research owed a debt, never to be adequately paid, to the work of her colleagues and collaborators.

In 1965 she received the British Order of Merit, which had been given to only one other Englishwoman, Florence Nightingale. As Lytton Strachey observed, "It is bestowed because a recipient deserves it and for no other reason."

After her trip to Stockholm, Dorothy Hodgkin turned back to the work on insulin she had begun in 1935. She suffered from arthritis in her hands, which made difficult the handling of tiny crystals. But she never let this condition interfere with her research. Friends and colleagues deeply admired her courage and perseverance.

Determining the structure of insulin was a formidable task because many of the 1000 atoms in an insulin molecule

were difficult to track down.   She found, however, that she
could accurately locate them if she introduced foreign atoms
to push them out of place.   Taking X-ray pictures of the
crystals, she then used a computer to work out the positions
and types of atoms that caused the distortions in the beginning.
In 1969 she announced at a National Committee for Crystallography meeting in New York that she had finally discovered the
structure of insulin.

For several years Dorothy continued to put in a laboratory week at Oxford.   Thomas retired as a fellow of Balliol
and lecturer in the government of new states and gave his
time to writing in a country house in Warwickshire.   While
pursuing her professional interests, Dorothy also gave loving
care to her aged mother-in-law.   She was happy that her
children and grandchildren had settled in England.

In 1980 the Hodgkins came again to the United States
to lecture in various places in their separate fields.   Thomas'
health, however, had become precarious.   He did not take
well to the English winters and spent the last months of his
life in the Sudan and Greece, where he died in 1982.

In 1984 Dorothy Hodgkin still devoted much time to
writing scientific papers and attending scientific meetings.
She was much sought after as a lecturer and invariably gener-
ated enthusiasm.   "I believe," she continued to say, "that
there is still a great deal of excitement in X-ray crystallography.   There are still crystals with complexities which challenge us."

A Sensitive Measure

ROSALYN YALOW

In Building C of the big Veterans Administration Hospital in the Bronx, New York, Dr. Rosalyn Yalow had long put in a "normal 70-hour week." So she was already at her desk at seven o'clock on the morning of October 13, 1977, when a long-distance call came from Stockholm. The caller, Professor Rolf Luft of the Caroline Institute, informed her that she had just been awarded half of the Nobel Prize in Physiology or Medicine. The other half of the Prize, she learned, had gone to Dr. Roger Guillemin of the Salk Institute in La Jolla, California, and to Dr. Andrew Schally of Tulane University and the Veterans Administration Hospital in New Orleans. Soon after the announcement, Dr. John D. Chase, the VA's chief medical director, proudly declared, "Dr. Yalow and Dr. Schally have added greatly to the stature of American medicine, and their Nobel award is the greatest recognition ever accorded the VA medical research program."

All three researchers had helped unravel mysteries of the endocrine system, which--it has been said--acts as a kind of Mission Control through its myriad glands and the hormones they secrete. Rosalyn Yalow was being honored "for the development of radioimmunoassays of peptide hormones." Radioimmunoassay (RIA), combining aspects of nuclear medicine and immunology, measures minute quantities of substances in the blood. Radioactive isotopes as markers had been used in medical research before. The Yalow work was a specific application of radioactive isotopes in a new investigative area. Working in separate laboratories with separate teams and sometimes in hot competition, Schally and Guillemin had used the RIA technique in making major discoveries about the peptide hormone production of the brain. A hormone is a chemical substance produced by the body to regulate the activity of a specific organ. Many hormones are peptides, substances consisting of short chains of amino acids. Proteins, on the other hand, are long chains of amino acids.

Rosalyn Yalow

To reporters, Professor Luft marveled that the new
lady laureate had already been in her office a couple of hours
when he spoke to her and had even cooked breakfast before that.
He commented, "She's a woman of extraordinarily sharp intellect
--she's won all the scientific honors in the United States." He
added, "She's a good cook, too," for he was well aware that
she had always kept a kosher kitchen.

The news took Rosalyn Yalow completely by surprise.
"For the first hour ... I had no reaction--I was absolutely
stunned." Then she began to relax and enjoy herself and reflect on her 30 years with the VA Hospital. She had been
working on a paper before the message came from Stockholm.
Smiling broadly, she put it aside in the excitement. Soon her
husband Aaron, a physics professor at Cooper Union, and their
25-year-old son, Benjamin, a systems programmer at the
Computer Center of the City University of New York, ran in
to congratulate her. Her office filled with flowers, and somebody brought champagne. Missing from the happy family circle, however, was the Yalows' daughter, Elanna, who was
pursuing a doctorate in educational psychology at Stanford University in California. Within hours of the news, Elanna and
her fiancé, Daniel Webb, made plans to honeymoon in Stockholm during Nobel Week. Still another family member heard
the report with great pride--Rosalyn's 92-year-old mother in
the Bronx.

Rosalyn Yalow was the first woman after Gerty Cori
to win the Nobel Prize in Physiology or Medicine, which has
always recognized the twentieth century's major achievements
in medicine. Theodore L. Sourkes once profiled a winner in
this field: "Behind and around him or her there is always a
constellation of scientists who have taken part in the same
work. Their preliminary researches have made it possible,
or their subsequent efforts have made it more fruitful. The
winner of the prize is therefore not only a discoverer in his
or her own right, but a representative--by virtue of an outstanding contribution--of those who have worked toward the
same or a similar goal." So, appropriately, Rosalyn Yalow's
associates and the young research scientists, whom she had
always called "my professional children," swirled about her
too.

The mood of the office party was euphoric. But at
various moments everybody was thinking about the man who
was not there--Solomon Berson, Rosalyn Yalow's associate
for 22 years. "The tragedy in today's Nobel award," she

reflected at one point, "is that Dr. Berson did not live to
share it." He had died unexpectedly in 1972.

Reporters also crowded in. The Bronx, Rosalyn Yalow
told them, was her world. She was born in the South Bronx
on July 19, 1921, to Simon and Clara (Zipper) Sussman. Clara
came from Germany to the United States at the age of four,
and Simon, whose forebears were Russian, was born on New
York's Lower East Side. Neither went beyond grade school,
but there was never any doubt that Rosalyn and her older
brother Alexander would go to college. Simon had a paper
and twine business.

Rosalyn grew up in a Jewish neighborhood in the part,
she informed a television interviewer, "that's now a disaster
area." In the 1970s, abandoned building fires, many of them
deliberately set by vandals or gangs, very nearly finisned
destroying the South Bronx. Block after block was leveled
or reduced to ruins.

During better days Rosalyn Sussman, a precocious,
stubborn, and determined child, went to P. S. 51 and P. S.
10. She had learned to read before entering kindergarten.
Every week, since there were no books in the Sussman home,
Alexander faithfully escorted his young sister to the public
library. By the seventh grade Rosalyn was devoted to mathematics. At Walton High School a teacher named Mr. Mondzak
stirred her interest in chemistry.

Then at Hunter College, professors Herbert Otis and
Duane Roller diverted her to physics. To the young college
student nuclear physics seemed the most exciting field in the
world. As an undergraduate she enthusiastically read Eve
Curie's just-published biography of her mother Marie and
ever after recommended it to every young aspiring woman
scientist. In her junior year Rosalyn heard Enrico Fermi
give a colloquium on the recently discovered process for
splitting the uranium nucleus (nuclear fission), which was to
lead not only to nuclear weapons but also to the ready availability of radioisotopes for medical research.

In September 1940, Rosalyn was in the last half of her
senior year at Hunter. Her practical-minded parents wanted
her to be an elementary school teacher. But, still stubborn
and determined, she dreamed of a career in physics even
though she knew that good graduate schools were not eager to
accept and give financial support to a woman in that field.

Yet she persisted, encouraged by her professors. Since she
was an excellent typist, she was offered a part-time job as
secretary to a leading biochemist at Columbia's College of
Physicians and Surgeons and was promised it might help her
get into graduate school. She herself had to promise to learn
stenography. After graduating from Hunter in January, 1941,
as the first woman physics major, she enrolled in business
school. Fortunately, an offer of a teaching assistantship in
physics at the University of Illinois arrived a few weeks later,
and Rosalyn tore up her steno books. She kept her secretarial
job, however, till June. That summer she took some additional physics courses at New York University and in the fall
left for Champaign-Urbana.

        The very first day of graduate school pretty, dark-
haired Rosalyn Sussman met a young student from Syracuse,
New York. Aaron Yalow later recalled that he had detected
a Bronx accent and had made some "snide remarks." Nonetheless, a courtship began, and on June 6, 1943, they were
married.

        Attending the first meeting of the Faculty of the Col-
lege of Engineering, Rosalyn discovered she was the only
woman among 400 members. The Dean informed her she
was the first woman there since 1917. Quickly she saw the
point. The draft of young men into the armed services just
before America's entry into World War II had provided an
opening for her.

        Except for a night course at City College and the two
summer courses she had just completed, Rosalyn had never
had boys in her classes from junior high school on. Also
because Hunter offered a physics major for the first time only
when she was a senior, she felt her preparation had been
less thorough than that of the other graduate students. Therefore she took some undergraduate and graduate courses in
physics and at the same time was a teaching assistant. Because she had never taught before, she carefully observed a
gifted young instructor in his classroom to learn the tricks
of the trade. Rosalyn earned her M. S. in 1942 and her Ph. D.
in 1945 with an experimental thesis titled, "Doubly Ionized
K-shell Following Radioactive Decay." It had demanded long
hours in the laboratory, where she became skilled at making
and using apparatus to measure radioactive substances. When

        When Aaron's thesis was delayed, Rosalyn returned
to New York alone to work as assistant engineer (the only

woman engineer) at Federal Telecommunications Laboratory,
a research laboratory for ITT. Aaron arrived in New York
in the fall of 1945, and the young couple lived first in an
apartment in Manhattan and then in a small house in the
Bronx.

In 1946 Rosalyn went back to Hunter College to teach
physics to veterans enrolled in a pre-engineering course.
By now she was intensely interested in medical research.
Moonlighting from the physics department, she accepted a
part-time job as a consultant in the new Radioisotope Section
of the Bronx VA Hospital in 1947. Thirty years later Rosalyn Yalow would say, "I'm very proud of the fact that in a
sense the VA was the first organization to appreciate the
importance of radioisotopes in medicine. The VA provided
me with laboratory facilities and the opportunity to grow
when I was very young." From that same perspective she
also remarked, "I think one must decide very early in one's
professional life the extent of dedication and commitment one
is prepared to make for a successful career. We have all
heard that as Edison once said, 'Genius is one per cent inspiration, ninety per cent perspiration.' For the lesser
among us to have an impact the per cent of perspiration may
be even higher--and whether we like it or not women, even
now, must exert greater total effort than men for the same
degree of success."

Radioisotope research derives from the discovery of
artificial radioactivity by Irène and Frédéric Joliot-Curie,
the discovery of the neutron by James Chadwick, and the development of the cyclotron by Ernest Lawrence (Nobel laureate in 1939). At first, however, cyclotron-produced isotopes
were prohibitively expensive for civilian investigators. But
by 1946 the United States government reactor in Oak Ridge,
Tennessee, was preparing less costly radioisotopes, such as
radioactive iodine, used for the treatment of thyroid cancer.

Work in the Radioisotope Unit focused on the application of radioisotopes to clinical diagnosis, therapy, and investigation. To the idealistic Rosalyn the ready availability
of radioisotopes seemed to provide "a torch to light the way
to investigative medicine."

In 1950, the year that Rosalyn Yalow started working
full-time at the VA Hospital, the first internist connected
with the unit resigned, and Solomon Berson, a 32-year-old
doctor, then completing a residency at the VA Hospital, was

appointed in his place.   Four years later he became chief of
the service.

          Rosalyn Yalow and Sol Berson did their early studies
on the use of radioiodine in the study of thyroid physiology
and the diagnosis of thyroid disease.   They went on to measure the amount of blood in the circulation by injecting radio-
isotopically labeled substances into the blood and taking sam-
ples after the injected material had been mixed uniformly.   If
the relative amount of red cells was low, it was possible to
determine whether the deficiency was caused by an absolute
decrease in their number (true anemia) or by an increase in
plasma volume (causing such diseases as cirrhosis or heart
failure).   The team moved on to develop mathematical analyses and experimental methods for studying the rate of re-
moval of serum proteins from the blood stream and determining their rates of synthesis and degradation.

          The partnership turned out to be a remarkable labora-
tory match.   "He wanted to be a physicist, and I wanted to
be a medical doctor, " Rosalyn Yalow would remember.   They
complemented each other in many ways.   She was a skilled
physicist, chemist, and mathematician.   He had a vast clinical knowledge.   Both were brilliant investigators, imaginative
but critical.   Sol was a dreamer who wanted to revolutionize
medical research, and the 1950s and 1960s were a most exciting period in the VA laboratory.   Eventually Rosalyn was
named assistant chief of the service.

          She and Sol next applied their methods to the distribu-
tion and degradation of a smaller protein (or peptide hormone)
--insulin.   General theory held that diabetes was caused by
an absolute deficiency of circulating insulin.   Yalow and Berson administered radioactive-labeled insulin intravenously to
diabetics and nondiabetics.   Surprisingly nearly every diabetic had a slower rate of disappearance of labeled insulin.
Slow disappearers had a history of previous insulin therapy.
The conclusion was that the insulin might be bound to antibodies in the blood which developed in response to exposure to
a foreign substance, the beef-pork insulins used.   The team
now developed new and highly sensitive methods to quantitate
the concentration of insulin-binding antibodies in the circulation.   As Rosalyn Yalow later wrote, "We soon appreciated
that the same methods used to quantify antibody could be
used reciprocally to measure antigen, in this case the circulating insulin.   Thus the radioimmunoassay (RIA) principle
was formulated as a serendipitous fall-out from an unrelated

study which asked a question concerning degradation of insulin in diabetics. " The year was 1959. To the team's disappointment the editor of a leading medical research journal rejected their paper because he would not believe that insulin could induce antibodies. (Eventually the paper was published.) RIAs of blood, other fluids, and tissues followed.

Meanwhile diabetes research was directed into new tracks and given new dimensions. The practical application of the concept was the measurement of insulin in human plasma. An early use of the technique showed that adult diabetics, unlike diabetic children, do have some insulin in their bodies, but are unable to use it to control the blood sugar level.

The RIA of a natural hormone involves the preparation of a solution containing a known amount of the radioisotope-labeled form of this hormone and the antibody to this hormone. When the natural form of the hormone, in unknown amount, is added to the solution, a portion of the labeled hormone is displaced from the hormone-antibody complex. The portion displaced is proportional to the unknown amount of the natural form added. Separation of the hormone-antibody complex from the solution allows the amounts of labeled hormone to be measured in each portion.

Twice Rosalyn Yalow took "four days off" from work-- for the birth of Benjamin in 1952 and Elanna in 1954. Meanwhile the Yalows moved into a house less than a mile from the VA Hospital. Until Ben was nine and Elanna seven, there was live-in help and thereafter gradually decreasing part-time help. Rosalyn's schedule was arduous, but careful organization and a greatly supportive husband were key elements in her successful roles as wife, mother, and scientist. Of Aaron she said, "He has never created conflicts between my role as a wife and my professional life. " On the subject of marriage she once commented, "It's true that women are different from men. If you want to be a good wife, you have to work a little harder. " The Yalow children, who attended public schools and the Bronx High School of Science, were raised on their mother's philosophy: "A child must learn from the cradle that upward mobility depends on what people themselves do. "

From time to time the developers of RIA trained a limited number of Fellows in their laboratory. According to Rosalyn, "We chose not to have a lab any larger than we could manage with our own hands. " They did, however, ad-

vise many investigators on the RIA technique, which began
to be used in laboratories throughout the world.

This technique is so sensitive that a Swedish scientist
has noted it is like detecting the presence of half a lump of
sugar in a lake about 62 miles wide and long and 30 feet deep.
Throughout the years Yalow and Berson and their associates
set their names to a series of brilliant, now classical papers
describing RIAs in detail.

Sol Berson was named senior medical investigator of
the VA in 1963. Then in 1968 he was appointed chairman of
the department of medicine of Mt. Sinai School of Medicine
in New York, with which the VA had become associated the
year before. Although he retained his VA title, he could no
longer be a full-time investigator. Still he remained, as
Rosalyn said, "a complete partner." In April 1972 he died
while attending a medical meeting in Atlantic City, New Jersey. Just before leaving for the conference he had stopped
in at the laboratory. A year later at Rosalyn's request it
was renamed the Solomon A. Berson Research Laboratory.
She was appointed director. In 1972 a talented young physician named Eugene Straus joined the laboratory as a fellow.
In the next few years he became a clinical investigator and
Rosalyn Yalow's chief collaborator. She had been chief of
the Nuclear Medicine Service, as the Radioisotope Unit was
now called, since 1970. In 1968 she too had become affiliated with the Mt. Sinai School of Medicine as research professor. Six years later her title was changed to that of distinguished research professor.

In spite of the great loss of Dr. Berson, Rosalyn
Yalow never faltered in her continuing research. The year
of Berson's death she became the first woman and the first
nonphysician to be appointed senior medical investigator at
the VA Hospital. Before, she had received many honors
with Dr. Berson; now she received them alone. As her reputation spread, she was elected to the National Academy of
Sciences. Next to the Nobel Prize, this is considered the
greatest honor that can be given to any American scientist.
Between 1974 and 1977 she received five honorary doctorates.

She was, of course, wearing many hats. Outside the
lab she served as advisor to important medical committees
and as a member of the editorial boards of important journals.
She was also an incisive lecturer, much in demand.

In 1976 she became the first woman to win the prestigious Albert Lasker Award for basic medical research.   To
help with a hospital party in honor of that occasion Dr. Yalow
brought roast turkeys from home and stood in the middle of
a meeting peeling potatoes and making potato salad while fellows reported to her.

The RIA test, the Nobel citation noted, "was accomplished by a spectacular combination of immunology, isotope
research, mathematics, and physics." By 1977 it was used
to measure the concentrations, not only of hormones, but of
hundreds of vitamins, viruses, enzymes, drugs, and other
substances to help determine changes between normal and
diseased states. Thanks to this sensitive measure, doctors
could now diagnose conditions that previously escaped detection because established methods had been too crude to measure the minute changes in the amount of hormones that dras-
tically affect a person's health.

Hundreds of blood banks used the test to remove blood
contaminated with a hepatitis virus from use in transfusion.
The test also detected human growth hormones. Because it
had been used in cancer research to detect the life history
in a mouse of a leukemia-causing virus long before a tumor
was evident, Dr. Yalow predicted in 1977 that "in the decades
to come the impact of radioimmunoassays on other fields as
varied as toxology, virology, and cancer detection will equal,
if not exceed, its effect on endocrinology."

In the next seven years after she won the Nobel Prize,
Rosalyn Yalow was given 22 special awards and 34 honorary
doctorates from American universities and colleges and from
universities in Argentina, Canada, Belgium, and France. It
was an astonishing record. She continued to publish important
papers and served on editorial boards and in consultant capacities. After leaving the Mt. Sinai School of Medicine, she was
distinguished professor-at-large at the Albert Einstein College
of Medicine, Yeshiva University, New York, for the year
1980. The next year she acted as chairperson of the Department of Clinical Sciences, Montefiore Medical Center in the
Bronx. All this while she continued as senior medical investigator at the VA and director of the Sol Berson Research
Laboratory at the VA Hospital.

In 1982, Rosalyn Yalow declared that a Nobel Prize
was both an honor and a responsibility. Because of the in-

creased visibility, a laureate could inform or misinform.
She felt deeply her responsibility to inform the public on topics
in which she could claim expertise. One of the issues she
spoke and wrote on frequently was "whether political and regu-
latory decisions concerning risk, particularly potential risk
associated with low-level radiation, should be based on public
perception or on science." She always argued for science.

Another issue she kept pushing was the role of women
in science. Often she observed that among the scientists,
scholars, and leaders of the world, women were not represented in reasonable proportion to their numbers in the community. Women had not achieved to an extent consistent with
their abilities largely because of "professional and social discrimination." But looking to a happier future, Rosalyn Yalow
was careful to point out that "negative population growth, particularly among our gifted, does not serve the common good.
Greater effort must be made by society to assume quality
care for the children of mothers having aspirations other than
remaining in the home while their children are in their developmental years."

Shortly before she went to Stockholm, Rosalyn Yalow
had addressed another responsibility:

> We cannot expect that in the foreseeable future
> women will achieve status in academic medicine
> in proportion to their numbers. But if we are to
> start working towards that goal we must believe
> in ourselves or no one else will believe in us; we
> must match our aspirations with the guts and
> determination to succeed; and for those of us who
> have had the good fortune to move upward, we must
> feel a personal responsibility to serve as role
> models and advisors to ease the path for those
> who come afterwards. We should not ask for
> reverse discrimination, but simply for equality of
> opportunity--so that those of us who wish can
> reach for the stars.

A Modern Mendel

BARBARA McCLINTOCK

Barbara McClintock did not have a telephone in her apartment. Her radio first brought her the news that she had been awarded the 1982 Nobel Prize for Medicine or Physiology for her discovery of mobile genetic elements. The bespectacled, crop-haired scientist, barely five feet tall, murmured, "Oh, dear." Then she set off for her morning walk through the woods near Cold Spring Harbor Laboratory on Long Island. Along the path she gathered walnuts to be used in baking cookies. Later, still in her customary attire of dungarees, man-tailored shirt, and oxfords, she told reporters, "The prize is such an extraordinary honor. It might seem unfair, however, to reward a person for having so much pleasure over the years, asking the maize plant to solve specific problems and then watching its responses."

At 81, Barbara McClintock was the third woman to be awarded an individual rather than a shared Prize in scientific categories. So she entered the company of Marie Curie and Dorothy Crowfoot Hodgkin, both winners in Chemistry. She was the first to win unshared honors in Medicine or Physiology. Her pioneering work in the mechanism of genetic inheritance, cited by the Caroline Institute, had been published, however, more than 30 years before.

Barbara McClintock's notion that genes could jump around on chromosomes was long ignored by orthodox scientists. In 1953 the discovery of the double helix structure of deoxyribonucleic acid (DNA), the molecular basis of heredity, gave some support to her theory. Then in the 1960s further advances in molecular and microbial genetics proved her right. Her discovery of transposable genetic elements in the maize plant is considered to be at the very root of current research in genetic engineering.

The Nobel Committee of the Caroline Institute mentioned

Barbara McClintock

the resemblance of her work and habits to those of Gregor
Mendel, the Austrian monk who discovered the rules of inheritance in the 1860s. Working in solitude, he performed controlled experiments in his pea patch and postulated that inherited characteristics are carried by tiny particles now called
genes. His theories, however, were not appreciated until
almost 40 years later.

Like Mendel, Barbara McClintock has preferred to work
in solitude and like him, she did not win immediate recognition for her most brilliant research. In her private life, too,
she has been a loner. As she has explained, she was never
closely associated with family members and never felt a strong
necessity for a personal attachment of any kind.

It was a pattern shaped in her early years. She was born
on June 16, 1902, in Hartford, Connecticut, the third child of
Thomas Henry McClintock, a homeopathic physician and his
wife, Sarah Handy McClintock.

Motherhood put considerable pressure on Mrs. McClintock, who had a somewhat tense relationship with her youngest
daughter. The other two girls, Marjorie and Mignon, were
more submissive than independent Barb. After Malcolm (Tom),
the only son, was born in 1904, the strain between Barb and
her mother increased. From time to time, until she was of
school age, the little girl was sent to live with her paternal
aunt and uncle in New York.

When Barbara finally came home again, she still refused to let her mother hug her. A special and different
child who craved solitude, she was an avid reader. Sometimes
though she played baseball and football and climbed trees with
boys in the neighborhood. But, very bright and full of intellectual curiosity, she preferred to sit alone "thinking about
things."

In 1908 the family moved to the semirural Flatbush
section of Brooklyn and the children attended the local elementary school. To Dr. McClintock and his wife school did not
seem too important, and he told the principal that his children
were not to be given homework and would not be forced to attend classes if they did not want to. Once Barb missed a
whole semester.

Like her father, she delighted in machines and tools
and quickly acquired mechanical skills. By the time she en-

rolled in Erasmus High School, the family was spending summers at the far end of Long Island. Running on the beach,
she discovered a special "flying or floating" technique that
she later learned was used by the "running lamas" of Tibet.
As she told Evelyn Fox Keller 70 years later: "You stood
quite straight, and your back felt completely straight and you
practically floated. Each step was rhythmically floating,
without any sense of fatigue and with a great sense of eu-
phoria."

During World War I, Dr. McClintock went overseas as
a military surgeon, and left his wife in sole charge of the
household. Afraid that too much education would keep her
daughters from marriage, Mrs. McClintock discouraged them
from attending college. After brief acting experiences in the
theater, Marjorie and Mignon dutifully became brides.

Barbara, however, had become excited about physics
and chemistry in high school and dreamed of going to college.
After graduation she worked in an employment agency, spending evenings and weekends at the library. Impressed by her
single-mindedness, her parents finally gave her permission
to attend college, and she enrolled as a biology major in the
College of Agriculture at Cornell University in Ithaca, New
York. Since plant breeding, the major she wanted, was not
available to women, she chose botany.

She was elected freshman class president and was socially active in her first two years. She was known for her
dry wit. Though some of her dates resulted in emotional at-
tachments, she realized that they could not last and decided
that marriage was not one of her life's requirements. Some
years later she told a colleague that she had met only two
men, both geneticists, worth having as husband, but that
neither was available. In her senior year and during some
of her graduate work she played banjo with a jazz group.

But her laboratory work had become paramount. By
her junior year she was taking graduate courses in genetics.
The young woman who received a B.S. degree in 1923 then
registered as a graduate student in the botany department
with a major in cytology (in chromosome work) and minors
in genetics and zoology. She followed her M.S. (1925) with
a Ph.D. (1927). She had already acquired a reputation for
intuitive brilliance and painstaking methodology. Meanwhile
she had served as a graduate assistant in the botany department from 1924 to 1927. On completion of graduate studies,
she was appointed instructor.

The decade of the 1920s were particularly stimulating times at the College of Agriculture. Faculty members like Rollins Emerson were breeding maize or Indian corn (<u>Zea</u> <u>mays</u>) with its variegated kernels and doing research on the inheritance of variegation.

Studies of cell structure and division now supported Mendel's theories. Genes, which are responsible for all inherited traits, are located on chromosomes, threadlike structures found in the nucleus of each cell of an organism. Genes are not visible and their properties and location must be determined by indirect methods. Chromosomes can be seen through the microscope as rod-shaped structures when the cell is ready to divide, a process called mitosis. Before division begins, chromosomes are duplicated. During mitosis, each chromosome, that now has two identical strands (chromatids), begins an elaborate process. New cells that are formed receive one strand from each pair and have a set of characteristics exactly like that of the original cell. With the exception of the sex chromosomes, chromosomes in each pair are similar, but quite different from those of other pairs. Thus each member of a pair will possess identical genes at corresponding sites, called loci. The genes are responsible for individual characteristics. Chromosomes are not of the same length, and when stained appropriately, may show characteristic bands, shortening, or constrictions.

In the formation of gametes or reproductive cells a somewhat different process, meiosis, occurs. First each chromosome duplicates, as in mitosis. Then the first meiotic division separates whole (duplicated) chromosomes and thus produces an equal division of the gene pairs that occupy the specific sites or loci on the chromosomes. Two cells are produced, each containing half the original number of chromosomes. Such a division is followed by a second division, this time similar to mitosis. The two chromatids of each duplicated chromosome now separate. The result is four cells, each with half the number of chromosomes (called chromatids until they duplicate). Genes located on one chromosome usually but not always stay together on the same chromosome. They are said to be linked. But the linked combinations can be separated by breaking and rejoining the chromosome, a process known as "crossing-over."

Meiosis, which produces the gametes or sex cells, takes place in the anthers and ovaries of the higher plants. It results in the formation of cells having half the normal

number of chromosomes. These cells, located in flowers of
higher plants, divide again several times to produce male and
female "plants" (gametophytes). The pollen grain is the male
gametophyte. In the corn plant, when a pollen grain from
the tassel lands on the threads of corn silk hanging out of the
young ears, it sends out a tiny pollen tube that quickly goes
down the silk to an egg cell of the female gametophyte located
in the young kernel. A male cell from the pollen grain fer-
tilizes the egg cell. As the fertilized egg cell grows, the
whole kernel becomes a seed, enclosed in a tiny fruit.

The various colors of Indian corn kernels are dictated
by genes on the chromosomes. Barbara McClintock decided
to make the genetics of variegation her life project. Corn
was planted in the spring, and the budding kernels were fertilized according to a plan of genetic crosses. Summer was
the time for watching the growth. Winter meant analysis in
the laboratory of the results.

She placed pollen grains from the tassel under her
microscope, making various modifications in the aceto-carmine
smear method developed by John Billings so that she could observe individual maize chromosomes through replication and
division. In her first year of graduate school she had discovered how to identify individual maize chromosomes by
their distinctive morphological (structural) features. Because
of this breakthrough, chromosomal analysis could henceforth
be integrated with plant-breeding experiments. She was well
on her way to a distinguished career in cytogenetics, the
branch of biology that deals with the study of heredity and
variation by the methods of genetics and cytology (the study
of cells).

Now she began working with two fellow graduate students, Marcus M. Rhoades and George Beadle, who would
become famous corn geneticists. The trio pursued the study
of the morphology of maize chromosomes and the correlation
between visible genetic traits and the recently discovered cytological markers. In 1929 her brilliant research revealed
that all ten chromosomes of maize could be identified micro-
scopically. (Visible markers on each were identified.) So
she provided corn geneticists and cytologists with a way to
correlate chromosome structure with the development and
subsequent appearance of the corn kernels.

From 1929 to 1931 she published nine papers. In the
latter year with a young colleague, Harriet Creighton, she

wrote "A Correlation of Cytological and Genetical Crossing-Over in Zea mays," published at the recommendation of the famous geneticist, Thomas Hunt Morgan, in Proceedings of the National Academy of Sciences. Their experiment proved the widely held assumption that chromosomes exchange genetic information and physical material when they cross over early in meiosis. The crossovers correspond to the breaking off and mutual exchange of broken chromosomal segments during one stage of the first meiotic division. This paper has been described as a cornerstone of modern genetics.

That same year Barbara McClintock was awarded a fellowship by the National Research Council, spending two years at the California Institute of Technology, in Pasadena, California. First, however, she went to the University of Missouri in Columbia, where X rays were being used to induce genetic mutations that facilitated the investigation of genetic structure. X-ray-irradiated pollen grains show marked changes in chromosome arrangement.

Next came a year as a Guggenheim Fellow at the University of Freiburg. The German experience was not happy. Barbara later described herself as "disturbed and utterly panicked" by the rise of Nazism, and she returned to the department of plant breeding at Cornell. Again she met with sex prejudice. No faculty appointment was then available to a woman. Some 30 years later Cornell did appoint her Andrew D. White Professor-at-Large. In 1935 she and Rhoades published an important paper, "The Cytogenetics of Maize," hailed as the highest point attained up to that time of identifying cytological markers.

Two years later she was established as an assistant professor in the botany department at the University of Missouri. During the Missouri years, Barbara McClintock published a series of papers explaining how broken chromosomes reanneal. The teaching experience, however, was not pleasant. In spite of her brilliant research, the university authorities considered her too independent and too much of a maverick. She disliked formal classes and committee work. Once when she had forgotten her office keys, she climbed up an outside wall and crawled through a window. A hidden photographer caught her act, confirming university suspicions of her idiosyncrasies. At Missouri, women occasionally won promotion, but academic advancement was not available to a maverick. Barbara requested a leave of absence without pay and promptly left.

She spent the summer of 1941 at the Cold Spring Harbor Laboratory on Long Island, working with her friend Marcus Rhoades. Toward the end of the year the Carnegie Institution of Washington, D. C. offered her a position in its Cold Spring Harbor genetics laboratory. Here she has remained, currently as a Distinguished Service Member. "If I had been at some other place," she said later, "I'm sure that I would have been fired for what I was doing because nobody was accepting it."

But in recognition of her earlier work Barbara McClintock became the third woman ever elected to the National Academy of Sciences. As she wrote a fellow geneticist: "... I was stunned. Jews, women, and Negroes are accustomed to discrimination and don't expect much, I am not a feminist, but I am always gratified when illogical barriers are broken.... It helps all of us." With news of her nomination, the University of Missouri tried to woo her back, but she refused any offer. Having served as vice-president of the Genetics Society in America in 1939, she became its president in 1945. The summer after her election to the academy and a productive visit to Stanford University near Palo Alto, California, Barbara returned to the cornfields on Long Island.

Having found patches of color in the leaves of a bunch of experimental Indian corn seedlings--unlike anything she had seen before--she watched their growth with interest. As early as 1941 she had described changes at specific sites in the size and form of chromosomes. In another moment of great intuitive insight she saw regularity in these patches and speculated that something was regulating the rates of mutation. Comparing the variant specimens with their parent plants, Barbara believed that she was observing something called "transposition." In this process, genetic material that she called "controlling elements" was moving from one place on a chromosome to another, making the color of kernels of one generation different from that of the preceding one.

In 1951, at a Cold Spring Harbor symposium, she presented her work, the result of painstaking recordkeeping and microscopic analysis. She was the first to recognize that there are two types of genes--structural genes and other genes that regulate their activity, "controlling elements" in her nomenclature. They regulate by inducing instability at particular sites (or loci) on the chromosome. One "controlling element," called the Dissociator (Ds) gene, is found at

the site of a broken chromosome. (The broken chromosome
piece may be reinserted at a different place on the chromosome.) Even when Ds is present, there will be no breakage
unless another controlling element (Ac or Activator) is present at another particular location on the chromosome. In
other words, Ac "tells" Ds to break at a certain place. Ac
also directs Ds to move to another place or to "jump." To
make the situation yet more complex, another gene, the
Structural gene (SG) becomes active and causes the developing
corn cells to make (or not to make) the colored pigment.
Depending on the instruction from Ac, Ds moves to or away
from SG, and either allows or suppresses the pigment manu-
facture. In general, the structural genes remain at their
original sites. The ultimate result of this jumping around
of the controlling or transposable elements is a variegated
bunch of kernels on an ear of Indian corn. Several jumps
will cause a speckled kernel.

"Chromosome Organization and Genetic Expression,"
the revolutionary paper Barbara McClintock presented, was
met by general disbelief if not incomprehension and bewilder-
ment. The same fate befell her further elaboration of her
findings in 1956. As the Nobel Committee later pointed out,
in 1951 possibly five geneticists in the world understood her.
She was considered heretical. Genes were believed to be
fixed on the chromosome like so many beads on a string.

Because of the frigid reception, Barbara McClintock
did not seek wide publication of her results. She was content to see her elaborations in the annual reports of Cold
Spring Harbor Laboratory symposia. Meanwhile she maintained a full laboratory schedule, but did take time off from
1958 to 1960 to train some Latin-American cytologists.

For more than a decade stony silence met her theory
of transposable elements. The self-reliant Barbara McClintock was not interested in doing battle to win acceptance and
understanding. She was convinced that eventually they would
come. "If you know you're right," she once said, "you don't
care. You know that sooner or later it will come out in the
wash." After Watson and Crick discovered the structure of
DNA and a whole new age of molecular biology began, tran-
position was rediscovered, and Barbara McClintock's findings
were no longer ignored.

In her book about the reclusive scientist and her work,
Evelyn Fox Keller has argued that Barbara's unconventional
style of scientific thinking and unconventional methods of re-

search may help to explain why her greatest piece of research
was so long unrecognized. She did not follow logical and se-
quential thinking. Rather she worked with intuitive insight
and grasp. Keller calls the McClintock style "a feeling for
the organism." Barbara McClintock herself once said, "When
I was working with the chromosomes, I wasn't outside. I
was down there. I was part of the system."

Her own intuitive style and approach to science, and
a great reverence for nature, had long made her receptive
to Eastern practices. The Tibetan monks with their effort-
less running and their regulation of body temperature had
interested her particularly, and she had developed certain
techniques of mind control. Long before biofeedback became
popular, Barbara McClintock was experimenting with ways
to control her temperature and blood flow. Beyond Keller's
opinion, some colleagues have further suggested that Barbara
McClintock was not gifted at explaining her ideas through
writing.

The great breadth of her interests prevented any bitterness toward geneticists who for years opposed her "jumping genes" theory. Finally in the mid-1970s, when these
genes began to be discovered in bacteria, yeast, other plants,
and the fruit fly Drosophila, she was hailed as a scientific
prophet. Her work was seen to present insights into several
biological mysteries--not only the question of how whole or-
ganisms develop from single cells but how entirely new species can arise. Many scientists believe that the mobility of
genes may be the key to unlock the inner workings of everything from viral cancer to African sleeping sickness. It
may even explain how bacteria become immune to antibiotics.

Suddenly honors and praise poured over Barbara
McClintock. In one year, 1979, she received eight awards,
including a $60,000-a-year, tax-free lifetime grant from
Chicago's MacArthur Foundation and the prestigious Lasker
prize for basic research, worth $15,000. "I'm not a person
who likes to accumulate things," she protested. Still she
bought a new car and moved into a larger apartment.

In 1982 the Nobel Prize Committee hailed her once
obscure work as "one of the two great discoveries of our
time in genetics," the other being Crick and Watson's discovery of the double-helix structure of DNA. Watson, director of the Cold Spring Harbor Laboratory, gave a succinct
summing up: "[Barbara McClintock] is a very remarkable

person, fiercely independent, beholden to no one. Her work
is of fundamental importance. " Far earlier her friend Marcus
Rhoades had remarked, "I've known a lot of famous scientists.
But the only one I thought really was a genius was McClintock.
By God, she's good. There is no question about that. "

TIME LINES 1833-1984

1833 Alfred Nobel born (also Johannes Brahms, Gen. Charles G. Gordon, Edwin Booth)

1839-42 Opium War between Britain and China

1842 Nobel family moves to St. Petersburg

1843 Bertha, Countess Kinsky (Baroness von Suttner) born (also Edvard Grieg)

1844 Samuel Morse invents telegraph

1848 The Communist Manifesto; revolutions in France, Germany, Austria, Italy; Second Republic established in France

1851 Coup d'état of Louis Napoleon (Napoleon III) in France

1852 Napoleon III founds Second Empire

1854 Commodore Perry opens up Japan

1854-55 Crimean War

1858 Selma Lagerlöf born (also Beatrice Webb, Giacomo Puccini); Blessed Virgin appears to Bernadette Soubirous at Lourdes; transfer of India to Crown from East India Company

1859 Charles Darwin completes Origin of Species; Austria forced to give up leadership in Italian political affairs

1860 Jane Addams born (also Gustav Mahler, Ignace Paderewski, Hugo Wolf)

1861 Selma Lagerlöf suffers lameness

1861-65 American Civil War

1863 Poles revolt but are beaten back by Russians

1864 Alfred Nobel's young brother Emil killed in plant explosion; Prussia goes to war with Denmark over Schleswig-Holstein

1866 Seven Weeks' War; Gregor Mendel publishes explanation of laws of heredity

1867 Alfred Nobel patents dynamite; Marie Skłodowska (Curie) born (also Arturo Toscanini, Luigi Pirandello); Austria-Hungary Dual Monarchy created; Karl Marx completes first volume of Das Kapital; Maximilian executed in Mexico; Emily Greene Balch born

1869 Suez Canal opens; Dmitri Mendeleev develops periodic table of the elements

1870 Unification of Italy completed

1870-71 Franco-Prussian War; end of Second Empire in France and establishment of the Third Republic

1871 Grazia Deledda (Madesani) born (also Alexander Scriabin); Second German Reich established under rule of Hohenzollerns; Stanley locates Livingstone in Africa

1873 Herbert Spencer completes Study of Sociology

1874 Heinrich Schliemann excavates Mycenae and opens new science of archeology

1876 Countess Kinsky (Bertha von Suttner) briefly becomes Nobel's secretary-household manager; she marries Artur von Suttner, and couple leaves for Caucasus; Thomas Edison invents phonograph; Alexander Graham Bell invents telephone; Alfred Nobel begins 18-year liaison with Sophie Hesse

1877 Russo-Turkish War

1879 Henrik Ibsen's A Doll's House; Thomas Edison invents incandescent light

1882 Sigrid Undset born; Triple Alliance formed; British occupy Egypt

1885 Bertha and Artur von Suttner return to Austria from Caucasus

1886 Suttners meet Alfred Nobel in Paris

1889 Lucila Godoy y Alcayaga (Gabriela Mistral) born (also Charles Chaplin, Jean Cocteau, Adolf Hitler); Jane Addams founds Hull-House; Bertha von Suttner's Die Waffen Nieder; Austrian Crown Prince Rudolf commits suicide at Mayerling

1891 Nelly Sachs born; Selma Lagerlöf's Gösta Berlings Saga (also Thomas Hardy's Tess of the D'Urbervilles); Bertha von Suttner founds Austrian Peace Society; Marie Curie arrives in Paris

1892 Pearl Sydenstricker (Buck) born in the United States and taken to China at three months of age; Jane Addams and Emily Balch meet; Bertha von Suttner founds Die Waffen Nieder, peace journal, and meets Nobel in Zürich; Grazia Deledda's Fior di Sardegne

1894 Alfred Dreyfus deported to Devil's Island; war between China and Japan

1895 Marie Skłodowska marries Pierre Curie; Wilhelm Röntgen discovers X rays

1896 Alfred Nobel dies and leaves will providing for Nobel Prizes; Gerty Radnitz (Cori) born

1897 Irène Curie (Joliot-Curie) born; J. J. Thomson discovers electron

1898 Marie and Pierre Curie discover radium and polonium; King Umberto of Italy assassinated; Emile Zola writes J'Accuse letter over Dreyfus Affair; British take over Sudan; United States and Spain go to war over Cuba

1899 Bertha von Suttner attends Hague Peace Conference; Grazia Deledda marries Palmiro Madesani

1899-1902 Boer War

1900 Boxer Rebellion against Westerners in China; Grazia Deledda gives birth to first son, Sardus; Max Planck advances quantum theory; Sigmund Freud founds psychoanalysis

1901 First Nobel ceremonies in Stockholm and Kristiania

1902 Alva Reimer (Myrdal) and Barbara McClintock born;
Marie Curie isolates decigram of radium; Artur von Suttner
dies; Selma Lagerlöf's Jerusalem

1903 Marie Curie takes doctorate; she and Pierre share
Nobel Prize in Physics with Henri Becquerel; Wright
brothers fly first airplane; Entente Cordiale established;
Ernest Rutherford and Frederick Soddy set forth theory of
radioactivity; Grazia Deledda's Elias Portolu

1904 Grazia Deledda gives birth to second son, Franz;
Marie Curie gives birth to second daughter, Eve

1904-05 Russo-Japanese War

1905 Bertha von Suttner wins Nobel Prize in Peace and pays
first visit to America; Pierre Curie gives Nobel lecture;
Sweden's union with Norway dissolved; Einstein formulates
theory of relativity; unsuccessful revolution breaks out in
Russia; Emily Balch spends study year in Austria-Hungary

1906 Maria Göppert (Mayer) born; Pierre Curie killed by
dray; San Francisco earthquake and fire; Selma Lagerlöf's
Nils Holgerssons Underbara Resa gennom Sverige

1907 Norwegian women given suffrage

1908 Nelly Sachs meets "der toten Bräutigam"

1909 Selma Lagerlöf wins Nobel Prize in Literature; Gabriela Mistral's former fiancé, Romelio Ureta, commits suicide

1910 Dorothy Crowfoot (Hodgkin) and Agnes Gouxha Bojaxhiu
(Mother Teresa) born; Pearl Buck comes to United States
to attend college; Jane Addams' Twenty Years at Hull-
House; reappearance of Halley's comet; Emily Greene
Balch's Our Slavic Fellow Citizens

1911 Marie Curie wins Nobel Prize in Chemistry; Ernest
Rutherford makes nuclear model of atom; Sir Arthur Evans
completes excavation at Knossos site; Roald Amundsen
reaches South Pole in race with Robert Scott; Sigrid Undset's Jenny

1912 Sigrid Undset marries Anders Svarstad; Bertha von

Suttner makes lecture tour of United States; Max von Laue diffracts X rays within crystal; William Henry Bragg and William Lawrence Bragg begin work in crystallography; Republic of China established with Sun Yat-sen as president; Titanic sinks

1912-1913   Balkan Wars

1913   Sigrid Undset Svarstad gives birth to first son, Anders; Peace Palace dedicated at The Hague; Frederick Soddy develops theory of isotopic radioactive elements

1914   Radium Institute in Paris dedicated; Lucila Godoy y Alcayaga wins Poetic Games and takes name Gabriela Mistral; Gerty Radnitz (Cori) enters medical school; Dorothy Crowfoot (Hodgkin) is transplanted from Egypt to England; Pearl Sydenstricker (Buck) returns to China; Bertha von Suttner dies; Archduke Franz Ferdinand assassinated at Sarajevo; suffragettes riot in England

1914-18   World War I; Marie and Irène Curie do radiological work at front; Carl Cori serves on Italian front

1915   Jane Addams and Emily G. Balch attend Women's Peace Conference at The Hague and visit European capitals with plan of continuous mediation; Sigrid Undset gives birth to daughter, Maren Charlotte, who later is found to be retarded; Lusitania sunk

1917   Pearl Sydenstricker marries John Lossing Buck; United States enters war; Bolsheviks seize power in Russia; Jane Addams reviled for pacifist stand

1918   Poland proclaims itself independent republic; Poland and Germany grant women suffrage

1918-33   Weimar Republic in Germany

1919   Women's International League for Peace and Freedom organized in Zürich with Jane Addams as president and Emily Greene Balch as secretary-treasurer; Treaty of Versailles; Sigrid Undset gives birth to second son, Hans; Emily G. Balch's Wellesley professorship is not renewed because of her pacifism and politics; Austria gives women the vote

1920   Grazia Deledda's La Madre (also F. Scott Fitzgerald's

This Side of Paradise; Sinclair Lewis's Main Street; Edith
Wharton's Age of Innocence; H. G. Wells's Outline of
History); Gerty Radnitz receives medical degree and marries Carl Cori; American women granted suffrage; League
of Nations established

1920-22 Sigrid Undset's Kristin Lavransdatter

1921 Pearl Buck gives birth to daughter, Carol, and later
learns child is retarded; Dorothy Crowfoot (Hodgkin) enters
Sir John Leman School; woman suffrage adopted in Sweden;
Marie Curie makes triumphal tour of United States to receive gram of radium; Rosalyn Sussman (Yalow) born

1922 Gabriela Mistral's Desolación (also James Joyce's Ulys-
ses; Hermann Hesse's Siddhartha; T. S. Eliot's The Waste
Land); Carl and Gerty Cori emigrate to the United States
to begin research in Buffalo; Gabriela Mistral goes to Mexico to help reform educational system; Benito Mussolini
and Fascists march on Rome; Jane Addams's Peace and
Bread in Time of War

1923 Dorothy Crowfoot (Hodgkin) visits the Sudan

1924 Gabriela Mistral's Ternura (also E. M. Forster's A
Passage to India; Thomas Mann's The Magic Mountain);
Sigrid Undset enters Catholic church, Undset-Svarstad
marriage is annulled; Alva Reimer marries Gunnar Myrdal

1925 Sigrid Undset's Olav Audunsson i Hestviken; Irène
Curie takes doctorate

1926 Irène Curie marries Frédéric Joliot and couple takes
name of Joliot-Curie; Emily G. Balch goes on mission to
Haiti; Gabriela Mistral appointed Chilean delegate to League
of Nations committee; new constitution in Chile restores
presidential power

1927 Grazia Deledda receives Nobel Prize in Literature for
1926; Sigrid Undset's Olav Audunsson og Hans Børn; Irène
Joliot-Curie gives birth to daughter, Hélène; Sacco and
Vanzetti executed; Charles Lindbergh flies solo and nonstop
to Paris; Pearl Buck and family flee from Communists
advancing on Nanking; Alva Myrdal gives birth to son, Jan;
Barbara McClintock takes doctorate

1927-28 Selma Lagerlöf's Löwensköldska Ringen

1928 Sigrid Undset is awarded Nobel Prize in Literature;
Kellogg-Briand Pact is signed; Dorothy Crowfoot (Hodgkin)
visits parents in Palestine and enters Somerville College,
Oxford; Britain grants complete suffrage to women; Chiang
Kai-shek unifies China; Agnes Bojaxhiu (Mother Teresa)
leaves for Dublin

1929 Maria Göppert marries Joseph Mayer and takes doctorate; couple leave for United States; Great Depression
begins; Alva and Gunnar Myrdal go to United States as Rockefeller Fellows

1931 Jane Addams shares Nobel Prize in Peace with Nicholas Murray Butler; Gerty and Carl Cori receive appointments at Washington U. Medical School, St. Louis; Pearl
Buck's The Good Earth; Agnes Bojaxhiu takes name Sister
Teresa, teaches in Calcutta

1932 Gabriela Mistral begins consular duties; Irène Joliot-
Curie gives birth to son, Pierre; Dorothy Crowfoot (Hodgkin) goes to Cambridge to study with J. D. Bernal; James
Chadwick discovers neutron; Carl Anderson discovers positron

1933 Joliot-Curies produce artificial isotopes; Maria G.
Mayer gives birth to daughter, Marianne; Adolf Hitler
becomes chancellor of Germany; Barbara McClintock
goes to Germany as Guggenheim Fellow

1934 Marie Curie dies; Alva Myrdal gives birth to daughter,
Sissela

1935 Irène and Frédéric Joliot-Curie are awarded Nobel
Prize in Chemistry; Jane Addams dies; Pearl Buck is di-
vorced and marries Richard Walsh; German Jews outlawed;
Italy seizes Ethiopia

1936 Grazia Deledda dies; Gerty and Carl Cori isolate glu-
cose-6-phosphate (Cori-ester); Gerty Cori gives birth to
son, Thomas, Alva Myrdal to daughter, Kai; Pearl Buck's
The Exile and Fighting Angel

1937 Dorothy Crowfoot takes doctorate and marries Thomas
Hodgkin

1938 Dorothy Crowfoot Hodgkin gives birth to first son,
Luke; Pearl Buck is awarded Nobel Prize in Literature;

Gabriela Mistral's <u>Tala</u>; Hitler makes Austria part of
Germany; Maria Goeppert-Mayer gives birth to son, Peter;
Irène Joliot-Curie and colleagues perform experiment that
leads Hahn and Strassman to conceive idea of nuclear fission

1939 Fascists complete overthrow of Spanish Republic

1939-45 World War II; Sweden remains neutral; Poland par-
titioned for fourth time

1940 Nazi invasion of Norway and Denmark; Nazi invasion
of Belgium, Netherlands, Luxembourg; Selma Lagerlöf
dies; Nelly Sachs flees to Sweden; Sigrid Undset flees to
Sweden and then to the United States

1940-44 Germany occupies France; Frédéric Joliot-Curie is
leader in resistance movement

1941 Dorothy Crowfoot Hodgkin gives birth to daughter,
Elizabeth; Barbara McClintock begins association with Cold
Spring Harbor Laboratory

1942 Enrico Fermi and associates obtain first nuclear chain
reaction; Gabriela Mistral's close friends, the Stefan
Zweigs, commit suicide; Maria Goeppert-Mayer joins SAM
(atomic bomb project); Dorothy Crowfoot Hodgkin begins
work on penicillin

1943 Rosalyn Sussman marries Aaron Yalow; Gerty and Carl
Cori achieve test-tube synthesis of glycogen; Juan Miguel
Godoy, Gabriela Mistral's nephew and adopted son, com-
mits suicide; Betty Smyth (Williams) born

1944 Mairead Corrigan born; allies land in Normandy and
later halt German offensive

1945 Sigrid Undset returns to Norway; Gabriela Mistral is
awarded Nobel Prize in Literature; atom bombs dropped
on Hiroshima and Nagasaki; United Nations chartered;
Rosalyn Yalow receives doctorate

1946 Emily G. Balch shares Nobel Prize for Peace with
John R. Mott; Dorothy Crowfoot Hodgkin gives birth to
son, Tobias; French women achieve the vote; Sister Teresa receives call to serve the poor; first electric computer developed; UNESCO established; Cold War begins

1947 Gerty and Carl Cori share Nobel Prize in Physiology
or Medicine with Bernardo Houssay; British withdraw from
India; two nations, India and Pakistan formed

1948 State of Israel founded

1949 Sigrid Undset dies; Nelly Sachs's Sternverdunkelung
(also George Orwell's 1984); Chinese Communists take
control of mainland; Alva Myrdal named to United Nations
post

1950-53 Korean War

1950 Frédéric Joliot-Curie dismissed as head of French
Atomic Energy Commission because of political beliefs;
Rosalyn Yalow begins working with Dr. Solomon Berson;
Missionaries of Charity instituted; Sister Teresa becomes
Mother Teresa

1951 Irène Joliot-Curie dismissed from French Atomic Energy Commission; Barbara McClintock presents paper on
"jumping genes"; Alva Myrdal to UNESCO

1952 Rosalyn Yalow gives birth to son, Benjamin; Mother
Teresa founds Nirmal Hriday

1954 Gabriela Mistral's Lagar; Rosalyn Yalow gives birth
to daughter, Elanna

1955 Irène Joliot-Curie draws up plans for Orsay Labora-
tories; Maria Goeppert-Mayer and J. Hans D. Jensen's
Elementary Theory of Nuclear Shell Structure; Alva
Myrdal becomes Swedish ambassador to India

1956 Irène Joliot-Curie dies; Suez crisis

1957 Gabriela Mistral dies; Gerty Cori dies; Sputnik launched;
Nelly Sachs's Und Niemand weiss weiter; Common Market
formed; Vietnam War widens; Mother Teresa begins work
with lepers

1959 Nelly Sachs's Flucht und Verwandlung; Rosalyn Yalow
and Solomon Berson develop first radioimmunoassay

1960 Dorothy Crowfoot Hodgkin becomes Wolfson research
professor; Nelly Sachs returns to Germany for visit after
20 years in Stockholm; Richard Walsh dies; Mayers go to

University of California, San Diego; modern feminist movement begins to produce changes

1961   Betty Smyth marries Ralph Williams; Emily Balch dies

1962   Alva Myrdal appointed chief of Swedish delegation to
United Nations Conference on Disarmament

1962-65   Dorothy Crowfoot Hodgkin spends time in Ghana

1962-66   Nelly Sachs's Glühende Rätsel

1963   Maria Goeppert-Mayer shares Nobel Prize in Physics
with J. Hans D. Jensen and Eugene Wigner; President
John F. Kennedy assassinated; Betty Williams has son,
Paul; Mother Teresa founds Missionary Brothers of
Charity

1964   Dorothy Crowfoot Hodgkin wins Nobel Prize in Chemistry

1965   Dorothy Crowfoot Hodgkin awarded British Order of
Merit

1966   Nelly Sachs shares Nobel Prize in Literature with
Shmuel Agnon; Alva Myrdal becomes Swedish minister
of disarmament

1967   Arab-Israeli War

1968   Catholics march for civil rights in Northern Ireland

1969   United States landing on the moon; American involvement in Vietnam at its height; civil war begins in Northern
Ireland; International Association of Co-Workers of Mother
Teresa founded; Dorothy Crowfoot Hodgkin determines
structure of insulin

1970   Nelly Sachs dies; Rosalyn Yalow becomes chief of nuclear medicine at VA Hospital; Betty Williams gives birth
to daughter, Deborah; Mother Teresa begins opening centers abroad

1972   Maria Goeppert-Mayer dies; Dr. Solomon Berson dies;
British institute direct rule in Northern Ireland; Mairead
Corrigan goes to Bangkok

1973   Pearl Buck dies; Mairead Corrigan travels to Soviet
       Union to make film

1975   Dorothy Crowfoot Hodgkin is only Lady Laureate to at-
       tend seventy-fifth anniversary Nobel celebration; Vietnam
       War ends

1976   Maguire children are killed: Mairead Corrigan, Betty
       Williams, and Ciaran McKeown organize peace marches
       and rallies in Belfast, Londonderry, London, and in Eire
       on the banks of the Boyne; Betty and Mairead receive Nor-
       wegian People's Peace Prize

1977   Peace People move into Peace House; Betty Williams
       and Mairead Corrigan share delayed Nobel Prize in Peace
       for 1976; Rosalyn Yalow shares Nobel Prize in Physiology
       or Medicine with Roger Guillemin and Andrew Schally;
       Alva Myrdal's The Game of Disarmament

1979   Mother Teresa awarded Nobel Prize for Peace

1980   Anne Maguire commits suicide; Betty Williams resigns
       from Peace People

1981   Mairead Corrigan marries Jackie Maguire

1982   Mairead Corrigan-Maguire gives birth to son, John
       Francis; Betty Williams divorces Ralph Williams and
       marries James Perkins, resides in United States; Alva
       Myrdal shares Nobel Prize for Peace with Alfonso Garcia
       Robles

1983   Barbara McClintock wins Nobel Prize in Medicine or
       Physiology

1984   Mairead Corrigan-Maguire gives birth to son, Luke

BIBLIOGRAPHY

GENERAL

Bergengren, Erik. Alfred Nobel, The Man and His Work
(English transl. by Alan Blair). Edinburgh: Thomas
Nelson & Sons, 1962.

Faines, Oscar J. Norway and the Nobel Peace Prize. New
York: Columbia University Press, 1938.

McCallum, T. W., and Stephen Taylor. The Nobel Prizewinners and the Nobel Foundation, 1901-1937. Zürich:
Central European Times Pub. Co., 1938.

Marble, Annie Russell. The Nobel Prize Winners in Literature, 1901-1931. New York: D. Appleton, 1932.

Nobel: The Man and His Prizes, 3d ed. Edited by Nobel
Foundation. New York: American Elsevier, 1972.

Nobel Foundation. Code of Statutes. Issued 1901 with subsequent amendments. (English, French, German, Swedish eds.) Stockholm: P. A. Norstedt & Söner.

Nobel Foundation Calendar. Uppsala: Almqvist & Wiksell;
issued every other year.

Nobel Lectures. Amsterdam: Elsevier Pub. Co.:
    Physics, 1901-1962, 3 vols.; supplement, 1963-1970,
    1 vol.
    Chemistry, 1901-1962, 3 vols.; supplement, 1963-
    1970, 1 vol.
    Physiology or Medicine, 1901-1962, 3 vols.; supple-
    ment, 1963-1970, 1 vol.
    Literature, 1901-1967, 1 vol.
    Peace, 1901-1970, 3 vols.

Les Prix Nobel. Annual publication of Nobel Foundation.
    Stockholm: P. A. Norstedt & Söner.

Ramel, S. "Alfred Nobel and the Nobel Prize." Stockholm:
   Nobel Foundation (brochure).

Schück, Henrik, and Ragnar Sohlman. The Life of Alfred
   Nobel. London: William Heinemann, 1926.

Zuckerman, Harriet. Scientific Elite. Nobel Laureates in
   the United States. New York: The Free Press, 1977.

BERTHA VON SUTTNER

Abrams, Irwin. "Bertha von Suttner and the Nobel Peace
   Prize." Journal of Central European Affairs 22, 3
   (October 1962), 286-307.

Beales, Arthur F. The History of Peace. New York: Dial,
   1931.

Kempf, Beatrix. Suffragette for Peace (English transl. by
   R. W. Last of Bertha von Suttner: Das Lebensbild einer
   grossen Frau). London: Oswald Wolff, 1972.

Mayer, Edith P. Champions of Peace. Boston: Little,
   Brown, 1959.

Playne, Carolyn E. Bertha von Suttner and the Struggle to
   Avert the World War, London: Allen & Unwin, 1936.

Les Prix Nobel en 1905. Stockholm: P. A. Norstedt &
   Söner.

Suttner, Bertha von. Lay Down Your Arms (authorized
   transl. of Die Waffen Nieder). London: Longmans,
   1892.

_____. Gesammelte Schriften [Collected Works] in 12
   vols. Dresden: E. Pierson, 1906.

_____. Memoirs (authorized English transl. of Memoiren),
   2 vols. New York: Ginn & Co., 1910.

Most of Bertha von Suttner's papers and manuscripts
are in the Bertha von Suttner Manuscript Collection in
the Peace Archives of the United Nations Library in
Geneva, Switzerland. Communications from Bertha
von Suttner to Alfred Nobel are in the Nobel Archives
of the Nobel Foundation in Stockholm.

JANE ADDAMS

Addams, Jane. Newer Ideals of Peace. New York: Macmillan, 1907.

_____. Twenty Years at Hull-House. New York: Mac-
millan, 1910.

_____. Peace and Bread in Time of War. New York:
Macmillan, 1922.

_____. The Second Twenty Years at Hull-House. New
York: Macmillan, 1930.

_____. A Centennial Reader. Ed. Emily C. Johnson.
New York: Macmillan, 1960.

Addams, Jane; Emily G. Balch; and Alice Hamilton. Women
at The Hague. New York: Macmillan, 1915.

Bussey, Gertrude, and Margaret Tims. Women's International
League for Peace and Freedom. London: George Allen
& Unwin, 1965.

Davis, Allen F. American Heroine. New York: Oxford
University Press, 1973.

Farrell, John C. Beloved Lady: A History of Jane Addams'
Ideas on Reform and Peace. Baltimore: Johns Hopkins
Press, 1967.

Linn, James. Jane Addams: A Biography. New York:
Appleton-Century, 1935.

Les Prix Nobel en 1930. Stockholm: P. A. Norstedt &
Söner.

Tims, Margaret. Jane Addams of Hull-House. London:
Allen & Unwin, 1961.

EMILY GREENE BALCH

Addams, Jane; Emily G. Balch; and Alice Hamilton. Women
at The Hague. New York: Oxford University Press,
1973.

Balch, Emily G. Our Slavic Fellow Citizens. New York:
Chanter Publ. Co., 1910.

_____. Approaches to the Great Settlement. New York:
Husbach, 1918.

_____. The Miracle of Living. New York: Island Press,
1941.

Bussey, Gertrude, and Margaret Tims. Women's International
League for Peace and Freedom. London: George Allen
& Unwin, 1965.

Les Prix Nobel en 1946. Stockholm: P. A. Norstedt &
Söner.

Randall, John. Emily Greene Balch of New England: Citizen
of the World. Washington, D. C.: Women's International League for Peace and Freedom, 1946.

Randall, Mercedes. Improper Bostonian--Emily Greene
Balch. New York: Twayne, 1964.

Extensive collections of Jane Addams's and Emily
Greene Balch's papers can be found at the Swarthmore
College Peace Collection, Swarthmore, Pennsylvania.

BETTY WILLIAMS and MAIREAD CORRIGAN

Deutsch, Richard. Mairead Corrigan, Betty Williams. Wood-
bury, N. Y.: Barron's, 1977.

McKeown, Ciaran. The Passion of Peace. London: William
Heinemann, 1984.

Les Prix Nobel en 1976. Stockholm: P. A. Norstedt &
Söner.

MOTHER TERESA

Doig, Desmond. Mother Teresa. Her People and Her Work.
San Francisco: Harper & Row, 1980.

Muggeridge, Malcolm. Something Beautiful for God. New
York: Image Books, 1977.

Les Prix Nobel en 1979. Stockholm: P. A. Norstedt &
Söner.

Spink, Kathryn. Miracle of Love. San Francisco: Harper
& Row, 1981.

_____, ed. Life in the Spirit. San Francisco: Harper &
Row, 1983.

Teresa, Mother. A Gift for God. San Francisco: Harper &
Row, 1983.

_____. The Love of Christ. San Francisco: Harper &
Row, 1982.

_____. Words to Love By. Notre Dame, Ind.: Ave
Maria Press, 1983.

_____ and Kathryn Spink. I Need Souls Like You. San
Francisco: Harper & Row, 1984.

ALVA MYRDAL

Alva och Gunnar Myrdal i fredens tjänst. Stockholm: Raben
& Sjögren, 1971.

Barnaby, Frank. "Alva Myrdal," Scanorama, October 1981.

Lindskog, Lars G. Alva Myrdal. Stockholm: Svensk Radios
Förlag, 1981.

Link, Ruth. "Alva. Soldier of Peace," Sweden Now, 10
(1976).

Myrdal, Alva. The Game of Disarmament. New York:
Pantheon, 1977.

_____. Nation and Family. New York: Harper & Row,
1941.

_____, et al. Dynamics of European Nuclear Disarma-
ment. Chester Springs, Pa.: Dufours, 1982.

_____, and Gunnar. Kontakt med Amerika. Stockholm:
Bonnier, 1941.

294   Bibliography

_____, and _____. Kris i befolkningsfrågan. Stockholm: Bonniers, 1934.

_____, and Viola Klein. Women's Two Roles. London: Routledge and Kegan Paul, 1956.

Les Prix Nobel en 1982. Stockholm: P. A. Norstedt & Söner.

SELMA LAGERLÖF

Afzelius, Nils. Selma Lagerlöf--Den Foragelseväckande. Lund, Sweden: Gleerup, 1969.

Arvidson, Stellan. Selma Lagerlöf. Stockholm: A. Bonniers Forlag, 1932.

Berendsohn, Walter. Selma Lagerlöf, Heimat und Leben, Kunsterschaft, Werke, Wirkung, und Wert. Munich: A. Lagen, 1967.

Edstrom, Vivi. Selma Lagerlöf. Boston: Twayne Publishers, 1984.

Ingerslev, Frederik. Selma Lagerlöf: Et Personligheds og Typebillede. Copenhagen: Gyldendal, 1949.

Lagerlöf, Selma. The Story of Gösta Berling (English transl. by Pauline Bancroft Flach and W. H. Hilton-Brown of Gösta Berlings Saga, 1891). Stockholm: Fritzes Kunglig Bokhandel, 1950.

_____. Miracles of Antichrist (English transl. by Pauline Bancroft Flach of Antikrists Mirakler, 1894). Garden City, N. Y.: Doubleday, Page, 1916.

_____. Jerusalem (English transl. by Velma Swanston Howard of Jerusalem, 1901-1902). Garden City, N. Y.: Doubleday, Page, 1916.

_____. The Wonderful Adventures of Nils (English transl. by Velma Swanston Howard of Nils Holgerssons Underbara Resa gennom Sverige, 1906). New York: Pantheon, 1957.

_____. Mårbacka (English transl. by Velma Swanston

Howard of Mårbacka, 1922. Garden City, N.Y.: Double-day, Page, 1924.

_____. The Diary of Selma Lagerlöf (English transl. by Velma Swanston Howard of Dagbok, Mårbacka III). Garden City, N.Y.: Doubleday, Doran 1936.

_____. The General's Ring (English transl. by Francesca Martin of Löwensköldska Ringen, 1927-1928). Garden City, N.Y.: Doubleday, 1928. Also transl. as Ring of the Löwenskölds, New York Literary Guild, 1931.

Oterdahl, Jeanne. Herrgårdsflickan som Blev Världsberömd. Stockholm: Missionsforbundets Forlag, 1948.

Les Prix Nobel en 1909. Stockholm: P. A. Norstedt & Söner.

GRAZIA DELEDDA

Balducci, Carolyn. A Self-Made Woman. Boston: Houghton Mifflin, 1975.

Deledda, Grazia. Tutte de Opere; Romanze e Novelle. Ed. by E. Cecchi, 4 vols., Milan: Mondadori, 1941-1955.

_____. Elias Portolu (1903). Milan: Mondadori, 1973.

_____. The Mother (English transl. by Mary G. Steegmann of La Madre, 1920). New York: Macmillan, 1920.

_____. Cosima. Milan: Fratelli Treves, 1930.

Piromalli, Antonio. Grazia Deledda. Florence: Nuova Italia, 1968.

Les Prix Nobel en 1926. Stockholm: P. A. Norstedt & Söner.

Sachetti, Lena. Grazia Deledda: Ricordi e Testimonianze. Bergamo: Minerva, 1971.

SIGRID UNDSET

Bukdahl, Jørgen. Det Skjulte Norge. Copenhagen: H. Aschehoug, 1926.

Krane, Borghild. Sigrid Undset: Liv og Meninger. Oslo:
    Gyldendal, 1970.

Les Prix Nobel en 1928. Stockholm: P. A. Norstedt &
    Söner.

Steen, Ellisev. Kristin Lavransdatter; En Kritisk Studie.
    Oslo: Aschehoug, 1959.

Undset, Sigrid. Jenny (English transl. by W. Emme of
    Jenny, 1911). New York: Knopf, 1921.

_____. Kristin Lavransdatter (English transl. in 1 vol.
    by Charles Archer and J. S. Scott of the 3-part Kristin
    Lavransdatter, 1920-1922). New York: Knopf, 1969.

_____. The Master of Hestviken (English transl. by
    Arthur G. Chater of Olav Audunsson i Hestviken, 1925,
    and Olav Audunsson og Hans Børn, 1927). New York:
    Knopf, 1935.

_____. Stages on the Road (English transl. by Arthur
    G. Chater of Etapper, 1929, 1933). New York: Knopf,
    1934.

_____. The Longest Years (English transl. by Arthur G.
    Chater of Elleve Aar, 1934). New York: Knopf, 1934.

_____. Madame Dorthea (English transl. by Arthur G.
    Chater of Madame Dorthea, 1939). New York: Knopf,
    1946.

_____. Return to the Future (English transl. by Henriette
    C. K. Naeseth of Tilbake til Fremtiden, 1942). New
    York: Knopf, 1942.

_____. Happy Times in Norway (English transl. by Jane
    Birkeland of Lykkelige Dage i Norge, 1943). New York:
    Knopf, 1946.

_____. Catherine of Siena (English transl. by Kate Austin-
    Lund of Catherine av Siena, 1951). New York: Sheed &
    Ward, 1954.

Vinde, Victor. Sigrid Undset: A Nordic Moralist. Seattle:
    University of Washington, 1930.

Winsnes, Andreas H. Sigrid Undset: A Study in Christian
    Realism (English transl. by P. G. Foote). New York:
    Sheed & Ward, 1953.

PEARL BUCK

American Winners of the Nobel Literary Prize. Ed. by War-
    ren G. French and Walter E. Kidd. Norman: University
    of Oklahoma Press, 1968.

Buck, Pearl. The Good Earth. New York: John Day, 1931.

_____. Sons. New York: John Day, 1933.

_____. A House Divided. New York: John Day, 1935.

[This trilogy appeared as House of Earth, 1935.]

_____. Fighting Angel. New York: John Day, 1936.

_____. The Exile. New York: John Day, 1936.

[These two appeared as The Spirit and the Flesh, 1944.]

_____. The Child Who Never Grew. New York: John
    Day, 1950.

_____. My Several Worlds. New York: John Day, 1954.

_____. A Bridge for Passing. New York: John Day,
    1962.

Doyle, Paul A. Pearl S. Buck. Boston: Twayne Publishers,
    1980.

Harris, Theodore F. Pearl Buck. New York: John Day,
    vol. 1, 1969; vol. 2, 1971.

Les Priz Nobel en 1938. Stockholm: P. A. Norstedt &
    Söner.

Stirling, Nora. Pearl Buck: A Woman in Conflict. Piscata-
    way, N. J.: New Century Publications, 1983.

298   Bibliography

GABRIELA MISTRAL

Arce de Vásquez, Margot. Gabriela Mistral. (English
transl. by Helene Masslo Anderson of Gabriela Mistral,
1964). New York: New York University Press, 1964.

Figueira, Gaston. De la Vida y la Obra de Gabriela Mistral.
Montevideo: Talleres Graficos, Gaceta Commercial,
1959.

Gautier-Gazarian, Marie-Lise. Gabriela Mistral. Chicago:
Franciscan Herald Press, 1975.

Gumucio, Alejandro. Gabriela Mistral y el Premio Nobel.
Santiago: Editorial Nascimente, 1946.

Mistral, Gabriela. Desolación. New York: Instituto de las
Españas en los Estados Unidos, 1922.

_____. Ternura. Madrid: Saturnina Calleja, 1924.

_____. Tala (1938). Buenos Aires: Editorial Losada,
1946.

_____. Lagar. Santiago: Editorial del Pacifico, 1954.

_____. Obras Completas de Gabriela Mistral [complete
works]. Ed. by Margaret Bates. Madrid: Aguilas,
1958.

_____. Selected Poems of Gabriela Mistral (transl. and
ed. by Doris Dana). Baltimore: Johns Hopkins Press,
1971.

Les Prix Nobel en 1945. Stockholm: P. A. Norstedt &
Söner.

NELLY SACHS

Berendsohn, Walter A. Einführung in das Werk der dichterin
jüdischen Schicksal. Darmstadt: Agna Verlag, 1974.

Holmkvist, Bengt. Das Buch der Nelly Sachs. Frankfurt
am Main: Suhrkamp, 1968.

Lagerkrantz, Olav. Versuch über die Lyrik der Nelly Sachs.
Frankfurt am Main: Suhrkamp, 1967.

Nelly Sachs zu Ehren. Frankfurt am Main: Suhrkamp, 1961, 1966.

Les Prix Nobel en 1966. Stockholm: P. A. Norstedt & Söner.

Sachs, Nelly. Legenden und Erzählungen. Berlin: F. W. Mayer, 1921.

_____. Von Welle und Granit; Querschnitt durch de schwedische Lyrik des 20. Jahrhundert. Berlin: Afbau Verlag, 1947.

_____. In den Wohnungen des Todes. Berlin: Afbau Verlag, 1947.

_____. Sternverdunkelung. Amsterdam: Beimann-Fischer, 1949.

_____. Eli: Ein Mysterienspiel vom Leiden Israels. Malmö: Insell, 1951.

_____. Und niemand weiss weiter. Hamburg: Ellerman, 1957.

_____. Flucht und Verwandlung. Stuttgart: Deutsche Verlags Anstalt, 1959.

_____. Fahrt ins Staublose. Frankfurt am Main: Suhr-kamp, 1961.

_____. Glühende Rätsel. Frankfurt am Main: Suhrkamp, 1966.

_____. Die Suchende. Frankfurt am Main: Suhrkamp, 1966.

_____. O the Chimneys (English transl. by Michael Hamburger, Christopher Holm, Ruth and Matthew Mead, et al.). New York: Farrar, Straus & Giroux, 1967.

_____. The Seeker and Other Poems (English transl. by Ruth and Matthew Mead and Michael Hamburger). New York: Farrar, Straus & Giroux, 1970.

MARIE CURIE

Biglow, Eileen. Madame Curie. New York: S. G. Phillips, 1967.

Cotton, Eugénie. Les Curie. Paris: Seghers, 1963.

Curie, Eve. Madame Curie (English transl. by Vincent Sheean). Garden City, N. Y.: Doubleday, 1932.

Curie, Marie. Pierre Curie (English transl. by Charlotte and Vernon Kellogg). New York: Macmillan, 1923.

_____. Radioactivité. Paris: Hermann & Cie., 1935.

Perrin, Francis. Marie Skłodowska Curie Centenary Lectures Given in Warsaw, 1967. New York: Unipub Inc., 1968.

Lex Prix Nobel en 1903. Stockholm: P. A. Norstedt & Söner.

Les Prix Nobel en 1911. Stockholm: P. A. Norstedt & Söner.

Riedman, Sarah R. Men and Women Behind the Atom. New York: Abelard-Schuman, 1958.

IRENE JOLIOT-CURIE

Biquard, Pierre. Frédéric Joliot-Curie, The Man and His Theories (English transl. by Jeffrey Strachan). New York: P. S. Eriksson, 1965.

Chadwick, James. "Obituary, Mme. Irène Joliot-Curie," Nature, May 28, 1956.

Cotton, Eugénie. Les Curie. Paris: Seghers, 1963.

Curie, Eve. Madame Curie (English transl. by Vincent Sheean). Garden City, N. Y.: Doubleday, 1937.

_____. "Madame la Sécretaire" (translated from French). Living Age 351 (September 1936), 40-42.

Goldsmith, Maurice. Frédéric Joliot-Curie. Woodstock, N. Y.: Beekman Publishers, 1976.

Les Prix Nobel en 1935. Stockholm: P. A. Norstedt & Söner.

Riedman, Sarah R. Men and Women Behind the Atom. New York: Abelard-Schuman, 1958.

GERTY CORI

Letters to author from Dr. Carl F. Cori, 1976.

Les Prix Nobel en 1947. Stockholm: P. A. Norstedt & Söner.

Riedman, Sarah R., and Elton T. Gustafson. Portraits of Nobel Laureates in Medicine and Physiology. London: Abelard-Schuman, 1953.

Sourkes, Theodore L. Nobel Winners in Medicine and Physiology, 1901-1965. New York: Abelard-Schuman, 1953.

Yost, Edna. Women of Modern Science. New York: Dodd, Mead, 1960.

MARIA GOEPPERT-MAYER

Dash, Joan. A Life of One's Own. New York: Harper & Row, 1973.

Hall, Mary Harrington. "An American Mother and the Nobel Prize--A Cinderella Story in Science," McCall's, July 1964.

Letters to the author from Dr. Joseph E. Mayer, 1976.

Mayer, Joseph E., and Maria G. Mayer. Statistical Mechanics. New York: John Wiley & Sons, 1940.

Mayer, Maria G. "The Structure of the Nucleus," Scientific American, March 1951.

_____, and J. Hans D. Jensen. Elementary Theory of Nuclear Shell Structure. New York: John Wiley, 1955.

Les Prix Nobel en 1963. Stockholm: P. A. Norstedt & Söner.

Wilson, Mitchell. "How Nobel Prize Winners Got That Way: Science Laureates," <u>Atlantic Monthly</u>, December 1969.

DOROTHY CROWFOOT HODGKIN

"British Winner Is a Grandmother," <u>New York Times</u>, October 29, 1964.

Jefferey, G. A. "Nobel Prize in Chemistry Awarded to Crystallographer," <u>Science</u>, November 1964.

Letters to author from Dr. Dorothy Crowfoot Hodgkin, 1976.

<u>Les Prix Nobel en 1964.</u> Stockholm: P. A. Norstedt & Söner.

ROSALYN YALOW

<u>Methods in Investigative and Diagnostic Endocrinology.</u> Vols. 2A (Part I, General Methodology) and 2B (Part III, Non-Pituitary Hormones), ed. by Solomon Berson and Rosalyn Yalow. Amsterdam: North-Holland, 1973.

Kent, Leticia. "Winner Woman! Dr. Rosalyn Yalow," <u>Vogue</u>, January 1978.

Letter to author from Dr. Rosalyn Yalow, 1977.

<u>Les Prix Nobel en 1977.</u> Stockholm: P. A. Norstedt & Söner.

BARBARA McCLINTOCK

Keller, Evelyn Fox. <u>A Feeling for the Organism.</u> New York: W. H. Freeman and Company, 1983.

McClintock, Barbara. "Chromosome Organization and Genic Expression," <u>Cold Spring Harbor Symposia on Quantitative Biology</u>, 16 (1951).

————. "Controlling Elements and the Gene," <u>Ibid.</u>, 21 (1956).

<u>Les Prix Nobel en 1983.</u> Stockholm: P. A. Norstedt & Söner.

INDEX